The Threshing FLOOR

The Threshing FLOOR

Juanita Bynum

Charisma
HOUSE
A STRANG COMPANY

Most STRANG COMMUNICATIONS/CHARISMA HOUSE/SILOAM/FRONTLINE/REALMS/ EXCEL BOOKS products are available at special quantity discounts for bulk purchase for sales promotions, premiums, fund-raising, and educational needs. For details, write Strang Communications/Charisma House/Siloam/Realms/Excel Books, 600 Rinehart Road, Lake Mary, Florida 32746, or telephone (407) 333–0600.

THE THRESHING FLOOR by Juanita Bynum
Published by Charisma House
A Strang Company
600 Rinehart Road
Lake Mary, Florida 32746
www.charismahouse.com

Unless otherwise noted, all Scripture quotations are from the Amplified Bible. Old Testament © 1965, 1987 by the Zondervan Corporation. The Amplified New Testament © 1954, 1958, 1987 by the Lockman Foundation. Used by Permission.

Scripture quotations marked KJV are from the King James Version of the Bible.

Scripture quotations marked NIV are from the Holy Bible, New International Version, © 1973, 1978, 1984, International Bible Society. Used by Permission.

Appendix A and Appendix B in *The Threshing Floor* are from a special King James Bible by Matthew Ashimolowo. They are used by permission. For more information regarding this resource, contact Matthew Ashimolowo Media Ministries, London, England, or go to his Web site at www.kicc.org.uk.

Cover Designer: Bill Johnson
Author Photos: Keith Major Photography, Inc.
Editorial services by ASarah Publications (www.asarah.com)

International Standard Book Number: 978-1-59979-230-9

The Library of Congress has catalogued the previous edition as follows:

Library of Congress Cataloging-in-Publication Data

Bynum, Juanita.
 The threshing floor / Juanita Bynum.
   p. cm.
 ISBN 1-59185-803-8
 1. Prayer. 2. Public worship. I. Title.
 BV210.3.B96 2005
 248.3'2--dc22

                                     2005010392

08 09 10 11 12 — 9 8 7 6 5 4 3 2 1
Printed in the United States of America

To Pastor Matthew Ashimolowo...for your impartation into my life on the matter of prayer...because of you, I have been changed forever.

To Mother Estella Boyd...for her impartation of prayer

To Laura Lowery, from Love Oasis Christian Center in New York...for your impartation of the message "The Well Within"

Acknowledgments

I would like to give special thanks to:

- Dr. John H. Boyd Sr., for providing me with a place to cultivate my call to the mandate of prayer at New Greater Bethel Church. I will always have a special love in my heart for the altar of this house. My experience in prayer at New Greater Bethel has changed my life forever.

Contents

Prayer Is Universal

RAYER IS THE only thing that no one religion can claim possession of or origination of. It is not a denominational or religious experience. Prayer is an individual experience that takes place between the Creator and those whom He has created.

It does not matter what religion a person is a part of; prayer and meditation are the vital links for staying connected with God. If you do not possess a prayer life, there's no way you can understand the principles of everyday life that God is trying to teach you. So bear with me—especially if you are mature in the Lord and, as a result, are a more prolific reader—because prayer is a universal subject. It is an absolute necessity in every person's life. For this reason I am approaching it carefully, so that every person—whether a congressman or a prison inmate—can understand the principles of prayer and have a life-changing experience.

When I was first prompted to write this book about prayer, I went to bookstores to see what was already in the marketplace. Interestingly, there weren't a lot of books written on this topic. I believe one of the reasons is that most people feel the way I used to feel about prayer—they tend to shy away from it. When I first started praying, I had a difficult time, because I didn't really understand what was expected of me when I came into the "presence of the Lord." Prayer was truly a difficult process.

Why did the process of prayer seem so difficult for me? Society teaches us to mask or suppress everything we feel, but when we come to pray, we have to train ourselves to do the opposite. We must release everything that we feel. For me, that was a very difficult thing to do.

When we have become masters of suppressing our feelings, then society calls that *maturity*. You are considered a *better* person if you can suppress what you feel, not truly expressing yourself for who you are and what you believe. Society thinks that the successful person is one who can suppress his or her thoughts and feelings in order to get or to keep a job or to establish and keep a certain status in life.

Yet, the most "wonderful and mature" people—by the world's standards—often end up crashing emotionally at some point in their lives. It's possible to play that role for only so long. Why? Because as human beings, we have been created with real emotions and real desires. Somewhere along the line, the real person will come out. The real things we are feeling will be expressed and heard. When this time comes, if we don't choose a positive outlet for this expression, the results could be tragic.

I believe that is why many people are in prison right now. That's why we hear of women being sent to prison for killing their husbands or children. It's the reason husbands are in jail for killing their wives, and children are imprisoned for killing their parents. It explains our epidemics of rape, theft, and white-collar crime. All of these things have a common root. Many of the people who commit these crimes were conditioned never to express what they really felt—whether it was anger, bitterness, or even happiness. They were not given an outlet for expressing their feelings or for being intelligently heard and helped. They reached the boiling point, the moment when they could no longer stuff their feelings inside, and they exploded. As a result, other people—even people they loved—were hurt and possibly even lost their lives.

This happens when people are not able to find a place where they can trust enough to be able to express themselves completely.

You see, prayer is the posture from which trust can be established or restored, the place from which God can channel back to you the answer you seek or give you the resolve you need to handle whatever situation you may be going through.

As your trust in God grows, He will assure you more and more that you can come to Him about any situation or need. During this process, as you come to Him, you will develop a new level of communication, a positive outlet that yields positive results. You will discover that when you leave His presence, you don't have to worry about how other people feel about you. His presence has liberated you. Now that's real freedom of speech. That's true freedom of expression.

I'm strongly impressed to write this book because I went on such a journey. Today when people hear me talk about the spiritual things that I have encountered, they often tell me, "That's so powerful." But for me it was a process. It is still a process. No person on this earth will ever have a monopoly on prayer. Why? Prayer is a spiritual experience, and no one can predict or control the Spirit of God. Each time you find your place in prayer, you will have fresh, new experiences in your relationship with God.

Here is my threefold goal for writing this book:

1. I want to give you some foundational principles to help you understand how to approach God and to know when you're in His presence.

2. I want you to understand what to do when you find yourself there.

3. I also want to help you identify what you can expect to receive from God in the place of prayer and intercession.

When these three components come together, you have become a *praying person*, not simply a *religious person*. In Luke 18:1, Jesus gave the only requirement for prayer, making an emphatic point when He "spoke a parable to them, that *men always ought to pray* and not lose heart" (NKJV, emphasis added). Here's my point: The Bible doesn't say that people always ought to go to church. It doesn't say that people always ought to sing in the choir, be on the usher board, or teach a Sunday school class. It clearly says we "*always ought to pray.*" That mandate is reinforced by 1 Thessalonians 5:17, which says: "Pray without ceasing" (NKJV).

Though the command was given, I believe it's a small nugget that we've missed—and this nugget is the glue that binds people to the structure and practice of religion. It also helps us to distinguish between what has been put together religiously by man and what is actually a demonstration of the presence of the Lord.

I believe that once people truly become involved in prayer, they will find God—not merely religion and denominationalism. They will begin to understand that the only reason for religious structure is to give the world a way to experience, reverence, and honor God. Once we understand the purpose for religious structure, we will be better able to relate to the people who live within that structure. When someone offends us by saying or doing something that doesn't look like God, we won't be so quick to respond by rejecting God, thus throwing the baby out with the bathwater. We must not get rid of the presence of God in our lives just because we have been offended by people.

Prayer is the only vehicle available that allows us to view humanity—with all its faults—and still understand that God is perfect. Anyone who makes a decision to walk away from God's presence, walking outside of His instructions, will make mistakes and run into trouble. But by following the pattern for prayer that I will unveil in this book, any person can come right back into God's presence and correct the mistakes. You have the perfect opportunity to be given a second chance. Once back in His presence you can be completely forgiven.

I'm not trying to feed you religion or denominationalism. I'm not even trying to encourage you to go to church. I'm trying to encourage you to recognize that you can have a relationship with God right now.

Determine now to establish a time each day that you spend alone with God, expressing how you feel. Stay in His presence long enough to hear Him respond to you by telling you how He feels about you and how He can help you in your daily life.

When prayer becomes a reality in your life, you will find yourself doing things just to please God—and you will experience the Lord doing things to please you. It is within this process of prayer that you will find holistic emotional contentment. As you read this book, I believe you are going to find God as never before. His presence will fill the void in your soul, releasing all those feelings and emotions you have learned to suppress. There's a solution for you, a place where you can go in prayer whether you consider yourself to be religious or not—and it's going to be incredible. Remember, prayer doesn't just change things—prayer changes everything!

A Journey Into His Presence

HIS BOOK IS a journey into the presence of the Lord. It will give us our first look at what *church* is all about. As we look closely at the ancient religious customs originated by God when He established the first tabernacle in the wilderness for the children of Israel, God's pattern and purpose for prayer will be revealed.

God established a tabernacle through His servant Moses so that the Israelites could understand how to come into His presence. Through the design of the tabernacle and God's institution of the religious practices to be followed in His tabernacle, God illustrated what is required in order to be able to stand in His presence. The tabernacle demonstrates God's attributes and shows us how His blessings are made accessible to His people.

However, this book will also show you how the true meaning of the tabernacle has been distorted—even until today. We have strayed far away from how God ordained that worship of Him was to be expressed in the first tabernacle. In this book, I will break down major aspects of the tabernacle and create a pattern for you, one you can establish in your own life when you have finished reading and studying this pattern. You will be able to pray according to the pattern of the Lord wherever you are—at home in your bedroom or basement, in your car, or sitting in the pew at church.

Prayer develops what people commonly call "inner strength." Without that divine strength within—the presence of God residing in your life—you have no other recourse but to respond to the external pressures and temptations from without. If you lose that presence, as so many have, you will fall apart in crises and give up on life. The strength of your temple determines your outer response to life.

God designed the first tabernacle so that it was portable. He gave instructions for tearing it down, picking up the pieces, and moving it as the children of Israel went about their journey. Every piece of that structure was sanctified and sacred, and the Israelites respected it. They knew that if they kept God's tabernacle in order, the presence of the Lord would lead them with a cloud by day and a fire by night. His heavenly light would radiate down upon the ark of the covenant in the most holy place. But every part of the tabernacle—from the doorposts to the ark of the covenant in the most holy place—had to be in order. No matter where they went on their journey, that order could not change.

The Israelites were very careful about the way they handled the pieces, because they knew that if even one element was out of place, it could affect the glory of God. That tabernacle held the very presence of God. It was the first time in history that God had come and dwelt among His people. They knew that unless they paid careful attention to His instructions, they might not be able to maintain this wonderful, new relationship with God.

The tabernacle had been built to be mobile; it took people from one place to another, ever closer to God's ultimate purpose for their lives. Now I truly understand the wisdom of God in making the first tabernacle portable. Today we build churches that are always accessible to us. People come to these buildings, but they miss out on experiencing the glory and presence of God, because His presence no longer dwells in a building made of stone and wood. As a result, people fail to move ever closer to God's ultimate purpose for their lives because they have failed to understand that *we are the church*.

To hold the awesome presence of God Himself, we must have lives that are in order according to the pattern He gave us when He provided instructions for the building of that first tabernacle.

In 1 Corinthians 6:19, the apostle Paul tells us that "your body is the temple of the Holy Ghost" (KJV). In recognition of this, I want to help you see that the pattern established for the Old Testament tabernacle is the spiritual pattern for you and me—the New Testament "temples of the

Holy Spirit." Once you understand this principle, you can become the new tabernacle God desires. As the temple of the Holy Spirit, you must handle carefully the sacred pieces that you house, wherever you go and however you move. Be careful not to do anything that would adversely affect those pieces—because if you do, it will affect your relationship with God.

It isn't the *external things* people say about you, or the things people have done to you, that affect your relationship with God. It really doesn't matter how you have been offended, affected, or hurt in the past. Your relationship with God is determined by how you handle or mishandle the *internal pieces of the tabernacle He has established within you.*

This book puts the responsibility for your relationship with God where it belongs—*on you.* If you have ever desired to really know God, this is your perfect opportunity. You may be surrounded by external problems and troubles, but through God's pattern for prayer you can rise above every one of them as you become better acquainted with the Lord. Once this heavenly relationship has been sanctified, set apart, protected, and covered from within, you will be able to handle anything that comes from without.

I believe that's why Jesus confronted the religious status quo and pointed the people back to relationship with the Father. Think about it. Jesus was able to endure the cross because He prayed without ceasing. He had built a strong tabernacle within by maintaining consistent communication with the Father. Through prayer, He could be transfigured by the power of the Holy Spirit.

This is the bottom line: you can rise above natural circumstances and tap into the supernatural realm—where you will find love, peace, contentment, and the solution to every problem you face, if you will answer the call to pray. *That's why God has called me to bring you to the threshing floor, the place of total surrender to Him in prayer and intercession.*

Come with me…this journey is going to change your life for eternity.

CHAPTER I

Introduction to Prayer:
The Gate

*L*ET ME START by explaining what third-dimensional prayer is. When you have tapped into the third dimension (on the threshing floor), you have reached a place in prayer where you are assured that you're in the divine presence of God. It is a place where you are confident that not only are you praying to God, but also you're praying with an assurance that He does hear you, and in His hearing you, He is obligated to give an answer. So as we enter into the introductory stage of prayer, it is important for you to maintain the understanding that God is using the tabernacle to lay a foundation, a parallel pattern as to how we as believers are to enter into His presence. If you were to fly in a helicopter over the structure of the tabernacle and the roof was completely removed, from the air looking down, the entire structure of the tabernacle would appear to be in the shape of a cross.

The gate to which I am referring in this first chapter would be positioned at the foot of the cross. We enter the gate (as we enter the presence of the Lord) because this gate brings us back to the foot of the cross. It brings us back to the works of salvation.

As we move step by step in our understanding of the pattern of the tabernacle and the priestly garments, we are seeing symbolically what our posture should be in prayer. This study of the tabernacle structure will reveal on a spiritual level how we are to appear before the Lord in prayer.

As I describe the elements and priestly garments from the Old Testament, I want you to apply these descriptions on a spiritual level to the elements you pass through and the garments you wear in prayer today. Because on a spiritual level, the priests of the Old Testament and the priests of the New Testament—of which you are a part if you have been adopted into God's royal family—enter the same tabernacle and wear the same garments. The elements and garments do not change just because the age has changed. Instead, they have been transformed from a natural representation to a spiritual representation.

The measurements and patterns for the tabernacle in the Old Testament were extremely important to God. In the Book of Ezekiel, God commanded the angel to take up a measuring rod and measure the temple. He instructed the angel to measure every part of the structure to see if it had been constructed according to His will. The same measuring line will be taken up for every believer in the presence of the Lord to see whether or not we measure up—not just to be a people who pray for ourselves, but also that we would become fully capable of standing in the gap to pray for others.

The pattern that is set before you today will help you to understand that when you enter into prayer, God does not desire for you to wander aimlessly in the Spirit realm. He wants you to know exactly where you are positioned, because people are destroyed for lack of knowledge (Hos. 4:6).

God doesn't want you to go to prayer shooting in the dark, not knowing if you are in His divine presence. He doesn't want you to have to wonder if He is hearing your prayers. God wants there to be absolutely no doubt in your mind as to whether there is something in your life that is hindering the level of spiritual communication you desire to have with Him.

The pattern of the tabernacle was set forth for you to be able to see where you are in the realm of the Spirit and to identify whatever may be in you that could hinder your prayers so that it can be corrected. God has designed the tabernacle structure and the garments to make us aware of where we are and how we are dressed spiritually, because His desire is that our prayers would not be hindered. His desire is that it would not be a struggle for us to pray.

A PERFECT PATTERN

When you go to a tailor, he measures your body and then cuts out a pattern. If he cuts the pattern according to the wrong measurements, the garment won't fit. It may look beautiful, but you won't be able to wear it.

The same is true with God's presence. If you don't pray according to the pattern He has *cut*, He will not be able to participate in your prayers. God can't commune with you on a human level—that pattern is too small. His pattern for prayer allows us to commune with Him on a spiritual level. He is the master of prayer, so we must use His pattern. Why? Because only God knows the measurements of His Spirit (Rom. 8:27).

This means we must begin by understanding there are dimensions in God. To reach the third dimension—the place where God hears and answers your prayers—you must start by looking for the pattern God has established that enables you to enter His presence. Receiving answers to your prayers can be an everyday reality—but these answers don't come by luck, chance, or your own ability to pray. They come by following the pattern. By the time you finish this book, you will be able to look back to times in the past when you have received answers from God, and you will recognize that the answers came because you prayed according to God's pattern—even without knowing it.

On the other hand, God is sovereign. He can choose to answer an "out of pattern" prayer because He knows what the ultimate result will be. As He told Moses, God reserves the right to act after the counsel of His own will.

> I will proclaim My name, THE LORD, before you; for I will be gracious to whom I will be gracious, and will show mercy and loving-kindness on whom I will show mercy and loving-kindness.
> —EXODUS 33:19

We must keep this in our focus as we pray: we are after the counsel and the will of God—not our will. Isaiah 55:11 says, "So shall My word be that goes forth out of My mouth: it shall not return to Me void [without producing any effect, useless], but it shall accomplish that which I please and purpose, and it shall prosper in the thing for which I sent it."

So as you pray, know that God is merciful and acts according to His will, and learn how to position yourself to hear from Him. By looking for God's pattern, you will come into the fullness of prayer and relationship that He desires. If not, your time with Him will be inconsistent. At times you will be able to commune with God, and at other times you will become lost in the process. Sometimes you will see results, and other times you won't. Then frustration will set in and may stop you from praying altogether. If this happens, the enemy's weapon against your soul has worked successfully.

In this last hour, God is bringing a new confidence in prayer. He is making sure we know Him well, because His plans and His purposes are coming to pass in the earth. As we learn to pray according to His pattern, we will see results—*every time.*

RETURNING TO THE BEGINNING

Let's examine the beginning of this process. Jesus' model prayer in Matthew 6:9–13 (KJV) is the beginning of prayer, our divine table of contents.

> After this manner therefore pray ye: Our Father which art in heaven, Hallowed be thy name. Thy kingdom come. Thy will be done in earth, as it is in heaven. Give us this day our daily bread. And forgive us our debts, as we forgive our debtors. And lead us not into temptation, but deliver us from evil: For thine is the kingdom, and the power, and the glory, for ever. Amen.

This prayer outlines the steps into prayer. It also reveals the difference between someone who merely prays and one who has been called to be an intercessor.

Step 1. Acknowledgment of who God is

The Lord's Prayer not only demonstrates *when* to begin praying, but it also reveals the spiritual attributes of God, our heavenly Father.

The prayer opens with worship, acknowledging God as the King of the universe. He is *Jehovah-Tsidkenu,* our righteousness; *Jehovah-M'Kaddesh,* our sanctification; *Jehovah-Shalom,* our peace; *Jehovah-Shammah,* ever present with us; *Jehovah-Rophe,* our healer; *Jehovah-Jireh,* our faithful provider; *Jehovah-Nissi,* our banner; and, finally, He is *Jehovah-Rohi,* our loving shepherd. To be an effective intercessor, these same attributes should be at work in your life, enabling you to call upon Him on behalf of others.

Step 2. Acknowledgment of God's kingdom

The prayer acknowledges God's kingdom, which is behind the veil in the third realm, resting upon the ark of the covenant. It requests that God bring that portion of the kingdom toward man. "Thy kingdom come. Thy will be done in earth, as it is in heaven" signifies the intercessor's flesh dying on the altar of sacrifice. In other words, to be an effective intercessor you must be willing to give up what you want in order to do what pleases God.

Step 3. Application of God's Word

The Lord then taught us to pray: "Give us this day our daily bread." Jesus is the Bread of Life. He is the shewbread in the holy place, which is always fresh and endued with (the power of) the Word. So, to be an effective intercessor, you must live and pray according to the Word. As you do, God will sustain you. You will be able to endure in prayer long after others have given up and come out with a fresh word and perspective.

Step 4. Attentiveness to the work of God

"And lead us not into temptation, but deliver us from evil" speaks of maintenance—being held back from stumbling into evil traps and being sheltered from the attacks of the enemy. As an effective intercessor, your attention must be focused on God and upon doing His work. This keeps you in the *secret place* where the enemy cannot enter.

The door and coverings that enclose the holy place of intercession actually protect you from anything that tries to come in from the outer court.

Step 5. Affirmation of God in everything you do

When Jesus said, "For thine is the kingdom, and the power, and the glory, for ever," He was affirming the eternal, weighty, glory of God, which waits behind the veil in the third realm of prayer. To be an effective intercessor means to affirm God in everything you do. Then He will meet with you in the most holy place, and you will walk in heavenly wisdom and authority on earth.

Now that we have established our table of contents, it's time to examine God's pattern more closely.

UNFOLDING THE PATTERN OF THE LORD

We are now at the second step of studying the pattern of prayer. Take a moment and look at the diagram of Moses' tabernacle on the next page. You will see the following elements of the tabernacle:

- An entry gate on the east
- The outer court, where you find...
- The brazen laver
- The brazen altar
- The holy place, where you come through...
- The door, to...
- The golden candlestick
- The table of shewbread
- The altar of incense
- The veil, behind which you find...
- The ark of the covenant

Each element has a great significance to prayer. There are many people who have overlooked the significance of this tabernacle for years, thinking, *This is just the tabernacle of Moses, something God gave to him for Israel's time in the wilderness.* Not so. This tabernacle is a divine key into the divine presence.

THE GATE TO THE OUTER COURT

God established the tabernacle to be a dwelling place for His presence and glory. Part of this construction plan was the erection of a wall of white linen, built to enclose the outer court. On the east side of this pure, white boundary was the entry gate.

The twelve tribes of Israel were camped around the outside of the wall. Each tribe had been given a specific location to pitch their tents. But regardless of a tribe's location, every Israelite had to enter the tabernacle through the same gate. No one had special privileges—no one could claim rank, saying, "I'm a preacher," or "I'm a bishop," or "I know the right people." Nobody could slip in under the curtain.

In Ephesians 2:11–12, the apostle Paul described the desperate condition of Gentiles before the death of Christ. They had no access, no privilege, or no opportunity for entering into the *tabernacle* and experiencing the presence of God. Scripture described their hopeless condition: "Wherefore remember, that ye being in time past Gentiles in the flesh, who are called Uncircumcision by that which is called the Circumcision in the flesh made by hands; that at that time ye were without Christ, being aliens from the commonwealth of Israel, and strangers from the covenants of promise, having no hope, and without God in the world" (KJV).

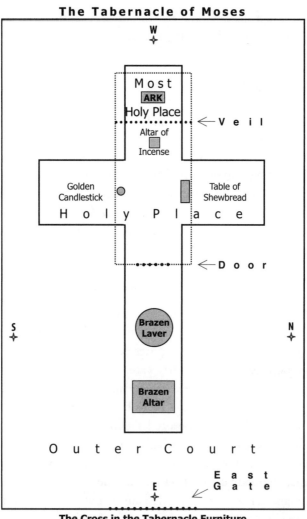

The Tabernacle of Moses

The Cross in the Tabernacle Furniture

But through the sacrifice of Christ at Calvary, everyone, Jew and Gentile alike, has access into an intimate relationship with God.

> But now in Christ Jesus ye who sometimes were far off are made nigh by the blood of Christ. For he is our peace, who hath made both one, and hath broken down the middle wall of partition between us; having abolished in his flesh the enmity, even the law of commandments, contained in ordinances; for to make in himself of twain one new man, so making peace; and that he might reconcile both unto God in one body by the cross, having slain the enmity thereby: and came and preached peace to you which were afar off, and to them that were nigh. For through him we both have access by one Spirit unto the Father.
>
> —EPHESIANS 2:13–18, KJV

When this took place, it was declared that there was no more hopelessness at being denied access at the gate. When the Israelites approached the tabernacle by way of these white curtains, the curtains symbolized entering into the righteousness of God. In the same way spiritually, as you enter prayer, you should begin to examine yourself in light of that pure, white curtain. By looking at this linen, you are to be reminded that your life doesn't compare to the purity of the wall that surrounds the tabernacle, symbolizing the righteousness of God. Isaiah 64:6 describes the vast difference between our best attempts at being *humanly good* and the awesome righteousness of God by saying:

> For we all have become like one who is unclean [ceremonially, like a leper], and all our righteousness (our best deeds of rightness and justice) is like filthy rags or a polluted garment; we all fade like a leaf, and our iniquities, like the wind, take us away [far from God's favor, hurrying us toward destruction].

If you were to take a walk around the entire circumference of the white linen wall of righteousness, you would recognize that you could never become as purified as these garments (outside of His righteousness). However, if you keep moving, you will eventually arrive at the gate to the outer court. *What is it about this gate that is so important to our prayer life?*

Jesus is the gate into the presence of God. In John 10:7–11, Jesus

11

said, "I assure you, most solemnly I tell you, that I Myself am the Door for the sheep. All others who came [as such] before Me are thieves and robbers, but the [true] sheep did not listen to and obey them. I am the Door; anyone who enters in through Me will be saved (will live). He will come in and he will go out [freely], and will find pasture. The thief comes only in order to steal and kill and destroy. I came that they may have and enjoy life, and have it in abundance (to the full, till it overflows). I am the Good Shepherd. The Good Shepherd risks and lays down His [own] life for the sheep."

This signifies that Jesus is the only way into the presence of God. He told us clearly, "I am the way, the truth, and the life: no man cometh unto the Father, but by me" (John 14:6, KJV). We must never lose focus on these three points: Jesus is our *way*, our *truth*, and our *life*.

The multicolored curtains of the gate

According to Exodus 27:16, there were curtains that were interwoven into this gate. These curtains were multicolored. Let's take a look at how Scripture describes this gate: "And for the gate of the court shall be an hanging of twenty cubits, of blue, and purple, and scarlet, and fine twined linen, wrought with needlework: and their pillars shall be four, and their sockets four" (KJV). These colors represent the works of Christ, something we should keep in clear view as we approach God in prayer. John tells us: "In him was life; and the life was the light of men" (John 1:4, KJV). Jesus is the life that lights our souls, like the glory that shines in the most holy place.

If you don't understand the symbolism of the colors of the curtains of the gate, you may get off track in your praying right from the start. If you miss it here, you may never reach the Father in the most holy place.

You come to God the Father by acknowledging the works of the Son. It's amazing how many people miss it right here. After God called me to intercession and I began to lead Tuesday prayer at my church, it was interesting to see how we approach the throne of God. I began to realize that *we have been deceived!* We think we can come to God any way we want and that He will *automatically* hear us.

One morning while in prayer, I heard the Lord speak in my spirit, saying, "Do you know how common the church has become when they *think* they are talking to Me?" If you get *common* with God, you will end up talking to yourself. God is not common. There are too many stages between the gate and the most holy place for anyone to think they can talk to Him like a common man.

We must be taught how to effectually approach God so that we can receive answers to our prayers. First of all, we learn to approach God by worshiping at the Beautiful Gate. There are four colors represented here: white, blue, purple, and scarlet. The *white,* fine-twined linen represents *the righteousness of Jesus Christ.* The Gospels record how He suffered to become righteousness for us. *Blue* represents *Christ as the heavenly one.* He is the living Word who was with God in the beginning and later became flesh so that all who believed in Him would be saved. (See John 1:12–14.) *Purple* represents *His royalty and kingship*—the promised Messiah from a royal lineage who fulfilled the prophetic Word to God's people. (See Matthew 1.) Finally, *scarlet* represents *Jesus' ultimate sacrifice* on the cross, the shedding of His blood. (See Mark 15.)

When you enter into prayer through the East Gate, you are acknowledging the four works of Jesus Christ as expressed in the Gospels. You cannot approach God correctly unless you go through His works! If you come to God any other way, you are disregarding the fact that He came to earth, was crucified on the cross of sacrifice, rose from the dead, and now sits at the right hand of the Father as King of kings and Lord of lords! How can you ignore this? How can you ignore that He's making intercession for you right now, according to Romans 8:34?

Let me break it down further. Jesus stands between the things of God in the outer court and the world. He is the gate, so this is His first act of intercession for us. As we approach the gate, He stands there and says, "You don't know Me as your personal Savior. You are not saved. All that is behind Me within these courts are treasures of the will of My Father that you can freely have. So I'm going to stand in this gate and wait until you get here. I'm going to be your way in. If you cannot believe My works at the gate, you certainly will not be able to comprehend Me in the gate, nor will you be able to perceive Me behind the veil. You cannot skip this step and be successful in prayer."

To pass through the gate, you must accept His works as part of your life. To enter into the things of God, you must be thankful for what He has done. "Enter into his gates with thanksgiving, and into his courts with praise: be thankful unto him, and bless his name. For the Lord is good; his mercy is everlasting; and his truth endureth to all generations" (Ps. 100:4–5, KJV). Countless people have never heeded the cry of God's voice saying, "Come to Me, all you who labor and are heavy-laden and overburdened, and I will cause you to rest. [I will ease and relieve and refresh your souls.]" (Matt. 11:28). This is why we must always enter His courts with thanksgiving. Psalm 65:4 says, "Blessed (happy, fortunate, to be envied) is the man whom You choose and cause to come near, that he may dwell in Your courts! We shall be satisfied with the goodness of Your house, Your holy temple."

HAVE YOU RECEIVED CHRIST?

If you have not accepted Christ as your personal Savior, you cannot be thankful for what Christ has done. This is why you must accept His works before you can enter through the gate. You have to receive Christ and acknowledge His works, or you won't even be able to get into the front yard—and forget about going behind the veil! If you haven't received Christ, that's out of the question.

If you are going to meet with God, you have to come through Jesus' works, which are represented by the gate. In other words, you have to be saved. If you think you can receive the counsel of God without making any commitment to Him, you are operating in deception. God doesn't hear your prayer! Hear what the Lord declared to the children of Israel: "Behold, the Lord's hand is not shortened at all, that it cannot save, nor His ear dull with deafness, that it cannot hear. But your iniquities have made a separation between you and your God, and your sins have hidden His face from you, so that He will not hear" (Isa. 59:1–2).

This is a tough pill to swallow, but those who are His have been washed in the blood of the Lamb.

Many people in church may look like they are saved. They may even walk around praying in tongues. But what does the blood test say? Have they been washed in the blood? If not, God will look at them and say, "You're not Mine." You may ask how I could say that an individual is

been constituted a Priest, not on the basis of a bodily legal requirement [an externally imposed command concerning His physical ancestry], but on the basis of the power of an endless and indestructible Life.

—HEBREWS 7:14–16

Jesus' priesthood didn't come from the order of man, but from the third realm where God dwells in eternal light. (See Hebrews 7:14–15.) He "has been constituted a Priest, not on the basis of a bodily legal requirement [an externally imposed command concerning His physical ancestry], but on the basis of the power of an endless and indestructible Life. For it is witnessed of Him, You *[meaning Jesus]* are a Priest forever after the order (with the rank) of Melchizedek" (vv. 16–17).

Jesus came "after the order of Melchizedek" because there was no history of Melchizedek's ancestors. There were no records of his beginning or end—he just walked off! It's much the same with Jesus. Though you can read about His parents, Mary and Joseph, and trace His natural lineage back to Abraham, you can't trace the origins of God. And since Jesus is the Son of God—and God has no beginning or end—you can't trace eternity! You also can't predict Christ's future, because God isn't limited to natural time.

No one knows Jesus' spiritual end, because He has no end, and no one can understand where He began, because He was with the Father before the foundation of the world. (See John 1:1–2.)

It was a legal requirement that a priest come from the line of Aaron. But in order to establish Jesus as our great High Priest, God canceled this tradition to perfect His eternal plan (Heb. 7:18). When Jesus came, He reconciled us to God and introduced us to the Holy Spirit, because He came from the third dimension! He canceled the old, Levitical requirements by adopting the lineage of the tribe of *Judah*, which means "praise." The Law could never make anyone perfect. "But instead a better hope is introduced through which we [now] come close to God" (v. 19).

So you see, God's purpose in canceling the old order was to give us an opportunity to draw near to Him—not to sit in church and simply repeat the Lord's Prayer, thinking we have arrived! Jesus has one goal: to give us a living, breathing, vital relationship with the Father.

The priest's service was so vital to man's forgiveness that God could not afford for it to be hindered or stopped just because a priest died...so He appointed an everlasting one. *This is why you can become an effective intercessor.*

> And it was not without the taking of an oath [that Christ was made Priest], for those who formerly became priests received their office without its being confirmed by the taking of an oath by God, but this One was designated and addressed and saluted with an oath, The Lord has sworn and will not regret it or change His mind, You are a Priest forever according to the order of Melchizedek. In keeping with [the oath's greatest strength and force], Jesus has become the Guarantee of a better (stronger) agreement [a more excellent and more advantageous covenant]. [Again, the former successive line of priests] was made up of many, because they were each prevented by death from continuing [perpetually in office].
>
> —HEBREWS 7:20–23

Think about this point for one second: He was born; He died on the cross to redeem us; when He died, our sins were washed away. He rose to get all power, but He forever lives to make intercession for you and me. Jesus Christ, the perfect High Priest, continually makes intercession for us. He never stops praying! And God won't ever replace Him with another priest, so His spiritual service continues throughout eternity. Hebrews 7:24–25 goes on, "But He holds His priesthood unchangeably, because He lives on forever. Therefore He is able also to save to the uttermost (completely, perfectly, finally, and for all time and eternity)."

Let's pause here; *this is powerful.* When you enter the gate and pass through the four colors and works of Christ, you have thanked God for providing a perfect Priest. You have acknowledged His works, understanding that He has saved you to the uttermost! You have no doubt that Jesus "...is able also to save to the uttermost (completely, perfectly, finally, and for all time and eternity) those who come to God through Him, since He is always living to make petition to God and intercede with Him and intervene for them" (v. 25). There's no better way to enter the courts of God than through the Beautiful Gate of what Christ has done! Because if you can believe it for yourself, then you can believe it on behalf of someone else.

> [Here is] the High Priest *[at the Gate!]* [perfectly adapted] to our needs, as was fitting—holy, blameless, unstained by sin, separated from sinners, and exalted higher than the heavens. He has no day by day necessity, as [do each of these other] high priests, to offer sacrifice first of all for his own [personal] sins and then for those of the people, because He [met all the requirements] once and for all when He brought Himself [as a sacrifice] which He offered up.
>
> —HEBREWS 7:26–27

Jesus is completely without sin, and that is why we are able to go deeper in prayer. Even before you think to ask God, "Will You…?" "Can You…?" *Jesus is already there*, representing the power that you will receive from Him to walk deeper into the Spirit realm. This is amazing! His completed works give you assurance that God will hear and answer your prayers.

THE POWER OF THE GATE

There is mighty power in the Beautiful Gate, because it sets the groundwork for the rest of your journey. The *gate*, the *outer court*, the *door*, the *holy place*, the *veil*, and the *most holy place* work together in prayer. So, if you neglect this first gate, you will have neglected an act of God—which can negate a prayer He wants to answer before you ask. Let me explain. The Bible says that God knows what you need even "before you ask Him" (Matt. 6:8). For example, before you asked Jesus into your heart, God was already wooing and drawing you to the gate. God provided for your salvation before you asked Jesus to save your soul.

Remember, with God everything is already finished, so if you ignore the works of Christ in the gate, you could delay or abort other things God has already provided for you in prayer. On the other hand, if you acknowledge His works, God will do mighty things through your life of prayer in fulfillment of Isaiah 64:4–5.

> For from of old no one has heard nor perceived by the ear, nor has the eye seen a God besides You, Who works and shows Himself

active on behalf of him who [earnestly] waits for Him. You meet and spare him who joyfully works righteousness (uprightness and justice), [earnestly] remembering You in Your ways. Behold, You were angry, for we sinned; we have long continued in our sins [prolonging Your anger]. And shall we be saved?

In Acts 12, the power of the gate can be seen through the circumstances Peter faced when he was thrown in prison by Herod. Herod had begun to "afflict and oppress and torment some who belonged to the church (assembly)" (v. 1). After he killed James the brother of John, he discovered that his actions were "pleasing to the Jews" (v. 3). Ever seeking the approval of the Jews, during Passover week he then sought out and arrested Peter. The fourth and fifth verses of Acts 12 tell us that "when he had seized [Peter], he put him in prison and delivered him to four squads of soldiers of four each to guard him, purposing after the Passover to bring him forth to the people. So Peter was kept in prison, but fervent prayer for him was persistently made to God by the church (assembly)."

The fervent, effectual prayer of the righteous avails much! (See James 5:16.) Fervent prayer gets the job done, *not* sleepy prayer. In Acts 12:6, we read: "The very night before Herod was about to bring him forth, Peter was sleeping between two soldiers, fastened with two chains, and sentries before the door were guarding the prison." Peter was in a bad situation, but prayer—*gate prayer*—was going up to God by people who had received the finished works of Christ.

In verse 7 we see the nearly instantaneous effect of those gate prayers: "And suddenly an angel of the Lord appeared [standing beside him]…" Why did the angel suddenly appear? It was because of fervent, persistent, effectual prayer! "…and a light shone in the place where he was." This was a manifestation of the third realm in a prison cell! Remember, the angels *descend* and *ascend* around God's throne in the third dimension. So when they come to earth, divine light and supernatural power come with them! The verse continues: "And the angel gently smote Peter on the side and awakened him, saying, Get up quickly! And the chains fell off his hands."

When God removes your chains, all you have to do is get up! Why? Prayer has already been offered up to God on your behalf. It's already finished; you just have to receive it and move forward. "And the angel said to him, Tighten your belt and bind on your sandals. And he did so. And he said to him, Wrap your outer garment around you and follow me. And [Peter] went out [along] following him, and he was not conscious that what was apparently being done by the angel was real, but thought he was seeing a vision" (vv. 8–9).

This is the kind of stuff God plans to do for us in prayer: spontaneous, miraculous things! When we follow God's pattern, we'll think we're seeing a vision or a dream when the answer comes. But what happened next confirmed to Peter that his experience was not a vision—it was the miraculous answer to the Christians' gate prayers.

> When they had passed through the first guard and the second, they came to the iron gate which leads into the city. Of its own accord [the gate] swung open, and they went out and passed on through one street; and at once the angel left him. Then Peter came to himself and said, Now I really know and am sure that the Lord has sent His angel and delivered me from the hand of Herod and from all that the Jewish people were expecting [to do to me]. When he, at a glance, became aware of this [comprehending all the elements of the case], he went to the house of Mary the mother of John, whose surname was Mark, where a large number were assembled together and were praying.
>
> —Acts 12:10–12

Peter passed through the third realm to receive what God had provided for him through prayer. Let's not forget the reason he had been thrown into prison—he had faithfully served the Lord, so he came under persecution (Acts 12:1). Peter and the others who were praying for him had embraced the four works of Christ, so the groundwork was set. God translated him through to the third dimension—the *gate*, the *door*, and the *veil*—and delivered him out of bondage.

Let's review. Jesus said, "I am the way...," and *the way* is the East Gate! Every other gate must come under subjection to THE GATE. By acknowledging the works of Christ, you are releasing supernatural power for the future. Then when the enemy comes against you, God will reveal *the way* of escape (1 Cor. 10:13). Remember, it's already there—Jesus made the way at the cross!

If you are trying to enter a job or start a business, go through the gate. If you need passageway into a city, or perhaps a loan from a bank...the gate, "the way," is already there! When you come through this gate, all others must open of their own accord. When you take that first step to enter prayer by way of Jesus Christ, then everything you need has already been made available to you. You just have to finish the pattern to see the end result.

Whether you are entering the righteousness of God for the first time or going deeper in prayer to the holy place, you must go through the door of Jesus Christ. "So Jesus said again, I assure you, most solemnly I tell you, that I myself am the Door for the sheep" (John 10:7). Even when you prepare to enter the most holy place—you must go through the veil of Christ's completed works in the four Gospels.

There's no shortcut to effective prayer. You must pass through three dimensions to operate at the level God desires for you to be in the Spirit. At each entry, the gate, the door, and the veil, you must travel the same path—*JESUS*. At every level of prayer and intercession, Jesus is the only "way" to true communion with God.

So now you're standing at the Beautiful Gate. In passing through it, you will demonstrate thankfulness to God for giving His Son, Jesus Christ—your Savior and Lord. Then you will begin to walk deeper into the outer court of prayer, believing Jesus each step of the way. He said, "I assure you, most solemnly I tell you, if anyone steadfastly believes in Me, he will himself be able to do the things that I do; and he will do even greater things than these, because I go to the Father" (John 14:12).

Doing what Jesus did involves pressing further into the things of God...going further into the court to the brazen laver, and then to the brazen altar of sacrifice. So take some time at this gate. Make sure you really know Jesus and understand exactly what He has done for you—because once you walk into the court, God is going to take you to victory.

CHAPTER 2

The Early Stages of Prayer:
The Outer Court

*G*OD NEVER STOPS moving; He is always in transition. So when you walk into the outer court of prayer, He demands that you keep moving forward. You have entered God's presence through the gate of Jesus Christ, yet He wants you to go deeper.

When the children of Israel left Egypt, their journey started in the wilderness. It was actually a place of blessing—until they stayed too long. This *blessed* place soon became the *place of curses*. This reveals our third step: following God's pattern of prayer.

Once you enter the gate through the works of Christ, there will be several levels of prayer through which you must move to reach the place of total surrender to God in prayer and intercession. The first stage of prayer within the gate is *outer court prayer*. There are many people who enter the courts of the Lord, embrace *religion*, and never go deeper into His presence. God wants to lead us through the outer court into the holy place, and then finally into the most holy place where we will experience His glory and bring it back into the earthly realm. We must obey Him at every step to keep making progress.

God gave the boundaries and instructions for the outer court in Exodus 27:9–18. The outer court corresponds to the initial conversion experience. It sets the groundwork for you in the Spirit realm and allows God to continue building on that foundation. Anyone who receives Jesus can come into the outer court. It is a place of washing and repentance—a place we enter with thanksgiving for what He has already done.

The outer court was lit by natural sunlight. You have been offered eternal light through the plan of salvation, but you haven't yet received eternal revelation. You are still under the influence of *natural* light. So even though you are saved, you are constantly being exposed to natural elements. If you remain in the outer court, fleshly opinions and earthly circumstances will hinder your pursuit of God. Over and over again, you will be forced to accept the ways and conversations of mortal men.

The people of Israel gathered in the outer court. They discussed their opinions about God and other things—and it kept them from getting closer to Him. When the Israelites "murmured," complaining to each other about what they thought God was doing, their murmurings delayed their progress. Circumstances and relationships worsened. Judgment followed. Outer court chatter will hinder your prayers! It's OK to enjoy your new spiritual family, but keep pressing toward God. Honor God, worship Him, and keep moving forward.

You are on a journey to the most holy place via the holy place, where only priests can enter. Every believer can walk into the outer court. Everyone can pray in the name of Jesus—but an intercessor must be *qualified* by God to pray effectually on behalf of others.

Outer court pray-ers are inconsistent. They pray *whenever*. They cry out to God in emergencies, when it looks like something terrible is going to devastate them. They also stay in a *praise mode*. They admire God, but they never come into relationship with Him. As a result, they can't receive the revelation of His heart or the burden of what He desires to accomplish in the earth.

Outer court pray-ers never get to the stage where they declare: "Thy kingdom come..." Instead, they say, "I'm saved." "I know who God is." And they never pass through the courts into intercession because they don't know God well enough to understand His heart and agonize for Him in prayer.

Outer court pray-ers are focused on washing, cleansing, and material things. They live to say, "Give me...," "I need...," because they are still

24

in their own infant state of being cleansed. They are still unsure of who they are in Christ, so these *natural* believers spend most of the time praying for themselves.

Coming through the gate of Christ is a wonderful blessing. Acknowledging God as your Provider, Peace, Righteousness, Banner of Protection, and so on is even better. However, when you stay in this mode—admiring, worshiping, and hallowing His name—you stay focused on *what you need* instead of upon *who you are in Christ*.

"Give me this, give me that" prayers keep you focused on material things—God wants to move you into the supernatural.

To pass through this stage and become an intercessor (which means becoming God's ambassador), you have to move deeper through the court to the brazen laver and the brazen altar. This is where you begin to lay down your life for God, letting go of anything that is not His will. This is where He begins to qualify you to serve in intercession.

YOU ARE NOT OF THIS WORLD

When a United States ambassador is assigned to serve in a remote, impoverished part of Africa, something peculiar happens. The community may be impoverished, but he probably drives a Mercedes Benz and lives in one of the most beautiful houses you have ever seen. Why?

The ambassador lives in Africa, but he's not a citizen of that country. He and his family are citizens of the United States. Our country is obligated to give him and his family the kind of lifestyle they would enjoy in America. This requirement is not merely put in place just for their comfort, but also so that others can look at their lifestyle and see a picture of America. What do people see when they look at your lifestyle? Are you a true ambassador for Christ?

God has prepared great things for those who love and seek after Him with all their heart. The outer court is just the beginning. We have to move through it to become His ambassadors! We must obtain the things of God that others lack because they live in the inferior, earthly realm. They have to see heaven through us! Our lifestyle—the way we carry ourselves and the way we live—must exemplify our heavenly citizenship. We can't get caught up in the outer court.

When you have been born again, you are no longer a citizen of this world. You must mature beyond earthly things to become an ambassador for God. Then you will be able to take help from heaven and distribute it to those who live in a place that is *remote* from His kingdom. This is true intercession: standing in the gap for someone else. If you are not doing this in your time with God, you haven't entered into intercessory prayer—which is receiving the things of God, standing in the gap of intercession, and passing His Word on to people who need to receive Him.

YOU CANNOT STAY IN NATURAL LIGHT

The outer court is a wonderful place, but it only stays that way when you are passing through. You must get beyond bloops, bleeps, and blunders and move on to maturity, which is found at the brazen laver and the brazen altar in the heart of the outer court. (Take a moment to refer back to the diagram on page 10.) Then you will be qualified to enter the supernatural realm of intercession in the holy place.

You aren't supposed to stay under the influence of natural light, praying only what you see in the natural. God wants you to pray by divine revelation, which comes only from Him in the most holy place! If you stay in the outer court, you will never find true intimacy with God. You will live in the *praise section*, along with everybody else who just met Him. And because you are *comfortable*, you won't stretch your faith to know God on a deeper level.

In the outer court stage of prayer you see people who are crippled, sick, and depressed in spite of your prayers for healing, deliverance, and peace. What's wrong? *You can't pray effectually in the outer court!* You must pass through to maturity by surrendering yourself to God—and then His power will begin to fuel your prayers! Hebrews 6:1 says:

> Therefore let us go on and get past the elementary stage in the teachings and doctrine of Christ (the Messiah), advancing steadily toward the completeness and perfection that belong to spiritual maturity. Let us not again be laying the foundation of repentance and abandonment of dead works (dead formalism) and of the faith [by which you turned] to God.

It is terrible to walk into the outer court, acknowledging God for all that He is, and then selfishly neglect to offer this same opportunity to others. God has a purpose for His pattern of prayer—to bring you into a living, intimate relationship with Him so that He can partner with you to help others. You can't stay in the outer court! You must move forward to the holy place.

We see a pattern for the outer court experience in James 5:16, which says: "Confess to one another therefore your faults (your slips, your false steps, your offenses, your sins) and pray [also] for one another, that you may be healed and restored [to a spiritual tone of mind and heart]." Confessing to "one another" reflects the outer court experience of washing and cleansing, which takes place at the brazen laver.

The verse goes on to say, "...and pray [also] for one another...." After you undergo the washing and cleansing process, you can make intercession for somebody else, which takes place after you have been to the brazen altar. As we intercede for others, we discover that "you may be healed and restored [to a spiritual tone of mind and heart]." Look at the dynamic promise in the final words of that verse: "The earnest (heartfelt, continued) prayer of a righteous man makes tremendous power available [dynamic in its working]." This promise is yours—*after* you have confessed, *after* you have repented, and *after* you have walked in righteousness! Then you possess tremendous power.

Welcome to real intercession!

In that nugget of truth from the Book of James, God again confirms His pattern: the *outer court* person who approaches the brazen laver to wash now becomes the intercessor who maintains the *holy place*, keeping the temple in order by taking care of the elements (menorah, table of shewbread, and so on). This person then enters the *most holy place* where tremendous power is available—*dynamic in its working*—as a fully matured, consecrated intercessor in the third realm of intercession.

Elijah knew how to tap into the third realm for divine revelation, intervention, strength, and power. He was just like you and me, yet he was able to consistently move beyond his flesh. James 5:17 tells us that, "Elijah was a human being with a nature such as we have [with feelings, affections, and a constitution like ours]; and he prayed earnestly for it not to rain, and no rain fell on the earth for three years and six months."

What power! A natural man was able to control the weather *because he prayed consistently.* What an amazing example of a true ambassador in prayer!

You might be thinking, *I've been saved from sin, but it still looks so glamorous to me. I just keep slipping back into it.* Hear me. As long as you keep slipping back and forth, you will never move on to maturity. You will never become an *effectual intercessor.*

Not only was Elijah able to stop the rain, but he also had power with God to restore it again. In verse 18 we read, "And [then] he prayed again and the heavens supplied rain and the land produced its crops [as usual]." God makes this same level of power available to anyone who prays effectually—not just to evangelists or other people with titles. *Anybody* who passes through the outer court into the holy place and the most holy place is going to get his or her prayers answered. This praying person, *even you,* can alter the course of nature. This person can change lives! God is not a respecter of persons. He will do the same thing with you that He did with Elijah—if you follow the pattern.

A GLIMPSE OF GLORY

Our ultimate destination—the highest level of prayer and intercession—is the most holy place. When God gave instructions for building the tabernacle to Moses, He had one purpose in mind: He was creating a place where His presence could actually come to earth to dwell with man! In Exodus 25 we can read the specific instructions God gave the Israelites—even specifying the material elements He would allow to be used to build His house (vv. 1–7). Why did He give specific orders? This is why: "Let them make Me a sanctuary, that I may dwell among them" (v. 8).

God constructs everything by way of a pattern. And although He gave explicit details for how the Israelites were to build the outer court and holy place for His tabernacle, He didn't declare that He would meet with them in either of those places. God didn't declare that He would speak to us on the *cleansing* and *maintenance* levels of prayer. He didn't say that He would give us divine instructions, speak intimately about His Word, or discuss His purpose in the first and second realms. The most holy place alone houses His presence. It is there that He meets with man and hears the intercessions of His chosen priests for His people.

God gave very specific instructions for construction of the ark of the covenant, which would be placed within the most holy place. You can read these instructions in verses 10 through 21 of Exodus 25. But the most important instruction He gave is contained in verse 22:

> There I will meet with you and, from above the mercy seat, from between the two cherubim that are upon the ark of the Testimony, I will speak intimately with you of all which I will give you in commandment to the Israelites.

That verse is vital to God's pattern of prayer. Though we pass through the processes of outer court prayer (cleansing) and holy place prayer (maintenance), as described earlier in this chapter—God has not declared that He will meet with us in either of those places! It is in the third realm of prayer, between the cherubim on the mercy seat, that God declared, "*There I will meet with you....*"

You can experience a "presence" of God simply because you are in the outer court, but that doesn't mean you have entered into intercession. For example, when you come to God in prayer because you have a problem, but you haven't committed yourself to Him—you can feel His presence and think that you have met with Him. But actually, you are only feeling the residue of His glory, which is coming from the most holy place.

In Old Testament days when the high priest offered up the "most holy perfume" to God on the altar of incense, that offering was aromatic. The scent went throughout the tent of meeting, and an essence escaped into the outer court. This is why, even today, people in the outer court smell the incense of the Lord and think they have received God's blessing. In reality, they have only picked up the *residue* of His presence!

If you want God to speak intimately with you, if you want to receive divine revelation and impartation from Him, *you have to go to the third dimension.* You have to press beyond the sweet aroma that is coming from the altar of incense to enter the most holy place—where He will meet with you in His glory. *No matter what anyone tells you in the outer court, you have to hear from God, from between the two cherubim on the mercy seat, for yourself.*

Though you are saved and in the outer court, God is calling you to a deeper level of prayer. Follow Him. Pass through every level, every piece of furniture in the tabernacle, to enter the third realm of intercession. This is the level of intimacy with God where *anyone* whom He has qualified can enter and change the course of this world. As the result of your intercessory prayer, God can and will do mighty things in your life and in the lives of others.

In this chapter we found ourselves in the outer court of prayer. From there we were able to get a glimpse of the glory of God that awaits us if we faithfully move through the outer court, into the holy place, and on into the very presence of God in the most holy place. But each of these stages of prayer requires a deeper understanding of God's pattern of prayer. We do not want to get stuck in the outer court, satisfied with just a glimpse, just an aroma of God's glorious presence. In the next chapter we are going to take a close look at the brazen laver and learn to move deeper in prayer through this experience of cleansing.

CHAPTER 3

The Place of Washing:
The Brazen Laver

*A*s YOU BEGIN to walk through the outer court, you will encounter the brazen laver stage of God's pattern of prayer. Let me review. You have passed through the gate that represents the four works of Jesus Christ: His righteousness, divinity, kingship, and ultimate sacrifice on the cross. These four works of Christ allow you to enter His "courts" in prayer through expressing praise and thankfulness to God for what He has already done. You have kept moving forward through the outer court, drawing ever nearer to God. Now you are about to come to the stage where you will become *a reflection of Christ.*

The brazen laver is the place of sanctification. It is where the Word of God cleanses and begins to prepare you to serve in your priestly function as an intercessor. The laver is the first piece of furniture in the tabernacle and the first part of God's nature that embraces your life. Exodus 30:17–21 (KJV) says:

> And the LORD spake unto Moses, saying, Thou shalt also make a laver of brass, to wash withal: and thou shalt put it between the tabernacle of the congregation and the altar, and thou shalt put water therein. For Aaron and his sons shall wash their hands and their feet thereat: when they go into the tabernacle of the congregation, they shall wash with water, that they die not; or when they

come near to the altar to minister, to burn offering made by fire unto the LORD: so shall they wash their hands and their feet, that they die not.

Every priest was required to *wash* before performing any ministry. This tells us that prayer is not supposed to stay on the personal level. By washing their hands and feet, the priests were demonstrating total devotion to God's service. So what does this have to do with you? You have come into the outer court by receiving a personal relationship with Jesus. But now God wants you to keep moving forward. He wants you to pass through the *personal level* of prayer (through washing at the laver) in order to prepare you to pray for others.

If you're thinking, *I'm not a priest,* think again. When you receive Christ, you do not merely become a part of God's family—you become a part of His royal priesthood. This new work of the priesthood begins within you at the brazen laver. First Peter 2:1–5 describes this cleansing process that moves us from simply being a family member to becoming a priest in God's pattern of prayer:

> So be done with every trace of wickedness (depravity, malignity) and all deceit and insincerity (pretense, hypocrisy) and grudges (envy, jealousy) and slander and evil speaking of every kind. Like new-born babies you should crave (thirst for, earnestly desire) the pure (unadulterated) spiritual milk, that by it you may be nurtured and grow unto [completed] salvation, since you have [already] tasted the goodness and kindness of the Lord. Come to Him [then, to that] Living Stone which men tried and threw away, but which is chosen [and] precious in God's sight. [Come] and, like living stones, be yourselves built [into] a spiritual house, for a holy (dedicated, con-secrated) priesthood, to offer up [those] spiritual sacrifices [that are] acceptable and pleasing to God through Jesus Christ.

You have already tasted the goodness of God (through salvation) at the gate. Now you must let Him build His character in you. This is how He prepares you to do His work. Unlike the fivefold ministry gifts in Ephesians 4:11 (apostle, prophet, evangelist, pastor, and teacher), prayer has been given to "all men." You don't have to function in the fivefold ministry to pray. You are a priest! It doesn't matter how old you are in Christ or what you do in the church—God has called *you* to pray every day. Luke 18:1 tells us that "men ought always to pray, and not to faint" (KJV).

Since prayer is not just a personal relationship with God, but also a ministry, before you can minister on any level—*to yourself, to someone else, or unto the Lord*—you must first wash at the laver. This cleansing prepares you to minister.

In the fifth chapter of Ephesians, Paul speaks to husbands and wives, but this passage also paints a picture of the cleansing every believer must undergo as the bride of Christ:

> Wives, be subject (be submissive and adapt yourselves) to your own husbands as [a service] to the Lord. For the husband is head of the wife as Christ is the Head of the church, Himself the Savior of [His] body. As the church is subject to Christ, so let wives also be subject in everything to their husbands. Husbands, love your wives, as Christ loved the church and gave Himself up for her, so that He might sanctify her, having cleansed her by the washing of water with the Word, that He might present the church to Himself in glorious splendor, without spot or wrinkle or any such things [that she might be holy and faultless].
>
> —EPHESIANS 5:22–27

In practical terms, this passage tells us that Jesus gave up His life to sanctify us "by the washing of water with the Word." As soon as you come into the outer court, Christ leads you straight to the brazen laver, because He has already given Himself up to make you righteous.

Washing in the Word helps you to strip off the "old (unregenerate) self," which is your flesh (Col. 3:9). Until we wash at the brazen laver, we live "according to the flesh and are controlled by its unholy desires" (Rom. 8:5). In the outer court, we are still setting our "minds on and *[pursuing]* those things which gratify the flesh" (v. 5). *This is why you must wash.* The verse continues by saying, "... those who are according to the Spirit and are controlled by the desires of the Spirit set their minds on and seek those things which gratify the [Holy] Spirit." If we live by the flesh, we will "surely die" (Rom. 8:13). But if we are cleansed at the brazen laver, "... through the power of the [Holy] Spirit you are [habitually] putting to death (making extinct, deadening) the [evil] deeds prompted by the body, you shall [really and genuinely] live forever" (v. 13).

Our sanctification at the brazen laver is the work of the Holy Spirit. "He is the Life-giver" (John 6:63). Even though you are a believer, unless you submit to the washing of the Spirit at the brazen laver, you will be controlled by your lower nature. God can't use a fleshly intercessor. When the priests performed daily sacrifices, they burned the animal skins (outer flesh) "outside the camp." (See Leviticus 8 and 9.) There's no room for your flesh in prayer! You must wash at the laver to get cleansed and prepared for the next level of consecration.

A PERFECT CONSTRUCTION

In general, the tabernacle furniture was constructed with wood (representing humanity), and then overlaid with either copper or gold. Some items were solid gold or copper. The brazen laver was made of solid copper (translated as "bronze" or "brass" in some Bible versions). (See Exodus 30:17–21.)

Copper symbolizes *God's judgment*—so it reminds us that He's the final judge of whether or not we are spiritually clean. When we wash at the laver, it should also remind us there's a final judgment for those who reject the Word (John 3:18; Rev. 20:11–15). *We must not reject the cleansing.* Jesus is the Word "made flesh" (John 1:14, KJV). Once you receive Him as Savior at the gate, you must submit to Him as Lord at the laver.

In John 5:22, we find that "the Father judges no one, for He has given all judgment (the last judgment and the whole business of judging) entirely into the hands of the Son." As Lord, Jesus is able to begin transforming you into the image of God. You can't do this for yourself. Only Jesus can. I believe this is why the laver had no recorded measurements and no wood in its construction. The Word of God is absolutely unlimited in its ability to wash and cleanse you!

Nothing is too deep within for the laver to reach, too far in your past to erase, or too distant in your future to control. Its cleansing power is unlimited, so you can become exactly who God has destined you to be in His kingdom. You can be "fitly cleansed and prepared" to become an effective intercessor.

A PERFECT REFLECTION

In Old Testament days, the mirrors that women used were made from bronze. The brazen laver was constructed from the mirrors of the Israelite women (Exod. 38:8). I think it's interesting and somewhat cute that women provided the mirrors, because the spirit of vanity is portrayed more in women than in men. It is almost as though God moved upon these women to surrender this vanity and, therefore, overcome it. To me, this also represents a surrendering of what *you think* you look like to the Lord. Do you really know what "manner of man" you are?

When a priest approached the brazen laver, he saw his reflection in the water and a second reflection in the basin. There could be no mistake about *how he looked*. When you go to the brazen laver in prayer, God shows you a true reflection of who you are. By coming to Him, you are able to see your *natural* reflection and get a glimpse of what you are becoming as He imparts the Word into your life. He's beginning the process of "completing" your salvation according to 1 Peter 2:1–5.

This is where you become conscious of *doing* the Word that God *imparts* to you from the basin—where you decide to start living for God and become a true reflection of Him. It's where you decide to rise up from your prayer closet and begin to live what you believe. James 1:22–25 says:

> But be doers of the Word [obey the message], and not merely listeners to it, betraying yourselves [into deception by reasoning contrary to the Truth]. For if anyone only listens to the Word without obeying it and being a doer of it, he is like a man who looks carefully at his [own] natural face in a mirror; for he thoughtfully observes himself, and then goes off and promptly forgets what he was like. But he who looks carefully into the faultless law *[the Word of God]*, the [law] of liberty, and is faithful to it and perseveres in looking into it, being not a heedless listener who forgets but an active doer [who obeys], he shall be blessed in his doing (his life of obedience).

In other words, by stopping to wash at the laver you are in the perfect position to do something about what you see. *The twofold power of the brazen laver is awesome.* The Word helps you to see yourself as you really are while it enables you to obey the revealed Word. You behold yourself through the water of the Word and, at the same time, are sanctified from sin and iniquity. Jesus said in John 15:3, "Now ye are clean through the word which I have spoken unto you" (KJV).

Many people hear the Word but fail to understand they need *to do* what it says. They hang around in the outer court and then wander over to the brazen laver to wash—because *everybody else is doing it.* They say, "This is just something I'm supposed to do." But when they can't endure the washing, they run away from the laver to a place where they feel more *comfortable.* (They think that God is *supposed* to answer their prayers, even though they constantly break His pattern.)

No matter how far you run, you can't escape the washing! If only you would wash at the laver, it would reveal the truth about who you really are by reflecting the Word into your heart. Then you would understand: it isn't that people are *supposed* to wash—we *need* to wash! We can't go deeper in God until we are sanctified at the brazen laver.

If you have accepted Christ yet haven't become a *doer* of His Word, then you are probably the type of person that has to see in the natural to believe. *You won't be able to see in the supernatural realm until you submit to the washing!* Only then will you be able to admit how much you need God's help. Remember, the sun always goes down in the outer court—so in order to see your way in the Spirit, you have to operate in the supernatural by obeying the Word.

Do you believe that you are called to be an intercessor? Then you must submit to the washing, or you will be ineffective in prayer. Let the laver expose the sin and deception in your own life, allowing them it to be washed away so that God can use you to make intercession for others.

A PERFECT COMMUNION

Jesus, our High Priest, has already walked through every stage of intercession. So when we wash at the laver in prayer, we come into communion with Him. We discover that our Father brings "many sons into glory" and brings "to maturity the human experience necessary to be perfectly equipped" (Heb. 2:10). At the brazen laver, the washing of the Word sanctifies us and prepares us for the work of an intercessor.

> For the Word that God speaks is alive and full of power [making it active, operative, energizing, and effective]; it is sharper than any two-edged sword, penetrating to the dividing line of the breath of life (soul) and [the immortal] spirit, and of joints and marrow [of the deepest parts of our nature], exposing and sifting and analyzing and judging the very thoughts and purposes of the heart. And not a creature exists that is concealed from His sight, but all things are open and exposed, naked and defenseless to the eyes of Him with Whom we have to do. Inasmuch then as we have a great High Priest Who has [already] ascended and passed through the heavens, Jesus the Son of God, let us hold fast our confession [of faith in Him].
>
> —HEBREWS 4:12–14

We are a royal priesthood, joint heirs with Christ, so we must move through every stage of prayer by way of His sacrifice. Like the bread and wine of Communion, Jesus' body was broken and His blood was shed to "perfect" (mature) our spiritual walk. So as often as we *do* our priestly duty of prayer in remembrance of Him, we demonstrate the works that He has already done (1 Cor. 11:26). At the gate we *acknowledge* His works. At the laver we begin to *demonstrate* them.

So "as often as we do" our priestly duty of prayer (every day), we share communion with Him. In doing so, we reaffirm our love, trust, and commitment to Him—and He transforms us into the image of God by the mighty power of His Word.

YOU CANNOT STAY AT THE LAVER

Though you wash at the brazen laver, you cannot remain there. You are still in the outer court level of praying, so the only person you will be able to pray for is *you*. Remember, outer court prayer focuses on *self: your* wrongdoings, *your* limitations and failures, what *you* need to overcome, and so on. At this stage, it's still all about YOU.

As a matter of fact, the priests could not stay at the laver for very long each day before they started performing their priestly duties. In other words, don't resist God when He deals with areas of your life at the laver! Let the Word do a quick work in you.

If you remain satisfied praying only for yourself, then you are not moving forward in God's pattern of prayer—and you are still operating on the elementary level. You aren't supposed to stay on this level! Get clean and pass through this realm into the deeper things of God in intercession.

The priests washed daily at the brazen laver, so you should wash in the Word every day. As a *royal* priest, washing is a requirement. You don't wash one day and then skip washing the next. Priests couldn't skip days in performing their duties! Once they became priests, it remained their lifestyle until they died. Do you see this? Once you have been adopted into the royal priesthood, you are supposed to remain there for the rest of your time on earth.

You can't afford to miss one day at the laver, because in doing so you cancel the pattern of God for His bride, the body of Christ—and you interfere with a vital principle God has set into place. Whether you realize it or not, you are actually trying to change the pattern of heaven, and that is ignoring the work of our Savior! Failing to wash causes you to bypass Jesus Christ in going to God the Father, when He said, "No man cometh unto the Father, but by Me" (John 14:6, KJV).

Always remember the pattern. Jesus said, "I am the way, the truth, and the life…." If you skip "the way," you definitely haven't arrived at "the truth," and you certainly haven't reached "the life."

We must pray correctly in order to get results, and washing at the laver is vital in this process. At every step in God's pattern of prayer—from the outer court to the holy place and into the most holy place…*the Word is there.* You can't have a successful, effective prayer life without the Word of God.

CHAPTER 4

The Place of Sacrifice:
The Brazen Altar

*O*NCE YOU HAVE washed at the brazen laver, it is time to be purified at the brazen altar. This is the second stage of our outer court step in God's pattern of prayer. The brazen altar is where you let go of your will and embrace everything the Lord wants to do in your life.

Infant prayer says, "Give me this; give me that." But the mature prayer of sacrifice says, "God, I surrender to *Your* will...I want whatever *You* want." This stage says *yes* to God.

Let's review. You have entered prayer through the gate of Jesus Christ with thanksgiving and praise for what He has done. You have drawn near to God by moving through every distraction in the outer court. You have submitted to the "washing of the Word" at the brazen laver, and now you know exactly what "manner of man" you are. The transformation has begun.

You have come through "the way" (the gate), but you are still in the outer court realm of personal prayer. You have reached the "truth" level for your personal life, but your prayer experience isn't fully matured; you still have to be broken before the Lord.

WHAT IS AN ALTAR?

The word *altar* in the Hebrew means "a slaughter place." (See Exodus 27:1.)[1] In the Greek, it's called "a place of sacrifice."[2] The brazen altar is the place where *natural*, earthly things that hinder your walk with God are consumed by the fire of God. It's the place where you become a "living sacrifice." The apostle Paul defined this process of becoming a living sacrifice in Romans 12:1–3:

> I appeal to you therefore, brethren, and beg of you in view of [all] the mercies of God, to make a decisive dedication of your bodies [presenting all your members and faculties] as a living sacrifice, holy (devoted, consecrated) and well pleasing to God, which is your reasonable (rational, intelligent) service and spiritual worship. Do not be conformed to this world (this age), [fashioned after and adapted to its external, superficial customs], but be transformed (changed) by the [entire] renewal of your mind [by its new ideals and its new attitude], so that you may prove [for yourselves] what is the good and acceptable and perfect will of God, even the thing which is good and acceptable and perfect [in His sight for you]. For by the grace (unmerited favor of God) given to me I warn everyone among you not to estimate and think of himself more highly than he ought [not to have an exaggerated opinion of his own importance], but to rate his ability with sober judgment, each according to the degree of faith apportioned by God to him.

You are a priest unto God, a member of the royal priesthood of Christ. Therefore, you must wash and undergo the fire of consecration to qualify you for ministry. This is where you prove the new ideals and attitude you received at the brazen laver by laying down your life to embrace God's perfect will. Everything within you that does not line up with God's perfect will comes to an end at the brazen altar. They are set on fire and consumed in the Spirit.

What do I mean by *set on fire and consumed in the Spirit?* What does it mean to be offered up on the brazen altar as a sacrifice that has been set on fire? This terminology describes what it would feel like after you become committed to a life of prayer, when the Lord allows you to be confronted with certain situations that will become the very trying of your faith. You must always remember that once you confess and declare that you believe the works of Christ and what He has done in your life, then every work of the Lord in your life shall be tried by fire, as 1 Corinthians 3:13–15 says. Some works are made of straw, and other works are made of wood, but only that which endures the fire will qualify to be used of God.

For example, gold jewelry is forged by being placed in the fire. The goldsmith's purpose for doing this is to draw the impurities and black tar particles to the surface. Then he pulls the gold out of the fire, scrapes off the impurities and foreign particles, and puts it back into the fire. He does this repeatedly until he's gotten to the deepest interior of that lump of gold. During this process, everything that would cause this piece of jewelry not to shine, not to be declared as costly pure gold, is burned out so that the value of the gold increases.

God is doing this same purifying work in our lives. When we allow God to put us "in the fire" (in fiery situations), we are cooperating with everything He is doing in us. We are releasing every impurity that would hinder us from becoming a most valuable resource to Him and to His work. When these impurities are burned out of us, nothing in prayer can be hindered—because the forging process strengthens us to carry weight in the Spirit. This makes us valuable instruments in His hands, not shallow believers, but those who have been proven to be *the real deal*. When we come through this process, we are authentic intercessors. We are authentic prayer warriors.

A SOUND CONSTRUCTION

God gave Moses very specific instructions for the construction of the altar in Exodus 27:1–8. The altar was to be "five cubits square and three cubits high [within reach of all]" (v. 1). *Five* is the number of *grace*, and *three* represents the *Godhead*: Father, Son, and Holy Spirit. When you go to the brazen altar, you are submitting to (proving) the work of the Godhead—and you will be transformed through His Word! Though you come to the brazen altar strictly on God's terms, you will never be alone. Jesus has already perfected the fire, meaning He has already tempered the flame to facilitate each and every person that will enter. No two people go through the same trial. No one goes through the same fire. God tempers the flame so that it only burns up what He cannot use. It will not consume the part of you that He desires to use.

So this is not a destructive flame; it is a constructive one. Though this fire gets rid of the bad elements, it allows "that which remains" and "that which is good" to be formed and shaped until it adheres completely to His image. God will be with you, just as He was with Shadrach, Meshach, and Abednego when they were thrown into the fiery furnace. (Read Daniel 3:24–25.)

God gave specific measurements for the altar. "Make horns for it on its four corners; they shall be of one piece with it, and you shall overlay it with bronze. You shall make pots to take away its ashes, and shovels, basins, forks, and firepans; make all its utensils of bronze. Also make for it a grate, a network of bronze; and on the net you shall make four bronze rings at its four corners. And you shall put it under the ledge of the altar, so that the net will extend halfway down the altar. And make poles for the altar, poles of acacia wood overlaid with bronze. The poles shall be put through the rings on the two sides of the altar, with which to carry it. You shall make [the altar] hollow with slabs or planks; as shown you on the mountain, so shall it be made" (Exod. 27:2–8).

The brazen altar was formed out of wood and then overlaid in copper (translated as brass or bronze in some Bible versions). *Wood* represents *humanity*, and whenever humanity is involved, there are limitations. *Copper* symbolizes *judgment*, so the brazen altar is where God atoned for the limitations of man through the shedding of blood. In ancient Israel, priests sacrificed animals at this altar. Later, Jesus became the final sacrificial Lamb:

> But He was wounded for our transgressions, He was bruised for our guilt and iniquities; the chastisement [needful to obtain] peace and well-being for us was upon Him, and with the stripes [that wounded] Him we are healed and made whole. All we like sheep have gone astray, we have turned every one to his own way; and the Lord has made to light upon Him the guilt and iniquity of us all. He was oppressed, [yet when] He was afflicted, He was submissive and opened not His mouth; like a lamb that is led to the slaughter, and as a sheep before her shearers is dumb, so He opened not His mouth.
>
> —ISAIAH 53:5–7

Jesus was placed upon the wood of sacrifice. He went under the fire, died on the cross—*and He didn't open His mouth* (Rev. 13:8). This gives us hope! As you approach the altar of sacrifice, your ability to hold fast to your confession will be tested. But if Christ patiently endured, so can you. Many fail this test and are snared by their own words (Matt. 12:37). When you become a living sacrifice, you have to learn how to be silent before God and others. In 1 Peter 2, we are admonished to "bear patiently with suffering [which results] when you do right and that is undeserved," because "it is acceptable and pleasing to God" (v. 20). It is Christ's example that shows us how to do this, for "Christ also suffered for you, leaving you [His personal] example, so that you should follow in His footsteps" (v. 21).

When Jesus died, one of the Roman soldiers who crucified Him "pierced His side with a spear, and immediately blood and water came (flowed) out" (John 19:34). This not only confirmed Jesus as the Messiah, but I believe it also foretold of the brazen laver's (*water*) and the brazen altar's (*blood*) power in prayer. When you die to the flesh in prayer, the laver and altar enable you to rise up in the Spirit and walk into the holy place.

God is saying, "You must daily put yourself on the brazen altar in prayer, because if you don't put your flesh on the altar and offer yourself up as a sacrifice, then you will be limited in what you can do for Me." What is your *flesh?* Everything you think and feel except that which is a result of the will of God and His Word within you.

Sacrifice always comes before service. Many people are serving God in the sanctuary—preaching, praying, prophesying, and laying on hands— but they haven't been to the brazen altar! They haven't stopped at the place of sacrifice and given everything to God... *they are still controlled by their own will.*

In the Garden of Gethsemane, Jesus prayed until "His sweat became like great clots of blood dropping down upon the ground" (Luke 22:44). He laid down His will and said, "Father, if You are willing, remove this cup from Me; yet not My will, but [always] Yours be done" (v. 42). At this moment in the realm of the Spirit, Jesus had made it to the brazen altar. He lay before God and said, "In My flesh, I don't want to do this. I can't do this... nevertheless... I want what You want. Yes, Father! I'm not going to let the limitations of My flesh keep Me from the supernatural operation of My spirit."

Before you can operate in the Spirit realm, in prayer or otherwise, you must stop at the brazen altar, saying, "God, whatever it is, I lay it down." Jesus is already there, with amazing grace to bring you through the fire.

> For we do not have a High Priest Who is unable to understand and sympathize and have a shared feeling with our weaknesses and infirmities and liability to the assaults of temptation, but One Who has been tempted in every respect as we are, yet without sinning.
> —HEBREWS 4:15

Too often, we pray for others from the outer court. Let me give you clarity again from the Holy Spirit—if you haven't gone into the holy place and the most holy place, the only person you can pray for is YOU. You haven't entered into the realm of intercession! You are still in the mode of self-sacrifice.

When you pray for a loved one from the outer court (and you want a certain answer from God), it's easy to pray without stopping by the brazen altar. You try to enter the throne room of God, telling Him what to do, when, instead, you should be saying, "Lord, let Thy will be done." Allow me to say this: if you pray this way, you are not praying according to God's will!

Let's say you pray something like, "God, do something with my son . . . he's on my last nerve. If You're not going to save him, just kill him; just do whatever You have to do." *What kind of prayer is that?* God hasn't told you to pray for people "by any means necessary." So when your son has an accident and loses an eye . . . *you* have to lead him around! And you can't complain because YOU prayed for it to happen!

Let go of your will. Put yourself on the brazen altar, and God will lead you to the second and third realms in prayer. You won't carry your thoughts, ways, and ideas to His throne—you will receive divine knowledge and revelation from Him as to how you should pray. This is why you must go beyond outer court prayer.

AN EQUAL SACRIFICE

The brazen altar was three cubits high, which symbolized the Godhead. It also matched the height of the ark of the covenant, which rests behind the veil in the most holy place. The base of the ark was two and one-half cubits, but it extended to three cubits when they mounted the cherubim on top of the cover. Take another look at the diagram of Moses' tabernacle on page 10; it will help you to see what I am describing here.

I believe this indicates that the glory of God will be equal to the sacrifice you make on the brazen altar. If there's no communion with God at the altar, you won't have a match or connection in the most holy place. To be effective in prayer, your sacrifice must measure up to the level of glory you want to experience with God in intercession. The apostle Paul talked about this balance of sacrifice and glory in Romans 5, when he said, "So that, [just] as sin has reigned in death, [so] grace (His unearned and undeserved favor) might reign also through righteousness (right standing with God) which issues in eternal life through Jesus Christ (the Messiah, the Anointed One) our Lord" (v. 21).

He goes on in chapter 6 to define the balance of sacrifice and glory even more, saying that God's favor and mercy cannot multiply and overflow in our lives if we remain in sin (vv. 1–2). In verses 4 and 5 we see a balance clearly expressed: "We were buried therefore with Him by the baptism into death *[at the brazen altar of prayer]*, so that just as Christ was raised from the dead by the glorious [power] of the Father, so we too might [habitually] live and behave in newness of life *[before the ark of the covenant]*. For if we have become one with Him by sharing a death like His, we shall also be [one with Him in sharing] His resurrection [by a new life lived for God]."

Too many believers want great power with little or no sacrifice. We don't want to give up everything on the brazen altar! We don't want to die or submit to anything! And we don't want to give up living in sin. But we want to experience everything in the third dimension of prayer (in the most holy place). We will never get it! Why? When we ignore the works of Christ, we disregard the pattern of God.

The danger comes when you think you are operating in the light of God, but in reality you are still functioning in *natural* light (because you are still in the outer court). In the outer court, in natural light, daylight ends, and night comes. That means sometimes you are able to see your way, and sometimes you can't. Sometimes you can see the victory, and sometimes you can't.

This is why sometimes you can shout, "I'm on my way; I can make it." Then at other times, you can't see your way out of a hat. *You are trying to dwell in the outer court.* You have to wait until the sun comes up again, until your natural senses kick in. For example, you wait *to receive* your paycheck in order *to see* that your bills are paid. When you are dwelling in the outer court, you will always have to wait for *earthly* proof before you can believe you have the victory.

In the third realm, the light is *supernatural.* It always shines, because it comes from the Shekinah glory of God. We always have victory in the third dimension of prayer! How do I know this? How can *we* know this is the pattern of God? We see a demonstration of the Shekinah glory of God at the first consecration service for the temple (Lev. 9:23–24). When Moses and Aaron came out of the tabernacle after meeting with God in the most holy place, "the glory of the Lord [the Shekinah cloud] appeared to all the people [as promised]. Then there came a fire out from before the Lord and consumed the burnt offering and the fat on the altar; and when all the people saw it, they shouted and fell on their faces."

Yes, the original flame that lit the brazen altar came directly from heaven! *The Chumash* states that the fire "went into the Holy of Holies and from there it went out to the Golden Altar and then to the Outer Altar, causing the incense and the sacrificial parts to go up in smoke."[3]

Do you see the pattern? In his first consecration service for Israel, Aaron performed the sacrifices according to the pattern God revealed to Moses (Lev. 1–8). He followed God's pattern, and the glory of God was revealed to all the people. *God consumed the sacrifice and atoned for Israel's sins.* After this "day of obedience," the priests were instructed that the "fire upon the altar shall be kept burning on it; it shall not be allowed to go out" (Lev. 6:12). Each morning they were to burn wood on it and make a sacrifice.

From that day forward, wood, which represents humanity, kept the fire burning. In other words, God requires us to lay ourselves on the brazen altar every day and say, "Whatever doesn't please You, Lord, burn it up. Consume my will, desires, emotions—anything that doesn't line up with Your will." We are the wood that keeps God's fire burning on the altar . . . *continuously,* so that the fire from the brazen altar can also extend to our golden altar (altar of incense). We'll learn more about the golden altar in chapters ten and eleven.

THE HORNS OF HELP

Even still, God doesn't expect you to sacrifice without His help. He provided for you by putting four horns on the corners of the brazen altar—which represent *salvation, strength,* and *power!* So when you lay on the altar of sacrifice, you receive salvation, strength, and power from Him to do His will. You become resilient in prayer and strong in intercession. Why? Your flesh is being consumed in the fire of God, so it can't hinder your prayers.

When you go into the holy place, you will be fully matured in prayer. You will be able to make effective intercession for someone else because you won't be in doubt about your own walk. The battle is over once you receive God's will on the brazen altar, because it is there you will receive salvation, strength, and power. Luke 1:68–69 says:

> Blessed (praised and extolled and thanked) be the Lord, the God of Israel, because He has come and brought deliverance and redemption to His people! And He has raised up a Horn of salvation [a mighty and valiant Helper, the Author of salvation] for us in the house of David His servant . . .

God has raised up the "Horn of salvation" as a mighty and valiant Helper! This reveals the missing ingredient in many of our prayers, and also why many of our prayers are not answered. Salvation is one of the horns on the brazen altar! When the fire of purification is consuming your flesh (meaning when you are being challenged to walk in right standing with God in the midst of temptation), you must remember your salvation. You must go back to the four completed works of Christ and learn to praise Him in the fire. Salvation helps you while you pray.

Why do so many of us try to make intercession without any help from

God? How do we walk past our Helper, slip under the white linen curtain on the side of the court, and sneak into the tabernacle thinking we are going to receive something from Him? *We are praying without help!* How do we think we can get in the door and beyond the veil without the blood sacrifice?

You can't pray effectively when you ignore the works of Christ! The process of *completing* your salvation and maturing in prayer is sealed by Christ's finished work—*the Lamb who was slain before the foundation of the world*—on the brazen altar. Jesus' blood gives you salvation, strength, and power to live and pray according to the will of God.

This also ties in to the four horns on the altar. The number *four* represents *the earth and its elements*—the four winds and the four corners of the earth. So Christ's power to help you in prayer is unlimited! It extends to all four corners of the earth. (There are also four horns on the golden altar in the holy place, which helps us to understand that this kind of help follows us from one level in God to the next.)

Jesus completed the pattern of prayer to be our help in time of need. His sacrifice was great and can't be ignored—we must embrace it. We must willingly go into the purifying fire of God with faith that Christ will help us. Romans 11:22 admonishes us to "note and appreciate the gracious kindness and the severity of God: severity toward those who have fallen, but God's gracious kindness to you—provided you continue in His grace and abide in His kindness; otherwise you too will be cut off (pruned away)."

The judgment of God will begin "with the household of God . . . it begins with us" (1 Pet. 4:17). Peter asks the question, "What will [be] the end of those who do not respect or believe or obey the good news (the Gospel) of God? And if the righteous are barely saved, what will become of the godless and wicked?" (vv. 17–18). It is so important that we recognize our need to "work out" our own salvation at the brazen altar, fearing God and honoring Christ's sacrifice.

> Therefore [because He stooped so low] God has highly exalted Him and has freely bestowed on Him the name that is above every name, that in (at) the name of Jesus every knee should (must) bow, in heaven and on earth and under the earth, and every tongue

[frankly and openly] confess and acknowledge that Jesus Christ is Lord, to the glory of God the Father. Therefore, my dear ones, as you have always obeyed [my suggestions], so now, not only [with the enthusiasm you would show] in my presence but much more because I am absent, work out (cultivate, carry out to the goal, and fully complete) your own salvation with reverence and awe and trembling (self-distrust, with serious caution, tenderness of conscience, watchfulness against temptation, timidly shrinking from whatever might offend God and discredit the name of Christ). [Not in your own strength] for it is God Who is all the while effectually at work in you [energizing and creating in you the power and desire], both to will and to work for His good pleasure and satisfaction and delight.

—PHILIPPIANS 2:9–13

Are you seeing the revelation? Only in Jesus' name—our salvation—can we lie on the altar and complete the process of purification! Trusting Him in the fire strengthens our faith to do His works and enables us to pray for others. Then when we make intercession, and God answers our prayers, we won't become proud and forget the name that put the horns of salvation, strength, and power on the altar of sacrifice. Like Paul, we must assert: "For I am not ashamed of the Gospel (good news) of Christ, for it is God's power working unto salvation [for deliverance from eternal death] to everyone who believes with a personal trust and a confident surrender and firm reliance, to the Jew first and also to the Greek. For in the Gospel a righteousness which God ascribes is revealed, both springing from faith and leading to faith [disclosed through the way of faith that arouses to more faith]" (Rom. 1:16–17).

Unless we have worked out our own salvation through faith in Christ on the altar, we will not have the faith to pray for others. It is the man and woman whose faith has made them just and upright who are able also to live by faith (Rom. 1:17).

Let's review... you come through the gate (of the four works of Christ) at salvation, and you receive faith to consistently *do* His will at the brazen altar. Faith in God comes supernaturally when you lay down your life and grab hold of the horns. You lay down your will and receive completed salvation; you receive help that gives you faith to become a "living sacrifice." This Helper is going to be with you at every level of prayer and intercession.

Salvation defeats the enemy! In the Book of Joshua, chapter 6, the children of Israel marched around the walls of Jericho and blew a trumpet in obedience to God's command. (In those days, a ram's horn was used, which represented *salvation*.) When the Israelites heard the trumpet, they "raised a great shout"...and the walls fell to the ground (v. 20). The people heard their Helper, and they could see the enemy falling. *Need I say more?*

When God told Abraham to sacrifice his only son, Isaac, Abraham had to break tradition, go against his own will, and sacrifice on an altar he had built himself (Gen. 22:2, 9). Abraham had to walk out the pattern of God—which God later repeated by sacrificing His only Son, Jesus Christ—in order to cut the New Covenant and complete the pattern once and for all (John 3:16). Abraham saw a ram caught in a thicket and offered the ram for a burnt offering instead of his son. He received his helper *only after he had put his son on the altar.* By obeying God, Abraham completed his call to become the "father of many nations" (Gen. 17:4).

In another example, King David had grown old, and it was time for him to pass his throne on to one of his sons. His son Adonijah had determined that he should be the next king and had, in fact, grabbed the throne and was reigning without David's knowledge. However, God had already promised the throne to Solomon. When David was told of Adonijah's actions by Bathsheba and Solomon, he rose from his bed and said he would choose the next king that day. (See 1 Kings 1:28–40.) When Adonijah heard that David now knew of his deceit and intended to name his successor, he greatly feared. He knew his father had placed Solomon on the throne that very day, and Adonijah feared for his life because of his deceit.

In fear, he fled to the tabernacle where he grabbed the horns of the altar and cried out, "Let King Solomon swear to me first that he will not slay his servant with the sword" (v. 51). When Solomon heard of his actions, he told his servants: "If he will show himself to be a worthy man, not a hair on him shall fall to the ground; but if wickedness is found in him, he shall die" (v. 52). When Adonijah was brought before Solomon, the king did not harm him, but told him to go to his house (v. 53).

Why was Adonijah saved? It was because he grabbed hold of the horns of the altar—his help! When Adonijah feared for his life, he grabbed the horns…he threw himself on the altar of sacrifice.

God lit the fire on the brazen altar, and this same fire was used to light the golden candlestick and to keep the altar of incense burning in the holy place! In other words, the *fires of intercession* will reflect your level of sacrifice on the brazen altar. Your submitted life keeps the fire burning. If you don't keep yourself on the altar like fresh wood that is laid upon it daily, the fire will go out. If this happens, you won't have any *illumination* of God's Word in the hard place as well as in the holy place.

You cannot make effective intercession without the illumination of sacrifice. It determines the depth and weight of your worship, as well as your spiritual insight. Now let me ask, what are you willing to put on the brazen altar and give up to God?

BEWARE OF STRANGE FIRE

Only the fire of God is worthy to be used in His tabernacle—in His pattern for prayer. There is no place for strange fire to be brought in from another source. The sons of Aaron, Nadab and Abihu, lost their lives because they attempted to offer unholy fire before the Lord. Leviticus 10:2–3 says, "And there came forth fire from before the Lord and killed them, and they died before the Lord. Then Moses said to Aaron, This is what the Lord meant when He said, I [and My will, not their own] will be acknowledged as hallowed by those who come near Me, and before all the people I will be honored. And Aaron said nothing."

Strange fire taints the work of the sanctuary even today. We have *images* of worship, praise, altars, sanctification, and holiness, but we are denying the power thereof (2 Tim. 3:5). Like Aaron's sons, we are ignoring the pattern to enter God's presence. This explains why many in the church are operating in *strange fire* and struggling in their walk with God.

I believe this is why we hear so much *strange worship*—songs that identify with the world and carnal worship. People have not sanctified their will on the altar. Like Nadab and Abihu, they have taken their own censers (their own lives), put their own mixture of incense inside, and lit it up. They have created their own personal mixture, which they call *true worship*. All the while, God is saying, "I didn't light that fire. That's not the fire from the altar of sacrifice."

If you don't sacrifice at the altar before you minister, you are lighting a *strange* fire. Understand this: before God sent fire from heaven to light the fire in the brazen altar, Moses and Aaron had already lit it when they consecrated the tabernacle. They knew no other way to light it, and their actions were *acceptable* to God at that point. However, once the real fire came from God, man-made fire was no longer acceptable. (See Leviticus 9.) God had replaced it with His own supernatural fire.

Could this be why we don't pray with fervor? Is this why our prayers aren't "effectual"? Could this be the reason our prayers aren't "availing" much?

Strange fires can be seen everywhere in Christendom today. They have been lit by people who remain enslaved to their flesh while trying to serve the Lord. Unless you have sacrificed everything at the altar, you are trying to do exactly what you want to do, and you are living from your emotions—*and that's lighting your own fire.* Galatians 5:17 says:

> For the desires of the flesh are opposed to the [Holy] Spirit, and [desires of the] Spirit are opposed to the flesh (godless human nature).

If you don't lay every area of your will on the brazen altar, you will find yourself inside the holy place, where you will be fighting against God with your flesh instead of making intercession. God will tell you, "Turn left."

You will say, "Well, I feel led in my spirit to go right."

God will say, "I want you to stay right here and pray some more for this particular sister."

You will say, "Well, I feel kind of thirsty..."

Then He will respond, "No, I do not want you to drink yet, I want you to keep praying..."

And you will interrupt and say, "But God, I just want to get some juice..."

You didn't put your will on the brazen altar, so you go into prayer fighting against what God tells you to do! Then you get up and speak in tongues all the way to the refrigerator… *What!* You are walking in disobedience and rebellion.

To become a true intercessor, your will must be consumed on the brazen altar—because when you get inside the holy place, there will be room for only ONE WILL. This is why many are stuck at "Your will be done…" (Matt. 6:10). We are still warring against the will of God!

The apostle Paul knew this would happen, and he clearly described what would be the result:

> For these are antagonistic to each other [continually withstanding and in conflict with each other], so that you are not free but are prevented from doing what you desire to do. But if you are guided (led) by the [Holy] Spirit, you are not subject to the Law. Now the doings (practices) of the flesh are clear (obvious): they are immorality, impurity, indecency, idolatry, sorcery, enmity, strife, jealousy, anger (ill temper), selfishness, divisions (dissensions), party spirit (factions, sects with peculiar opinions, heresies), envy, drunkenness, carousing, and the like. I warn you beforehand, just as I did previously, that those who do such things shall not inherit the kingdom of God.
>
> —GALATIANS 5:17–21

Once after preaching in Bermuda, I decided to stay for a week of vacation. When my mother was getting ready to return home to the States, she said, "I'm going back to the States; don't you all get on those mopeds." Even after she had gone outside to get in a taxi, she came back in to where we were, looked straight at me, and said, "Nita, especially you."

She knew that I was a daredevil and might disobey her advice. So, *what did I do?* I hopped right on a moped, even though she had said not to do it. I rationalized to myself, *She's full of fear. I'm going to ride a moped. I'm going to find one on the beach right now.*

Needless to say, I had an accident and had to be rushed to the hospital for stitches. When I arrived at the emergency room, many of the people waiting to be helped recognized me from the meetings where I had preached during the past seven or eight days. They were saying, "There goes the prophetess; they need to help the prophetess." Everybody with me kept saying, "She needs to see a doctor."

The admitting nurse was sitting at her desk with her head down, writing. Everybody kept saying, "She needs to see a doctor." I was bleeding profusely. Then she lifted her head and calmly said, "What's your name?"

I was delirious…crying…and everybody else was upset. People behind us were saying, "She needs to see a doctor; she's bleeding!" Unaffected, the nurse repeated, "What's your name?"

I said, "Juanita."

"Last name?"

I replied, "Bynum."

Then she said, "Oh, you're the evangelist."

"Yes."

"What's your address?"

I was bleeding and blood was dripping on the floor, but that woman didn't care who I was. It was as though she were saying, "Before a doctor can see you, you have to go through admitting. I don't care about your title. At this point, I must follow the procedure before you can see a doctor."

Church, it's the same for all of us with God. We have to go through "admitting" before we minister in intercession! Get before the brazen altar and admit your sins to God! "I'm a liar, a thief…I'm jealous, envious, indecent…I don't do things right…I don't have integrity…" God can't help you until you go through admitting!

The first question you are asked in admitting is, "What's your name?" Can you say it? "Jealousy, envy, strife, confusion…" What's your name?

Don't reach for a sedative. Don't even think about taking a painkiller. The brazen altar is a death process, not surgery. God is putting you in the fire and burning up that sin! He's getting rid of that "strange fire" and replacing it with the fire of purification!

You may be thinking, *I don't understand why I go through so much.* Didn't you say that God called you to be an intercessor? All intercessors have to be purified in the fire *before* they can carry the fire. You have to know the power of the fire you carry! You can't carry the fire to save someone else's life, asking God to break the power of the enemy off of that person—until He has been able to get the sin out of you!

Are you going through the fire? Good! That means you are on schedule. Every time you get comfortable and shout, "Hallelujah," *BAM…*

something else hits. Every time you say, "I have the victory!" *BAM*, something else comes against you, somebody else gets on your nerves, and something else goes wrong. Why? God doesn't want you to think that you have arrived! In fact, in 1 Corinthians 10:12, Paul says, "Let anyone who thinks he stands [who feels sure that he has a steadfast mind and is standing firm], take heed lest he fall [into sin]."

But in the next verse, verse 13, we are given a promise for overcoming the temptations that every person will face:

> For no temptation (no trial regarded as enticing to sin, no matter how it comes or where it leads) has overtaken you and laid hold on you that is not common to man [that is, no temptation or trial has come to you that is beyond human resistance and that is not adjusted and adapted and belonging to human experience, and such as man can bear]. But God is faithful [to His Word and to His compassionate nature], and He [can be trusted] not to let you be tempted and tried and assayed beyond your ability and strength of resistance and power to endure, but with the temptation He will [always] also provide the way out (the means of escape to a landing place), that you may be capable and strong and powerful to bear up under it patiently.

Look in the mirror, wash, and then let God put you back in the fire of purification. Grab hold of the horns of the altar, where you will receive salvation, strength, and power! The apostle Paul learned to do that. He understood the purpose of temptation and knew the power of God to help him overcome. "And to keep me from being puffed up and too much elated by the exceeding greatness (preeminence) of these revelations, there was given me a thorn (a splinter) in the flesh, a messenger of Satan, to rack and buffet and harass me, to keep me from being excessively exalted. Three times I called upon the Lord and besought [Him] about this and begged that it might depart from me; but He said to me, My grace (My favor and loving-kindness and mercy) is enough for you [sufficient against any danger and enables you to bear the trouble manfully]; for My strength and power are made perfect (fulfilled and completed) and show themselves most effective in [your] weakness" (2 Cor. 12:7–9).

Knowing God's purpose and power enabled him to declare: "Therefore, I will all the more gladly glory in my weaknesses and infirmities, that the strength and power of Christ (the Messiah) may rest (yes, may pitch a tent over and dwell) upon me! So for the sake of Christ, I am well pleased and take pleasure in infirmities, insults, hardships, persecutions, perplexities and distresses; for when I am weak [in human strength], then am I [truly] strong (able, powerful in divine strength)" (vv. 9–10).

In Leviticus 9:24, when God's fire lit the altar, people fell on their faces in worship. When His fire begins to hit sanctuaries in this final hour, it will send people to the ground—and to the altar. I believe a day is coming when no one will have to make an altar call.

Not one of us has *made it*, no matter who we are or how long we have been saved. Yet God's grace (as symbolized by the number five, the width of the altar) and His will (as represented by the number three, the Godhead, the height of the altar) will carry us to the other side of sacrifice. Stay on the brazen altar until *God* takes you off it. Then you will be prepared to move to the next level of prayer in His strength and power. Beware—you will be returned to the brazen altar daily.

A Final Warning

You have been saved at the gate and washed at the brazen laver, and you have given up your will to God at the brazen altar. If you jump off the altar too soon, you will be in danger. There is a procedure I would like to show you concerning the tabernacle service. You must wait for the natural sunlight to go down in the outer court, because your sacrifices are supposed to burn on the altar until morning (Lev. 6:9), indicating that He burns not only the things that can be seen, but also the things in the dark, hidden places. Don't jump off the altar while your sins and limitations are still being consumed!

While the natural light is still shining, you can sense that you are in communion with God because He has allowed the sun to shine. That can cause you to think that you have been purified. You may even be able to see how to get to the door of the holy place. But once the sun goes down, all you will be able to see is the consuming fire from the altar. Don't rush this process.

God commanded the priests to keep the fire burning on the brazen altar. If you jump off too soon, not only could you fall back into sin, but also the fire could go out. You must wait on God's perfect timing to rise from the altar and head toward the holy place.

You must complete the work of the outer court and keep moving to the next level in prayer. If you fall, get up and start again. Do whatever is necessary to follow the pattern of the Lord. Keep moving, because the Bible says that when we fall, we have to do our "first works" over again (Rev. 2:5, KJV). Jesus told us to work "while it is day: the night cometh, when no man can work" (John 9:4, KJV).

You can't move forward when you are in spiritual darkness—you can't see where you are going! So stay on the brazen altar *until God takes you off.* Then you can move on to the holy place, where the fires of your "completed" salvation bring supernatural illumination in prayer.

CHAPTER 5

The Foundational Garment:
The Tunic of Righteousness

*W*HEN GOD GAVE instructions to Moses for the building of the tabernacle, He also gave very specific directions for the garments that Aaron and his sons were to wear as they performed their duties as priests in the tabernacle. So in this chapter, we will also see that God used the priestly garments to demonstrate that He never contradicts Himself. How so? Because each priestly garment harmonized with the materials and colors that God instructed Moses to use in the holy place and in the East Gate.

The same colors and materials that were used to construct the tabernacle were also required clothing for the priests. What does this mean to us today? Whatever we are experiencing in prayer ought to be a portrayal of our everyday lifestyle. Like the tabernacle, these garments represented a spirit of excellence that God desired to manifest in the lives of every believer...especially those who had been called to prayer.

As I explain the garments, you will see that by the time we are preparing to go into the holy place, the garments, structure, and furniture in the holy place must all work together in order to bring about successful results in prayer.

Let's start by looking at how we are made the righteousness of God and at our responsibility for maintaining our righteousness after we have been washed and have offered ourselves to God as a living sacrifice.

It is important that we understand the Word and Spirit always work in harmony. They *complement* and *complete* each other. God works powerfully within the realm of agreement. Jesus said, "Again I tell you, if two of you on earth agree (harmonize together, make a symphony together) about whatever [anything and everything] they may ask, it will come to pass and be done for them by My Father in heaven" (Matt. 18:19).

In verse 18, Jesus told the disciples, "Truly I tell you, whatever you forbid and declare to be improper and unlawful on earth must be what is already forbidden in heaven, and whatever you permit and declare proper and lawful on earth must be what is already permitted in heaven." In other words, anything we do as a kingdom of priests must come from the third realm. You can't live like the devil and expect to hear God's Word in prayer. And you certainly can't declare anything in prayer, expecting it to happen, when you are out of agreement with God!

Are you in harmony with God? Is your life functioning according to God's pattern? If not, you will never see or experience His victorious glory. When you break the pattern, you ignore the works of Christ—*and His sacrifice was too costly to ignore.* Each piece of your new spiritual prayer clothing is custom-made according to God's measurements. You must be properly clothed (spiritually) for God to meet with you in prayer.

The tabernacle was built to God's specifications. Since God has declared that we are the temple of the Holy Spirit, we must also be built to His specifications. "Except the Lord builds the house, they labor in vain who build it; except the Lord keeps the city, the watchman wakes but in vain" (Ps. 127:1).

What is God building? Mark 11:17 says, "And He *[Jesus]* taught and said to them, Is it not written, My house shall be called a house of prayer for all the nations? But you have turned it into a den of robbers." *Watch out!* When you neglect the pattern of God and ignore the works of Christ, God calls you a thief! You have stolen the sacred things of heaven to build your own house and have robbed God's presence and supernatural blessings from among His people. If you go back to doing your own thing *after going through the fire,* you are a thief.

RECEIVING YOUR PRIESTLY GARMENTS

Let's start by reading God's instructions to Moses about establishing the priesthood and the priestly garments in Exodus 28:1–3:

> From among the Israelites take your brother Aaron and his sons with him, that he may minister to Me in the priest's office, even Aaron, Nadab and Abihu, Eleazar and Ithamar, Aaron's sons. And you shall make for Aaron your brother sacred garments [appointed official dress set apart for special holy services] for honor and for beauty. Tell all who are expert, whom I have endowed with skill and good judgment, that they shall make Aaron's garments to sanctify him for My priesthood.

The first thing that God told Moses was to "take Aaron and *his sons* with him." Aaron represents the office of the high priest, and his sons represent the lower priestly office. God told Moses to take them "from among" the children of Israel. This says we must first be *sons of God* before we can operate in the *office of the priesthood* and be able to go into the tabernacle to a threshing floor experience.

Anyone can come into the outer court through salvation, but not everyone honors God by being obedient. Only the obedient will be able to receive their priestly garments and ultimately enter the holy place in prayer. "Many are called...but few are chosen" (Matt. 22:14). The path of obedience requires that we enter the gate, wash at the laver, and sacrifice at the altar in obedience to God's pattern of prayer. That path of obedience allows us to pass from death into life and prepares us to be clothed for victory in intercessory prayer. Jesus spoke about this path of obedience in John 5, where He said: "Whoever does not honor the Son does not honor the Father, Who has sent Him. I assure you, most solemnly I tell you, the person whose ears are open to My words [who listens to My message] and believes and trusts in and clings to and relies on Him Who sent Me has (possesses now) eternal life. And he does not come into judgment [does not incur sentence of judgment, will not come under condemnation], but he has already passed over out of death into life" (John 5:23–24).

Once the garments of the priesthood and the tabernacle were complete, Moses held an inauguration ceremony. In Leviticus 8:1–9, we discover that God gave instructions to Moses about how to do this. He told Moses, "Take Aaron and his sons with him, and the garments [symbols of their office], and the anointing oil, and the bull of the sin offering, and the two rams, and the basket of unleavened bread; and assemble all the congregation at the door of the Tent of Meeting" (vv. 2–3). When Moses had assembled the Israelites at the door of the Tent of Meeting, he told the congregation, "This is what the Lord has commanded to be done" (v. 5). He then proceeded to prepare Aaron and his sons to put on the priestly garments. He began by washing them with water (v. 6), just as the Lord requires us to be washed at the brazen laver. Then he helped Aaron put on the garments of the high priest:

> He put on Aaron the long undertunic, girded him with the long sash, clothed him with the robe, put the ephod (an upper vestment) upon him, and girded him with the skillfully woven cords attached to the ephod, binding it to him. And Moses put upon Aaron the breastplate; also he put in the breastplate the Urim and the Thummim [articles upon which the high priest put his hand when seeking the divine will concerning the nation]. And he put the turban or miter on his head; on it, in front, Moses put the shining gold plate, the holy diadem, as the Lord commanded him.
>
> —LEVITICUS 8:7–9

The priestly garments represent everything we do after we enter the holy place. Whether it be worship and praise, preaching, baptizing, counseling—whatever we do—it must match who Christ is. He is the Gate of four colors: white representing *His righteousness*, blue showing forth *His divinity*, purple reflecting *His royalty*, and scarlet symbolizing *His ultimate sacrifice on the cross*.

Our works must match the works of Christ in the tabernacle. If they don't, God won't show up, and the people will lose His blessings. Being clothed in the right garments for intercession is vital. In Matthew 22:11–14, we discover that if we are improperly dressed, we can't even enter the King's presence—much less serve Him! "But when the king came in to view the guests, he looked intently at a man there who had on no wedding garment. And he said, Friend, how did you come in here without putting on the [appropriate] wedding garment? And he was speechless (muzzled, gagged). Then the king said to the attendants, Tie him hand and foot, and throw him into the darkness outside; there will be weeping and grinding of teeth. For many are called (invited and summoned), but few are chosen."

We are a royal priesthood, so we must dress accordingly, or God will allow "common men" to bind our hands and feet. Many times the enemy binds us in prayer (instead of us binding him and his works) because we are improperly dressed. And when this happens, we can't operate in the things of God or accomplish His will in the Spirit realm.

To be fully dressed for spiritual service you must wear the proper garments in prayer. It is critical that you wear the right spiritual clothing to come before the King. Otherwise, you will be bound in prayer.

I understand on a much greater level now why God requires us to be washed, purified, and properly dressed before we enter into the fullness of intercessory prayer. God commanded Moses to make special garments for the priests in the tabernacle service so that their clothing would be tailor-made to reflect the dignity of their office and the highest respect for Him. Let's look at how each piece of priestly clothing is important to your walk of prayer.

THE TUNIC OF RIGHTEOUSNESS

This foundational garment represents *the righteousness of God*. It is the reason every other piece of priestly clothing can fulfill its purpose. Let's look at how this garment was made:

> And you shall weave the long and sleeved tunic of checkerwork of fine linen or silk and make a turban of fine linen or silk; and you shall make a girdle, the work of the embroiderer. For Aaron's sons you shall make long and sleeved tunics and belts or sashes and caps, for glory and honor and beauty. And you shall put them on Aaron your brother and his sons with him, and shall anoint them and ordain and sanctify them [set them apart for God], that they may serve Me as priests. You shall make for them [white] linen trunks to cover their naked flesh, reaching from the waist to the thighs. And they shall be on Aaron and his sons when they go into the Tent of Meeting or when they come near to the

altar to minister in the Holy Place, lest they bring iniquity upon themselves and die; it shall be a statute forever to Aaron and to his descendants after him.

—EXODUS 28:39–43

All priests wore white tunics, but only the high priest wore additional garments over his tunic. Notice that the tunic is what allowed the priests to minister in the holy place; it allowed them to come before the presence of the Lord and not die. The tunic was the first piece of clothing Moses placed upon Aaron (Lev. 8:7). This garment matched the wall that surrounded the outer court, as well as the white linen thread that was part of the first tabernacle covering. (We will study this more in chapter nine.)

Let me clarify. Though all of the priests wore trunks and tunics, Aaron's sons (the lower priests) wore the tunic as their main garment. Aaron wore it underneath his other priestly clothing, which confirms there's more than one level in prayer. Aaron's sons were allowed to serve in the outer court and in the holy place, but not in the most holy place. The other Levites performed duties in support of the tabernacle and the priesthood, but they were forbidden to touch the *sacred vessels* of the sanctuary or the brazen altar (Num. 18:23).

I believe God is saying that you must put on this tunic as the foundation of everything you do in prayer. For you to be prepared to take up the burden of the Lord, your nakedness must be covered, just as the tunic and trousers covered Aaron and his sons. Once you are saved and have become a Christian, you are supposed to come into the house of prayer (the tent of meeting) already washed and purified, your tunic in place. You are responsible for maintaining your salvation, for being sure you have this foundational tunic in place in your prayer life. Your first responsibility is to maintain the temple that is within you.

If you attempt to do the work of an intercessor without the tunic of righteousness in place, you will bring iniquity into the house of God. As a result, God will not be able to use you to help anyone else. You cannot come to church on Sunday to get blessed, and then leave the church and go right back to living in sin until the next time you come to the church building. If you do, each time you enter the church you bring iniquity, bad attitudes, lying spirits, and deception—expecting God to clean it up. God is saying to His people, "When am I going to get a holy people to walk into the house of meeting with their inner tabernacle clean, so that I can give them some instructions?"

This isn't an unreasonable request. Jude 24–25 says, "Now unto him that is able to keep you from falling, and to present you faultless before the presence of his glory with exceeding joy, to the only wise God our Saviour..." (KJV). God is able to keep you from continually falling into sin! Understand this: when you backslide, you have *chosen* to fall to iniquity. That's why there are so many people in the church who are always up and down, in and out of fellowship. If you have been redeemed, yet you continue to sin, you are coming to the altar of God *filled with those things from which you should be free!*

In Romans 12:3, the apostle Paul warns us to be very careful to maintain this tunic of righteousness when he says, "For by the grace (unmerited favor of God) given to me I warn everyone among you not to estimate and think of himself more highly than he ought [not to have an exaggerated opinion of his own importance], but to rate his ability with sober judgment, each according to the degree of faith apportioned by God to him."

When God calls you into service, He gives you a level of faith that matches your spiritual assignment. When He speaks to you from the third realm and puts you in your assigned place, you will stay covered by His righteousness if you continue to function at that level of service. But too many believers aspire to be high priests without having the faith to operate on that level. We must learn to be content and productive for God right where we are. Remember... "For therein [in the gospel of Christ] is the righteousness of God revealed from faith to faith: as it is written, The just shall live by faith" (Rom. 1:17, KJV).

It is vital that you learn to reject your human senses and to embrace the righteousness of God. Your spiritual underclothing—the white linen trunks and tunic—helps you do this by keeping your nakedness covered, that is, your human nature without God. When you come into the presence of the Lord, these white garments will remind you that God doesn't need anything *sensual* from you. It is the tunic of righteousness that will help you to walk the path of obedience after you have washed at the laver and sacrificed at the altar. *Maintaining the righteousness of God in your life will initially be your biggest struggle in prayer.* You will need to learn to stop relying on your own human senses, because it is your righteousness that makes Satan tremble. Why? James 5:16 says, "The earnest (heartfelt, continued) prayer of a righteous man makes tremendous power available [dynamic in its working]."

God doesn't need anything from your five senses: what you can *see, smell, taste, hear,* or *touch.* These earthly senses are useless in the spiritual realm of prayer, because while you are praying for someone's healing, your senses will be telling you that person is still sick. Your senses will tell you that a person is still bound. Your five senses will look at impossible circumstances and say, "I've never seen anyone else survive this . . . a person in the last stages of AIDS can't be healed."

This is why God puts a covering—a blinding—over your earthly nature by giving you the white tunic and trousers. When He is preparing you to enter the realm of the Spirit, your earthly senses are no longer needed.

Covering the private parts also covers the part of our nature that puts gender confidence in our innate abilities as either a man or a woman. Being male or female doesn't make anyone *strong enough* to become an effective intercessor. Everyone must draw strength directly from the nature of God.

Christ's divine nature covers our old nature. The apostle Peter tells us that Jesus our Lord has "given unto us all things that pertain unto life and godliness, through the knowledge of him that hath called us to glory and virtue: whereby are given unto us exceeding great and precious promises: that by these ye might be partakers of the divine nature, having escaped the corruption that is in the world through lust" (2 Pet. 1:3–4, KJV).

But it is as we walk in obedience to God that He empowers us to "add to your faith virtue; and to virtue knowledge; and to knowledge temperance; and to temperance patience; and to patience godliness; and to godliness brotherly kindness; and to brotherly kindness charity" (vv. 5–7, KJV).

If all these things remain in you, your prayer life will be fruitful. *If you maintain your inner tabernacle, you will always come out of your prayer closet in victory.*

But Peter also warns us of the results of not staying behind the covering of God's righteousness by walking in disobedience. He says, "But he that lacketh these things is blind, and cannot see afar off, and hath forgotten that he was purged from his old sins" (v. 9, KJV). Peter is describing the person who has forgotten that he has already been washed and cleansed from sin at the brazen laver and the brazen altar. Peter implores us to "give diligence to make your calling and election sure: for if ye do these things, ye shall never fall" (v. 10, KJV).

In other words, when you are spiritually blind, you can't be in the holy place or in the most holy place. Why? Because you lack the divine nature of God. You can't serve a divine God from your lower nature. There's no match in the Spirit, because light will not fellowship with darkness. That means when you pray, God won't show up. Don't minimize the value of your white tunic and trunks.

The most powerful part of the passage in 2 Peter 1 is verse 11, which reveals what happens when you guard your garments of intercession:

> For so an entrance shall be ministered unto you abundantly into the everlasting kingdom of our Lord and Saviour Jesus Christ.
>
> —KJV

When you are clothed in your white linen tunic and trunks, it creates a match in the Spirit realm and an entrance into the second and third dimensions of prayer (which happen inside the tabernacle). When you advance into these realms of prayer on behalf of others, you will come out having obtained for them the fruit of the kingdom: "... righteousness, and peace, and joy in the Holy Ghost" (Rom. 14:17, KJV).

ARE YOU BEING CALLED TO HIGHER GROUND?

In learning about the priestly garments, God wants us to discern the difference between a person who merely prays and one who understands that he or she has been called to intercession. Many people think that some believers are ordained to pray, and others aren't. First Thessalonians 5:17 tells us that we ought to "pray without ceasing" (KJV). I believe that every Christian is called to prayer, but there comes a season in our lives when we are called to higher ground.

The Lord has allotted time in the realm of the Spirit for spiritual growth. This progress cannot be measured in natural years. Some believers have been saved for many years, yet they still act like they are only two years old spiritually. When you were a child, your mother tied your shoes, put a bib on you, and did everything for you. As you came of age, you started cleaning your own room, working a part-time job, and paying your own bills—because with growth comes another level of responsibility.

In the Spirit realm, the Lord is now maturing many believers beyond their natural ages because the hour is so short. However, you must remember that once you allow God to mature you in character and to place a mantle of prayer upon your shoulders, you cannot choose to go back to being a spiritual baby when you hit a bump in the road. Things don't work that way in God's kingdom. It would be better never to touch God's mantle or come into the knowledge of the hidden mysteries of God (the power of righteousness), than to turn and look back. You might as well have never even touched it. Why do I say this? You are responsible for everything that you hear from God, whether you obey what you hear or not. A person may die as the biggest crack addict in the world, but that person will still be judged by God for what he or she heard from God during his or her lifetime. God has made sure that no one leaves this earth without having had a chance to know the right way. If you die in sin, it's because you choose to do so.

Once you come into the knowledge of Jesus Christ, you automatically become an enemy of Satan. When you walked to the altar, repented of all of your sins, and became a believer by faith, Christ came to live within you. During this supernatural encounter, God allowed your heart and mind to be shifted into the supernatural realm so that you could hear and believe in Him. Everything you did in the past was wiped away. You can no longer go back to living from the realm of your flesh.

Once you become an enemy of Satan, you must receive your spiritual clothing, take up your weapons, and learn how to use them. It's crazy to inherit an enemy and not learn how to fight! Too many Christians are saved, yet they live defeated lives because they never rise up against the enemy's attacks. And because they don't know how to fight back, they find themselves constantly talking about what the devil is doing. If this describes you, it's time to reverse your thinking.

You need to stop talking about the devil and worrying about his attacks against you. Luke 10:19 gives us this marvelous promise: "Behold! I have given you authority and power to trample upon serpents and scorpions, and [physical and mental strength and ability] over all the power that the enemy [possesses]; and nothing shall in any way harm you." Too many believers are being destroyed—while they are sitting in church—because their inner tabernacle is empty. They live in a state of confusion, and they have no strength to take up the call of intercessory prayer.

I recently took on the responsibility of caring for one of my nieces. When she first arrived at my home (although she's definitely a Bynum), she was acting like she was crazy and generally ignorant about her heritage. When a person isn't aware of his or her bloodline and what that affords, that individual must be retrained to think like an heir.

Not long ago, my niece asked, "When are you going to give me a key?" When I hesitated, she pressed in, "You act like you don't trust me. I can put it around my neck."

At that point I had to help her understand that she was only thirteen. She wasn't ready to have a key to my house where there are countless treasures inside. I said, "No, you can't have a key until I see that your mind has been changed."

As an intercessor, you must be trained in maintaining the discipline of your inheritance. This will teach you how to discern every spirit. You will be able to look at a situation and see it for what it is in the eternal realm. More than this, when the enemy is trying to make you think a situation is going to turn out one way, you will already know the answer because you belong to the kingdom of God.

How do you get this vital training? *You get dressed to get in His presence.* Now that you have come through the outer court levels where anyone can enter—the lame, the broke, the busted, and the disgusted, a new life of prayer is ready to open before your eyes. Remember that the outer court is for people who always have to be washed and rewashed for the same sins and iniquities. Three years after coming through the gate of salvation, they are still saying, "Oops," about the same issues God dealt with when they first came into the kingdom. Believers who are satisfied with this lower level of living will wait on the outside of the mysteries of God until the high priest comes out of the most holy place once a year to declare that their sins have been forgiven. They will wait until others can tell them about their experiences in the presence of the Lord. That's tragic.

Then there are people who go to the next level of prayer in the holy place, but they only enjoy being entertained by the light and the bread. They never go beyond receiving somebody else's teachings about having a supernatural, face-to-face relationship with God. These are the people who always need someone else to pray for them—they never graduate to praying for others. They say, "Pray for me," because their heart is outside the tabernacle, and the level of their righteousness doesn't allow their vision to go all the way to the divine presence for themselves.

These are the people who will lie and still shout in church. They will sleep around and still stand in the choir and sing. These people are so unclean that they will curse and do all kinds of damnable things without feeling a tinge of conviction. They attend church, but they won't come anywhere near the most holy place. They express a reverential fear of God without having a relationship with Him.

When you are in relationship with God, you fear Him because of the greatness of who He is; yet you love Him tenderly and deeply. When part of you forgets about how much you love Him and wants to do wrong, the other part of you says, "I'm afraid to do wrong." Do you know why? When you have truly been in God's presence, you know by experience who He is. That authenticates everything you experience in the supernatural and forms a foundation that influences your everyday decisions. When you truly know God, your love for Him will always bring you into balance.

This reveals the problem with many people in the church—*they have never had an experience with God.* They have never had an experience where they couldn't stop weeping under His power, or they couldn't stop speaking in tongues. They have never had an experience where a light came into the room and the power of God shook their bodies to the extent that they could only lie still under His awesome power. The bottom line is this: *until you have a real experience in the presence of the Lord, you don't really have a relationship with Him.* Instead, your relationship is with your preacher or your favorite evangelist. Some people even relegate their relationship with God to audiocassettes or tapes to which they have listened or to books they have read.

When you are in the presence of God, your deepest desire is to hear what the Holy Spirit is saying. Once you realize that God alone has the answers for all your needs, then you will get a fresh word from Him. This process of growth breaks the infant spirit off of you.

When the Lord began to reveal these truths to me, I was determined to have that type of relationship with Him—*for real*. When you get to that place, you won't need to wait to come into a building to celebrate God. You will be able to shout all by yourself and sing songs of worship to God alone in your living room. And when you do go to church, people will see your passion and know that you have had an experience with God.

Too many believers are coming to the house of God to *get fire* instead of *bringing it*. They are stuck in the outer court and cannot go any further because they are not properly dressed. We must let God cover our sensualities with the linen trousers and our human nature with His tunic of righteousness, *or we won't go any further in the things of God.*

Do We Attain Perfection?

Keeping in mind that the things we read about in the Old Testament are a typology of what God expects of us spiritually, let's go to Hebrews 7:11:

> Now if perfection (a perfect fellowship between God and the worshiper) had been attainable by the Levitical priesthood—for under it the people were given the Law—why was it further necessary that there should arise another and different kind of Priest, one after the order of Melchizedek, rather than one appointed after the order and rank of Aaron?

We hear a lot about attaining *perfection* in the body of Christ today, so I feel it's necessary to address what the Lord gave me clarity about in prayer. Though the Bible talks about perfection and striving to be perfect, *we are not perfect*. When I read this passage, the Lord revealed to me that man's idea of perfection is doing everything right without ever making a mistake. Hear me. As long as you are in your natural body, you are going to make errors and mistakes.

The perfection of the Lord relates to having perfect fellowship with Him. When you were saved, you were made righteous without doing anything to receive it. After you have been given this gift, it is your responsibility to submit to divine training so that the rest of your body will line up with what you have been given on the inside.

Although you have been made righteous, most likely you have been living for many years with a certain pattern in your flesh. You may get up every day, smoke a cigarette, and then drink a cup of coffee. When somebody gets on your nerves, you may have developed a habit of cursing that individual out. If someone cuts you off in traffic on your way to work, you may have become accustomed to driving people off the road. When you do those things every day—and then suddenly you are given a gift that transforms you into the righteousness of God—you must understand that God has imputed His righteousness unto you. There's a good example of this in James 2:23:

> And [so] the Scripture was fulfilled that says, Abraham believed in (adhered to, trusted in, and relied on) God, and this was accounted to him as righteousness (as conformity to God's will in thought and deed), and he was called God's friend.

When you see the word *imputed*, it means *to be included within a certain space, place, or limit.* It is inclusive. It also indicates motion or direction from the outside to a point within. When something is imputed to you, it gives you an opportunity to move from a place on the outside to a new place on the inside. You don't even have to ask for it. *Imputed* means that you have been transitioned from one state to another by the One who lives vicariously through you.

Let me break it down further. *Imputed* also means to attribute or ascribe, proclaim, or declare that a person is righteous vicariously. What does *vicariously* mean? It is an act that is performed, received, or suffered in the place of another. It is an emotion that is felt or enjoyed through the imagined participation in the experience of others. In other words, Jesus came to the earth, stepped into your experience before you got here, and lived vicariously through your experience when He went to the cross. In doing this, He took your place and enabled you to get in His space. That's why the Bible says in 2 Corinthians 5:17, "Therefore if any man be in Christ, he is a new creature: old things are passed away; behold, all things are become new" (KJV).

Jesus died on the cross for our sins and made us righteous so that He would have a right to live in the earth realm and give us power to live through Him. That's why Jesus said in John 11:25, "I am [Myself] the Resurrection and the Life. Whoever believes in (adheres to, trusts in, and relies on) Me, although he may die, yet he shall live." Christ lives through every person who proclaims Him. You accepted that gift when you said, "Lord Jesus, come into my life. Save me. Live in me. As long as I live, I vow that I will serve You." Now Jesus has full permission to live in you and walk in the earth realm vicariously through you. And it doesn't stop there. You have a right to walk vicariously where Jesus walked. You can do what He did. You can cast out devils and lay hands on the sick—but you must stay in relationship with Him through prayer.

You need to maintain a prayer life so that you can ask Him what He wants to do through you. When I gave my life to Him, I died to myself. Now I ask Him every day, "What do You want me to do, God? What do You want me to say? Where do You want me to go? Whom do You want to heal through me? What demon (i.e., force) do You want to cast down?" Listen to me. You are not supposed to be sitting around getting beat up by the devil! Jesus defeated Satan once and for all. He died on the cross, rose from the dead, took the keys to death, hell, and the grave, and made an open show of the devil. You can walk in this same victory.

When you become a son or daughter of God, the Spirit of God will begin to lead you. I can be on my way to the store when the power of God hits me, and I end up laying my hands on someone and seeing that person get delivered. I don't have to work it up. I don't have to beg God—because I'm not the one doing the work. Christ is living vicariously through me.

You don't have to be in the ministry for Christ to break yokes of bondage through you. In the past, you had to be a bishop to pray for somebody. You had to be ordained before you could lay hands on somebody. And before you could give somebody a word from God, you had to get your prophet's license. Hear me! God is saying, "Not now. That's the old order."

Now you can go into the most holy place because Christ lives vicariously through you. You can walk in on your own. You don't have to go through the high priest. You can stand before the throne of God knowing that you are seated with Christ at the right hand of the Father. When this happens, you will be able to see what Jesus sees and know what He knows—because He is living in you.

When we have no vision, we fail to maintain our tunic of righteousness and keep our sensualities covered with our linen trousers. In the outer court, most people can't see anything but flesh, flesh, and more flesh. In the religious world, there are "religious" men operating within their five senses, so they are always trying to dominate and control by manipulating those who get elevated and those who don't. Psalm 75:6–7 says that promotion must come from God alone. He raises one person up and sits another person down—and the way you will be promoted is based upon your righteousness.

This is why the tunic is the foundational garment in prayer. That's why you must make sure that you are properly dressed before you start praying. Otherwise, you will be defeated before you get started. Why? Because if the devil does not see your robe of righteousness, he will give you a good old-fashioned whipping. Let me show you an example of what I am trying to tell you. In Acts 19:13–16 the seven sons of Sceva (who was the chief of the priests) tried casting a demon out of a man and didn't have the supernatural power to do it. The Bible tells us that they ended up running away naked and wounded. You can't just come to God any way you feel is right. That's why the Lord has revealed a pattern.

When you become an intercessor, cleanliness is a requirement. Revelation 1:13–16 describes how Jesus is dressed as He ever intercedes for us:

> ...And in the midst of the lampstands [One] like a Son of Man, clothed with a robe which reached to His feet and with a girdle of gold about His breast. His head and His hair were white like white wool, [as white] as snow, and His eyes [flashed] like a flame of fire. His feet glowed like burnished (bright) bronze as it is refined in a furnace, and His voice was like the sound of many waters. In His right hand He held seven stars, and from His mouth there came

forth a sharp two-edged sword, and His face was like the sun shining in full power at midday.

The fine radiant linen signifies righteousness. It represents the upright, just, and godly deeds and conduct of the saints—God's holy people. That's you and me. So you must put on your new white linen tunic (righteousness) if you are going to get into the presence of the Lord in prayer. Everything you are and ever hope to be has to be covered in righteousness.

Let me break this down. You can't keep doing all the things you used to do and still walk around saying that you are righteous. For example, if you've compromised yourself in a romantic relationship, you have to put on that linen garment that covers your intimate parts and say, "We're saved now. We don't do that. We're holy. We need to get married." Any other kind of thinking isn't attached to righteousness. Righteousness is purification. It's a life that trains every individual to live without sin.

When you put on your tunic of righteousness, that's your declaration. Since Jesus Christ is your righteousness, when you walk into the most holy place to battle in the Spirit, the devil will have to look at you and say, "Here comes Jesus..." And remember, at the name of Jesus every knee must bow. Every demon spirit has to become subject to you when they see you wearing the robe of righteousness. This is why Isaiah 61:10 says:

> I will greatly rejoice in the Lord, my soul will exult in my God; for He has clothed me with the garments of salvation, He has covered me with the robe of righteousness, as a bridegroom decks himself with a garland, and as a bride adorns herself with her jewels.

When Christ has clothed you in righteousness, you can become a mighty weapon against the enemy. But you must know your rights—you must know that righteousness has been imputed unto you and declare, "Greater is He that is in me than he that is in the world."

Let me help you with something. Let's say there are a lot of alcoholics and drug addicts in your family. You may believe, according to your genealogy and your family background, that you were never supposed to go to college, own a home, or do anything positive with your life. But then the Lord intervenes, breaks all the rules, and does something in your life that's never been done in the history of your family. *You can be assured that His righteousness is real.* Your life becomes a testimony to this fact.

WILL YOU WEAR YOUR TUNIC?

Are you going to let the devil defeat you and keep you in sin or under a generational curse from your family, when you can walk in righteousness and get anything that God has for you? Don't be like Esau who sold his birthright for a bowl of soup.

The devil knows that he can't do anything to stop your destiny unless you give up your righteousness. Hear me. If you give up your righteousness, you will give up your future. You won't be able to rebuke the devil out of a closet. He will look at you the same way he looked at the sons of Sceva in Acts 19:13–16. Remember what happened when they tried to cast out a devil. That demon jumped on them and said, "Jesus I know, and Paul I know, but who are ye?" (v. 15, KJV). All seven of them got stripped and whipped by the enemy. So you see, it doesn't matter how gifted you are. You may have a gift, a talent, or a great ministry, but the righteousness of God is the only thing that demons will respect in a human being.

If you have been saved and filled with the Holy Spirit, you must know that demons do not respond to just your tongues. Tongues are not new to the devil, so your prayer language, knowledge of Scripture, worship, dancing, and shouting do not scare him. What really frightens him is when he looks at you and is blinded by your righteousness.

The light that comes from the secret place is unbearable to the enemy. So when you go into prayer dressed in your tunic of righteousness, the devil has to feel around for you because he can't open his eyes and see—the light is too bright. When the enemy sees you walking in righteousness, it's like a person sleeping in a pitch-dark room for two days and then someone walking in and opening the curtains to a bright, sunny day. The light becomes so unbearable that he can't even recognize who is in the room. All he can see is the startling light.

Remember that James 5:16 tells us that the prayers of the righteous *availeth much*. The world is in trouble; our nation is in trouble; and people all around us are in trouble *because they don't have the answer.* You know how to get the answer, but you won't get it until you put on your tunic and live in the righteousness of God. When you have been called to be an intercessor, you are spiritually responsible for everyone you know. The way I see it, God didn't allow me to meet my beautician just for the sake of meeting her and getting my hair done. He made me responsible for her. Now I have to live righteously so that if she ever asks me for prayer, I will be able to get an answer on her behalf. It's time to put on righteousness so we can have an answer for every man, woman, and child.

If you train and discipline your flesh to walk in righteousness, the Bible promises that God will hear your cry and deliver you out of ALL your troubles. (See Psalm 34:17.) That means whatever you are going through, you are going to come out! Whatever the devil brings, it's not going to take you out. When you walk in the righteousness of God, no weapon that has been formed against you by the enemy shall prosper.

Let me close with Psalm 15:1–5:

> Lord, who shall dwell [temporarily] in Your tabernacle? Who shall dwell [permanently] on Your holy hill? He who walks and lives uprightly and blamelessly, who works rightness and justice and speaks and thinks the truth in his heart, he who does not slander with his tongue, nor does evil to his friend, nor takes up a reproach against his neighbor; in whose eyes a vile person is despised, but he who honors those who fear the Lord (who revere and worship Him); who swears to his own hurt and does not change; [he who] does not put out his money for interest [to one of his own people] and who will not take a bribe against the innocent. He who does these things shall never be moved.

Some people are satisfied with going to a building to worship God, but I want to dwell on His holy hill permanently. That means I'm letting God cover me in His righteousness and build a solid tabernacle in my spirit. "Church folk" are content to dwell in His tabernacle temporarily, but the righteous—that's you and me—shall dwell on the holy hill forever. God hasn't put you in a temporary position; He's birthing righteousness in you so that you can dwell permanently in a place of authority and victory over the devil.

The person who dwells permanently on God's holy hill is the one who lives uprightly and blamelessly and rejoices in doing things right. Even when someone fails to handle things correctly with you, you will do things right anyway. Don't forfeit what God is going to do in your life by retaliating against flesh and blood. The robe of righteousness elevates you to the class of "it doesn't matter," because if you do all of "these things" in Psalm 15:1–5, you shall NEVER BE MOVED. The devil can come, but he won't be able to shake you. Temptation may rise, but it won't move you. Tribulation may come your way, but it's not going to defeat you. Your destiny is "on the hill."

Take a moment to pray with me:

> *Lord, clothe me in Your righteousness. Take me to the hill. Do whatever You desire to do in me, Lord. I've been behind schedule. Give me a speed shot and put me back on schedule. Do whatever it takes to keep me on Your holy hill, Lord. I want to be holy. I want to be righteous. God, help me today. Train and discipline my flesh unto righteousness so that I can become the intercessor You have called me to be. In Jesus' name, amen.*

CHAPTER 6

The Garments of Completion

$\mathcal{B}$Y GIVING PRECISE, specific instructions for the making of the tabernacle and the priestly garments, God demonstrated that He is meticulous. He is a God of great detail. These Old Testament examples help us to understand in the midst of all that's happening in our lives, we can still (to this day) get into the divine presence in the most holy place.

As we consider the priestly wardrobe, we will continue to discover why the Lord saw fit to have the priests dress a certain way. Every item was associated with an element that was used in constructing the temple, because the tabernacle was never supposed to operate apart from the priesthood. When we understand this, we will also understand that it is not enough for the believer simply to attend church. As God's people, we must begin to become the church—especially if we are called to be intercessors.

First Corinthians 6:19 tells us that we are temples of the Holy Spirit. This means that once we have accepted Jesus as our personal Savior, there must be a priesthood inside our earthly temple. If there is no priesthood functioning within us, we become people who attend church but have no righteousness. As a result, we have no power or authority in our Christian experience. When the priesthood is present in you, then your temple becomes operational.

We have come through the gate and have accepted the works of Christ. We have repented of our sins and been washed at the brazen laver by God's Word. We have presented our bodies as a living sacrifice, holy and acceptable unto the Lord at the brazen altar. We no longer want to live as we lived in the past! We are clothed with the robe of righteousness—the first garment we receive when we are adopted into the royal priesthood.

You may be asking: "Where do I go from here? Is it time for me to move to the next level, which is to enter the holy place?" Your robe of righteousness prepares you to maintain the structure of your temple (your body), but if you intend to enter into the holy place, you must wear all the garments of the priesthood. We will now look more closely at these additional priestly garments.

THE SASH

After clothing Aaron with the tunic (robe of righteousness), Moses girded him with the sash. "He put on Aaron the long undertunic, girded him with the long sash..." (Lev. 8:7). There were two belts in the priestly garments. The first belt went over the tunic, and the second belt was part of the ephod, skillfully woven of the same colors (Exod. 28:8). The sash to which I am referring now is the sash or belt described in Exodus 28:39–40: "And you shall weave the long and sleeved tunic of checkerwork of fine linen or silk and make a turban of fine linen or silk; *and you shall make a girdle, the work of the embroiderer.* For Aaron's sons you shall make long and sleeved tunics *and belts or sashes and caps...*" (emphasis added).

When you put on the garments of intercession, this belt of truth goes on top of the tunic of righteousness. But unlike the belt of the ephod, it is still not visible to the naked eye. This belt girds your loins. It holds your tunic together underneath the robe of blue, the ephod, and the breastplate. Why do I call it the belt of truth? There were two belts in Aaron's sacred garments, just as the Word of God—the "Word of Truth" (2 Tim. 2:15)—is described as a two-edged sword in Hebrews 4:12. In order to walk in righteousness you must embrace truth and keep it girded about you.

This belt also symbolizes *readiness*—when you have it fastened, you are activated to be a servant. You are instant in and out of season, always ready to go to the world. Actually, this truth impacts you on two levels: because the Word of God is true, you are ready to go to work for God in prayer, and, second, it is constantly working in you and for you.

When I go into intercession with my belt of truth in place, I know that I will have days of lamenting, wailing, and weeping, yet I understand that I must simply speak the truth in prayer—which can only be done by speaking the Word of God.

When you are praying for someone, you won't have to say, "Lord, will You just save him? Lord, will You just heal him? Will You just get him off crack?" You are strapped with the Word of Truth. When you go to prayer, you are supposed to speak *the truth*, not the problem. Immature Christians pray the problem. When you become an intercessor, you pray the answer. Intercessors don't beg! Intercessors don't have to plead with God because we are speaking the truth of His Word.

An intercessor goes to God saying, "God, You said in Your Word that the fruit of my body shall be blessed. I decree it to be so in the name of Jesus. I decree that my son shall preach the gospel. I decree that the anointing of God shall be upon my daughter. I speak it in Jesus' name. No weapon that has been formed against them is going to prosper." An intercessor doesn't have to beg, because the Bible says that if we decree a thing, He shall bring it to pass (Job 22:28). When you operate in truth and decree a thing in the Spirit realm, you can be assured it is already done. You don't have to wait around for it to manifest in the flesh; you can move on and start praying for somebody else. You don't even have to look back, because you know that you have already decreed and declared it. You have asked according to the will of the Father, and you have asked in faith. You have come in the name of Jesus, are clothed in righteousness, and are belted with truth. How can you be a loser in prayer? The decreed Word of God must come to pass.

I'm not talking about trying to *name it and claim it*, and nothing ever happens. I'm talking about the intercessor who has come through the process, the person who has put on the robe of righteousness and girded his or her loins with truth. When you walk in righteousness and know your Word (Bible), you can decree what God has already declared in His Word and get results! Some days your feelings will tell you that God isn't going to perform His Word. Some days you will feel like the things you have been praying for aren't going to happen. Some days you may even feel like you are not even saved—but as an intercessor, you don't operate according to your feelings. You operate in the realm of the Spirit according to God's truth.

Say this right now: "I am girded about with truth. I don't care what lies the devil may speak. I know the truth. I don't care what the devil tries to tell me about myself. I know the truth. I don't care how many times I make a mistake. I know the truth. I know that my mistakes are training me in righteousness. I may make some mistakes, but truth is going to straighten me out. I may bump my head sometimes, but I'm coming out because I'm girded with truth."

You feel bad when you do something wrong because you are righteous. Unrighteous people don't feel anything. It's not the same for you. Conviction comes upon you because the belt of truth has started choking you. Every time you do something wrong, the belt of truth confronts it. It keeps pulling you tighter and tighter until you can't deny it. Hear me. When you are in training for righteousness, you don't have to be discouraged.

Conviction comes because righteousness has been imputed unto you, and your belt of truth is activating it. Therefore, you know that lies, fornication, and other works of the flesh have no business trying to jump on your outfit of righteousness and truth. When the devil says to you, "You won't ever be able to stop doing that...it's already a habit," you can say, "Not so! That's a habit of the flesh, and I'm being trained in righteousness. My fleshly body is being trained to walk according to my inner wardrobe."

What is the proof that you are qualified to be an intercessor? In 1 Peter 1:13, the Word tells us, "Brace up your minds; be sober (circumspect, morally alert); set your hope wholly and unchangeably on the grace (divine favor) that is coming to you when Jesus Christ (the Messiah) is revealed." In the King James Version, the verse says to "gird up" the loins of your mind. I found that *to gird* means "to hold firm in place and keep steady." *Loins* are located between the place where your ribs end and your pelvic bone begins. This area of the body is called the *seat of strength*.

When you go into intercession, only God knows how long you are going to be there, so your sash strengthens your loins. I remember going to Home Depot one day and noticing that a lot of the workers were wearing thick, black, girdle-like belts. I stopped a worker and asked, "Why do you have that around your waist? It seems like everybody's wearing them."

He said, "When you are standing on concrete for long periods of time, there's no shock or support for your feet. This band helps to support your legs and keeps you from getting tired. It supports you from the waist up."

A wood floor, on the other hand, gives a shock balance, although you couldn't see this effect unless you were looking at it with the help of a high-powered microscope. Floors give from the shock of a person's heel hitting the surface. When you walk on a concrete floor, there is no give. When a person's heel hits the concrete, the shock goes back up the legs and into the lower back. People who work for long hours on concrete floors wear braces to support the lower vertebrae, so that when the shocks come back up the leg there won't be any damage.

Once I understood this, I realized that when you are standing in intercession it's like standing on concrete, because you are standing in a hard place. And since only God knows how long you are going to be in prayer, you must go into His presence girded.

When you are standing in a hard place in prayer, and it looks like the devil isn't going to move, God will declare to you from His Word, "I'm not going let your mind go into shock. I'm going to help you gird up your mind so that you'll be able to stand—and you won't feel the pain because you're standing on My Word." Your garments enable you to speak the Word instead of moaning and complaining all the time. When your friends say, "You ought to give up on that situation, honey. It doesn't look like it's changing," you will be able to say, "That's all right, because I'm girded up. I'm built to take the shock. I have enough Word in my spirit."

When you gird up the loins of your mind, you can stand in a hard place for long periods of time. You will be shouting when it doesn't look like anything is happening in the natural. You may want to give up in your flesh, but when you have girded up the loins of your mind, every time you see or hear something negative, it won't shock you.

Every time the doctors give a bad report, it won't shock you. Every time the devil messes with your finances, it won't shock you. That's why you can declare that no weapon formed against you shall prosper. You are shock proof!

When you look at the human anatomy, the loins are defined as, "a: the upper and lower abdominal regions and the region around the hips; b (1): the pubic region; (2) the reproductive organs."[1] This speaks of reproduction. Proverbs 23:7 says, "For as he thinketh in his heart, so is he" (KJV). When your mind is girded with the Word, you have the ability to become creative and productive for God, and you will receive what the Word tells your mind that you can have. *By girding up the loins of your mind, you will protect what you reproduce in the Spirit.* Think about Creation. God stepped out in the midst of nothing and created a new world. This same God lives in you. Do you understand the significance of this in your prayer life?

Philippians 2:5 says, "Let this mind be in you, which was also in Christ Jesus" (KJV). This means that if God can think it, speak it, and it comes to pass—then you can gird up your mind, decree His Word in prayer, and see results! That's why the warfare is so heavy in your mind. That's why the devil tries to keep you depressed in your mind. He knows that when you begin to gird it up with the Word, you will be able to speak "those things which be not as though they were" (Rom. 4:17, KJV). Listen closely. You will reap from whatever you sow into your mind (Gal. 6:7). If you sow Nehemiah 8:10 into your mind, then you will be able to stand, knowing that "the joy of the Lord is your strength." You will be able to dance and rejoice when everything in your life seems to be going crazy.

THE ROBE OF BLUE

The next piece of clothing that Moses placed on Aaron was the blue robe, which represented position and authority (Lev. 8:7). This robe is also described in Exodus 28:31–35:

> Make the robe [to be worn beneath] the ephod all of blue. There shall be a hole in the center of it [to slip over the head], with a binding of woven work around the hole, like the opening in a coat of

mail or a garment, that it may not fray or tear. And you shall make pomegranates of blue, purple, and scarlet [stuff] around about its skirts, with gold bells between them; a gold bell and a pomegranate, a gold bell and a pomegranate, round about on the skirts of the robe. Aaron shall wear the robe when he ministers, and its sound shall be heard when he goes [alone] into the Holy of Holies before the Lord and when he comes out, lest he die there.

This robe is very important to us. Colors are extremely significant to God in prayer, because they were one of the ways that God chose to bring knowledge of Himself and the heavenly realm to the human race. That way, when we operate in the realm of the Spirit, the things we encounter won't be foreign to us.

Blue represents *covering authority*. It also represents *divinity* and *grace*. Why are all of these things important? You must go into prayer with a firm hold on your walk of salvation. This means that you will have matured in Christ and grown out of doing some of the things you used to do in your "flesh." You will have matured to the point that certain things no longer cause you to struggle spiritually. This is when you can say to yourself, *I'm not trying to live saved. I am saved. This is who I am, and I'm not going back. I'm not trying to find a sneaky way out of righteousness, and I'm not trying to straddle the fence. I'm not living so close to the world that people can hardly tell I'm saved.*

These are the people who say, "I've been there, done that, got a T-shirt for it, and don't want to go back. I already know that if I lie down to sleep with somebody, I'm going to feel bad when I get up. As a result, I will not be able to praise God for two or three Sundays."

That's right. You can find yourself falling into sin repeatedly, and you may already know from past experience how long it will take you to get back to God after you fall. You may be thinking, *OK, if I do this, it's going to take me two or three weeks to get back to church, and I'm going to feel a little hypocritical.* When you do make it back to church, that will be the week you play sick. When people ask you what's wrong, you will say, "Oh, I'm not feeling my best today…" The fact is, you really messed up, and you don't want to have to tell anyone what you did. Does this sound familiar?

You feel very awkward that first Sunday back at church. Then by

Wednesday night Bible study, you begin to get interested in the lesson. By Friday night, during deliverance service, you shed a few tears, but you still will not have broken all the way through. By Sunday, you will be able to give God a "sloppy agape" praise. Then by the next Sunday, you will have regained your strength—that is, until you mess up again.

As you mature in Christ, you will get to the point of recognizing the patterns, and you will say, *I don't even feel like going down that road. That's going to mean three weeks out of the pocket.* When you get to that point, the old sins will no longer even tempt you. You will just know: *I can't be bothered with this. I can't go there anymore. It takes too much energy to get back. I'm too old for this. I'm not six months old in the Spirit anymore.* At six months, you are foolish. At one year, you don't understand. Then at five years of age, you start to know better. By the time you reach seven or eight years, you can't even go there. You can't continue to do those things anymore.

When God calls you to be an intercessor, you must become a person who is finished with sin. This doesn't mean you will never make a mistake. But if you do, it will be because the devil has caught you off guard—because you already know better than to do it. When you are secure in your salvation, and the Word has girded up your mind, the devil will have to sneak up on you to cause you to sin. Because you are faithful to prayer and committed to the household of faith, the devil will only be able to deceive you if he comes up on your blind side.

When you have matured in this walk of prayer, you will come to the realization that every time you sin deliberately, you lose ground. You will know that you cannot get your job done as an intercessor until you have whipped every demon in your own life. Make certain that you have challenged every demon and fleshly temptation in your own life with the Holy Spirit's help before you go around declaring, "God has called me to be an intercessor." Make sure you are walking out your own deliverance with fear and trembling! (See Philippians 2:12–13.) If you don't, when you get to the veil of the most holy place, the devil will have launched a fiery dart to penetrate your mind and deceive you by saying something like, "How can you pray for anyone when you have unclean deeds in your own spirit?"

We discover why Jesus was able to set the captives free in John 14:30:

> The prince (evil genius, ruler) of the world is coming. And he has no claim on Me. [He has nothing in common with Me: there is nothing in Me that belongs to him, and he has no power over Me.]

That's why Jesus was able to bring down the enemy! And that's why you have been given authority in the third realm. Satan can't penetrate your robe of authority and stop what God is doing in your life. Do you see the pattern? The devil couldn't stop the plan of God through Jesus Christ. Yet because it was part of God's purpose and plan, the devil could persecute Jesus, whip Him all night long, take Him to the cross, and pierce His side. But he could not hinder our Lord's purpose *because there was no ground of evil found in Christ.*

When you go into intercession, the only weapon the devil should possess against you is your past—and he will never win the battle when he tries to play the "past" game with you. If he brings your past to your mind in prayer, then you have already won. When he brings your past before you, *remind him of his past!* Say, "I remember when you were thrown out of heaven, and everyone on earth took your place in praise and worship! I remember when Christ made an open show of you, stripped you of your authority, and took the keys of death, hell, and the grave away from you. Most of all, I remember that you live in hell—and you don't even control that, because Jesus has the keys!"

If you start talking like that, the devil has to flee from you. You can go into prayer remembering that Christ has given you power and authority to tread on the heads of serpents and scorpions and over every evil work of the devil. You can remember that nothing shall by any means harm you. You can tell the devil that he's trespassing and just making a bunch of noise, and the only reason he is able to do that is because you are still in the outer court. If you keep following the pattern of prayer, once you are in the holy place, you won't even be able to hear the devil.

God is trying to bring us all the way through the outer court where we are living and praying according to human customs, traditions, and denominationalism. He's leading us into the realm of the Spirit where the devil cannot follow us! The deeper we go in God, the fainter the enemy's voice becomes. In the outer court, the enemy's voice is loud in your ear, but the more you obey and activate your garments, the more you hear from God, the more distant the voice of Satan becomes. This means that you have progressed far enough in purification that the devil cannot follow you.

Going to another level of purification ordains you as an authentic intercessor. It equips you to travel into the Spirit realm where the enemy can't follow, because only the pure in heart can go this distance and see God (Matt. 5:8). Only the righteous, those who wear the tunic and sash and know how to put on the robe of authority, can tap into the deep realms of prayer and intercession.

The robe of blue also represents *divinity*. The intercessor who wears the robe of Christ's righteous divinity should remain in a position of *praying through* instead of *praying about*. We need to change our terminologies. So often we say, "I'm praying about it." The Lord has been dealing with me about that. Instead of saying, "I'm praying about it," I need to say, "I'm praying it through." When you are praying *about* something, it means that you are still waiting for God to do it. When you are praying something *through*, it means that you believe it was already done when you first declared the Word in prayer.

There's a huge difference between going *to* a door and going *through* it. I can go to a door and not go through that door to the other side. But when you declare that you are going through a door, then you are saying that you are in the process of coming through the other side to your destination.

When you embrace the divinity of God in your priestly robe, it means that the outcome of the situation you are praying through will have nothing to do with man. The answer will be the divine intervention of God, which you have already obtained in prayer. When you possess that divine spirit, you can know that crack cocaine is going to be broken off of somebody's life. Why? You possess the anointing that creates, re-creates, constructs, and reconstructs. Creativity lives inside of you. The same God who spoke and created the heavens and the earth is going to speak again, through you—and, as a result, people's lives, your church, and even your own spirit will never be the same. When you go into intercession you activate the divine spirit through your robe of blue.

You don't have to go into your prayer chamber hoping and wishing that God will hear your prayer. *You can go in knowing God will perform His Word.* Why? Because you already possess everything required for Him to turn it around. Hebrews 11:6 says, "But without faith it is impossible to please and be satisfactory to Him. For whoever would come near to God must [necessarily] believe that God exists and that He is the rewarder of those who earnestly and diligently seek Him [out]." When you possess the divine spirit, you can speak the Word, and things will begin to move and turn. The divine authority to heal sick bodies and change lives resides in you right now!

Not only does the priestly robe give you authority in prayer, but also it covers you while you pray. It protects you. The devil can't get a foothold in your spirit while you are praying because you have a soul tie with God! He may try to attack you on the outside, but he can never hinder what you have been called to do. God covers you as you remain in prayer.

Declare this right now: "I walk in authority. I walk with a divine spirit. I walk in divinity, and I am covered. The Spirit of the Lord is going to work through me, because I have submitted my life to God."

WHY DON'T YOU HAVE THE VICTORY?

What are the reasons why many of God's people do not have victory in prayer? The ingredients that lead to a lack of power in prayer are locked up in *discouragement* and *weariness.* In 2 Corinthians 4:1, Paul states these reasons clearly:

> Therefore, since we do hold and engage in this ministry by the mercy of God [granting us favor, benefits, opportunities, and especially salvation], we do not get discouraged (spiritless and despondent with fear) or become faint with weariness and exhaustion.

Discouragement and weariness will make you spiritless, despondent, doubtful, and full of fear. As an intercessor, the only way you can become discouraged and weary is when one or more of these ingredients have taken up residence in you. Paul tells us that this happens when we fail to renounce "disgraceful ways (secret thoughts, feelings, desires and underhandedness, the methods and arts that men hide through shame)" (v. 2). We are told to "refuse to deal craftily (to practice trickery and cunning) or to adulterate or handle dishonestly the Word of God" (v. 2). We are to state the truth openly, clearly, and candidly.

If you have not renounced trickery—writing bad checks, not paying your tithes, repeating gossip, stealing items from the tape table at church, cussing people out, getting mad because somebody's sitting in your favorite seat, and the like—then you are mishandling the Word of God. You have to renounce any "disgraceful ways" in your life if you expect to succeed in prayer. That's why some people who declare, "The joy of the Lord is my strength," aren't experiencing joy.

Instead of trying to declare joy when they come to the house of God without their tunic and robe, these believers need to go and put on their garments. In other words, they need to go back and repent to the person they just offended. Otherwise, they are mishandling the Word of God and using the Scriptures to try and justify their own shortcomings. And if one scripture doesn't apply, they will find another one: "Well, His grace is sufficient for me...His strength is made perfect in my weakness." If that doesn't work they will go to the old landmark, "He loves me."

While it's true that Jesus loves us, let me take you to Revelation 3:19 where He declares what His love is all about: "Those whom I [dearly and tenderly] love, I tell their faults and convict and convince and reprove and chasten [I discipline and instruct them]. So be enthusiastic and in earnest and burning with zeal and repent [changing your mind and attitude]." Jesus loves you when He cuts the fire out of you. He loves you when He rebukes and convicts you of sin. He loves you when He tells you your faults!

The real proof that God loves you isn't the fact that you can feel goose bumps during a service. It's not because you are crying. It's because He exposes your wrongdoings. He identifies the reasons why you have fear instead of faith. When you go to Him in prayer, He helps you to understand why you have been full of doubt and unbelief. Now you will love Him like never before! God shows His love by purifying you so your prayers won't be hindered.

YOU HAVE A DOUBLE PORTION OF PROTECTION

Let's move on. Exodus 28:29–32 tells us that the neckband of the priestly robe Moses gave to Aaron was reinforced. An extra band was woven around the neck opening to keep it from fraying or tearing. The construction of the neckband was so strong that if someone had tried to tear this robe off the high priest, it would have broken his neck. When we look at this symbolically, your robe of authority has been so designed that it can never be torn from you.

Because it symbolizes the office of authority and divinity, the robe becomes the strength of your relationship with God in prayer. Righteousness is your passageway, and the belt of truth is what enables you to stand, but when you get into the presence of the Lord, the enemy can never shake the authority of God. He cannot tear it away from you! Too many Christians are not aware of their authority in God; they do not realize they are walking in divinity and consecration by virtue of their spiritual garments.

When you guard the garments Christ has given you, you are the very symbol of authority to every enemy of the cross. This means that when you go into prayer clothed with authority, the enemy already knows that he cannot win. He knows that he cannot scare you out of praying by tormenting you with satanic visions and dreams, showing you demonic figures on the wall, causing you to hear strange voices, noises, and the like.

I have actually had some of these experiences—suddenly a door slams, but nobody is there. Suddenly, you feel a cool breeze, but no doors or windows are open. These are Satan's devices that he will use to chase you out of prayer. But when you pray wearing the spiritual robe of authority and are clothed in righteousness with the belt of truth girded tightly around you declaring that to the enemy—you won't be scared out of prayer. You won't come out until you have an answer from God.

That's why you should come into the presence of the Lord giving Him praise for the victory. When you look at your garments and see the works of Christ, and then look at the colors in the door of the tabernacle, you can declare that He's a redeemer. You know without a doubt that He's a deliverer, your Savior, who gives you authority over every demon spirit.

You enter His gates by praising God with authority: "God, I praise You because You're *Jehovah Jireh,* my provider." "Lord, I thank You because You are my righteousness." "God, I give You the glory because You are the banner that watches over me." "I thank You because You are *Jehovah Rapha,* my healer." Although you are coming to God to make intercession for someone who is sick in his or her body, before you get to the throne you have to start blessing God in the outer court. You begin by giving praises to Him because you know who He is.

You have to embrace His authority in your praise before you ever get to intercession. If you can't praise Him with authority, you won't be able to express His authority in prayer. Remember that "he is a rewarder of them that diligently seek him" (Heb. 11:6, KJV). Do you see the pattern? Believing that *He is* represents my praise of His authority. Once I reach the most holy place, then I begin to understand that *He is a rewarder* of them that diligently seek Him. But first I must believe that He is and praise Him in that way.

Don't waste time praying until you can believe God will do something. That's why many come out of prayer without answers. They came into prayer incorrectly! You have to come to the throne of grace boldly—not wondering timidly if God is going to perform His Word. I don't waste time wondering if God will do what He said. I come to prayer expecting God to tell me what to do next. There's a big difference in prayer when you know your authority.

If the Holy Spirit tells you to wake up every morning at 6:00 a.m. and hop on one leg, do it. I don't care who comes in your house and says, "Why are you hopping like that? That doesn't make any sense."

Just say, "That's all right. I know who God is, and He told me to hop like this, so I'm just doing it His way, not mine." If God tells you to do something during your time of personal prayer, do exactly what He says.

God chooses to work miracles in many different ways in order to prevent us from turning His power into a formula. Think about it. No two miracles in the Bible were exactly alike. In this God is saying, "I'm going to make you seek Me out, so that I can clothe you with righteousness, stabilize you in truth, and strengthen you with authority. Then I'm going to cause you to wait until I tell you exactly how I want to do it."

God will not allow anyone to gain a monopoly on His ways. No one is going to be able to control deliverance. Some people get delivered by laughing. He delivers others through tears. Some people get delivered by being put out in the street, and still others come into deliverance by being knocked out under the power of God on the floor. God's ways are beyond finding out!

When Jesus found out that Lazarus was dying, He didn't rush

because there was a human emergency. (See John 11:1–44.) When they came and told him, "Lazarus is dying! You'd better hurry up, Jesus, he's going to die!" Jesus was already busy doing what the Father was directing Him to do. He didn't say, "Get me a horse so I can get there fast; otherwise, Lazarus is going to die." Jesus knew His authority. Instead, this was His response: "When Jesus received the message, He said, This sickness is not to end in death; but [on the contrary] it is to honor God and to promote His glory, that the Son of God may be glorified through (by) it" (v. 4).

When Jesus arrived in Bethany four days after Lazarus died, He commanded the people to roll away the stone from Lazarus' grave. Then He "lifted up His eyes and said, Father, I thank You that You have heard Me. Yes, I know You always hear and listen to Me, but I have said this on account of and for the benefit of the people standing around, so that they may believe that You did send Me [that You have made Me Your Messenger]. When He had said this, He shouted with a loud voice, Lazarus, come out!" (vv. 41–43). And who said we shouldn't shout when we pray?

Jesus acknowledged the Father in praise and then declared life through His Word. He didn't let the fear of the flesh rush Him. As an intercessor, neither should you. When the devil tries to manipulate you with fear and intimidation, don't listen. Keep standing in prayer according to the will of God, knowing that the Spirit searches the mind of God and will reveal what you need to do.

God is telling you: "I'm breaking your codependency on people and perfect situations. I'm trying to help you to understand that I allowed your situation to get as bad as it has, because I'm tired of you depending on somebody else. Come to Me, and I'll give you rest."

God is trying to give you a robe of authority. Don't reject this robe. Don't try to take the easy way out. Recognize that God has allowed you to be placed in a deadlocked situation so that He can step in and give you power to overcome that situation. Don't be afraid of the deadlock! Don't rush to come up with your own quick solution. You don't have to rush or be upset when you are confronted with challenges on every side, because you know YOUR GOD. The same God who paid your car note off is going to pay someone else's rent. The God who healed your body is going to do the same for somebody else. If you know YOUR GOD, you can operate in your God-given authority!

As an intercessor and part of the royal priesthood, your job is not to worry and complain. Your job is to keep the presence of the Lord in the room. When the devil tries to frustrate you, just remind him that he can't do anything about what God has already done through your prayers. Operating in your authority means you can stand and declare that God has already made a way out of no way. Your job is to bless Him. Your job is to praise God, because when you let praise come out of your mouth you are telling the devil, "I'm not going to lose my authority."

Stop right now, and praise Jesus for being your authority. Give glory to God because He is your authority, and He cannot and will not ever be shaken. By blessing God, you are telling the devil that everything he tried against you didn't work. You still have power! You still have authority!

Thank God that your robe of blue gives you authority over the enemy, and nothing can tear it off of you. When the devil tries to pull you in some direction away from God's authority, your robe will not come off. If he tries to yank you another way, it is not going to budge. Though he may try to pull you down, tell lies about you, mess with your family, your finances, your mind, or your ministry—your mandate, or your robe of authority will never come off.

Having done all, you will be able to stand and give God the praise. Don't ever take your robe off by believing the lies of the enemy and relinquishing your authority. As long as you keep your robe on, you can take back everything the enemy has ever stolen from you.

THE EPHOD

After receiving a robe of blue, the next garment Aaron received was the ephod (Lev. 8:7). "He put on Aaron the long undertunic, girded him with the long sash, clothed him with the robe, put the ephod (an upper vestment) upon him, and girded him with the skillfully woven cords attached to the ephod, binding it to him." According to Exodus 28:8, the ephod consisted of gold (*deity*), blue/turquoise (*divinity*), purple (*the royal One*), scarlet (*servanthood* and *humanity*), and white fine-twined linen. Notice again that the ephod has an attached belt, so it provides a second level of girding for intercessory prayer; this belt was able to be seen by others.

The ephod clothes you in the garment that represents the mediator Jesus Christ and His power to become a servant. Before it was woven with the other colors, the gold cord had to be beaten out. Just so, when He clothes you with the ephod, it confirms the trials and tests you have overcome in order to get to this level. Your gold says, "I've already been through the fire and survived the worst of it. So I'm ready for whatever comes my way in prayer."

In Luke 12:35, Jesus told His disciples, "Keep your loins girded and your lamps burning." This scripture admonishes us to keep the oil of the Spirit, the anointing of God, upon us. He also told His disciples to be waiting expectedly, "like men who are waiting for their master to return home from the marriage feast, so that when He returns from the wedding and comes and knocks, they may open to him immediately" (v. 36). Why should we be waiting expectedly with our loins girded and our anointing in place? Verse 37 tells us the reason: "Blessed (happy, fortunate, and to be envied) are those servants whom the master finds awake and alert and watching when he comes. Truly I say to you, he will gird himself and have them recline at table and will come and serve them!"

When the Spirit of the Lord finds us girded, He responds by girding Himself to us—so that we can relax at His table. This means we have a part to play in the process of prayer. Our first step in the process is to surrender to God. Then we have to walk in prayer until the Spirit of the Lord comes and takes over. He girds Himself and begins to serve us, answering our prayers and ministering to us about what we have brought to Him.

As a kingdom of priests, we have been commanded to enter into His rest (Heb. 3:7–11). It is only when we rest in the Lord that we can serve others as He has served us. In John 13, we see an example of Christ girding Himself as a servant so that He could operate in the Spirit and serve the spiritual needs of others. It was just before the beginning of the Passover feast, and Jesus was very aware that the time had almost arrived for His sacrificial death on the cross. (See John 13:1–5.) He knew that once He returned to His Father in heaven, His disciples would be left without His earthly presence.

He met with His disciples for one last supper together. "So [it was] during supper, Satan having already put the thought of betraying Jesus in the heart of Judas Iscariot, Simon's son, [that] Jesus, knowing (fully aware) that the Father had put everything into His hands, and that He had come from God and was [now] returning to God, got up from supper, took off His garments, and taking a [servant's] towel, He fastened it around His waist. Then He poured water into the washbasin and began to wash the disciples' feet and to wipe them with the [servant's] towel with which He was girded" (John 13:2–5).

This example from John displays the *humility* and *servanthood* of Christ. As an intercessor, you must willingly take up the burden of the Lord—take on other people's situations or circumstances—and become a servant to them in prayer. We are not to be concerned about only the things that interest ourselves. We are to have the "attitude and purpose and [humble] mind" that Christ had (Phil. 2:5). He is our example in humility. How did He respond to the needs of others? In Philippians 2:6–8, we find the answer to that question: "Who, although being essentially one with God and in the form of God [possessing the fullness of the attributes which make God God], did not think this equality with God was a thing to be eagerly grasped or retained, but stripped Himself [of all privileges and rightful dignity], so as to assume the guise of a servant (slave), in that He became like men and was born a human being. And after He had appeared in human form, He abased and humbled Himself [still further] and carried His obedience to the extreme of death, even the death of the cross!"

In 1 Samuel 30:1–20, the Amalekites invaded Ziklag, burned it with fire, and took the women captive. When they saw the devastation, David and those with him wept until they could weep no more. Then David called for Abiathar the priest to bring him the ephod—and he cried out to the Lord. The Scripture says, "The Lord answered him, Pursue, for you shall surely recover all" (v. 8). David not only recovered all, but he also captured all the flocks and herds of Israel's enemy (v. 20). When David humbled himself under the priestly anointing of the ephod and inquired of the Lord, they took back everything that had been stolen from all of the people.

Christ's ephod helps you to serve others, especially those who are weak or of a lesser status—*by His grace*—to help the immature come to maturity. I have heard intercessors say, "God showed me this about a particular person," then they turn around and say, "But I don't have patience with that." If this is you, do you really think this attitude is pleasing to God? This attitude does not reflect that you are truly girded with the ephod of the Lord.

There were two onyx stones on the shoulders of the ephod. These stones were inscribed with the names of the twelve tribes of Israel, but they appeared in a different order than those on the breastplate. On the ephod, they were inscribed in the order of their birthright. But these same names were ascribed on an attached piece of the garment called the *breastplate* according to the will of God.

Let me clarify this by revelation. You may know something about someone and carry this burden on your shoulders. You may know how she was born in the Spirit, how she's doing right now, and be familiar with her family background (i.e., all of her uncles were alcoholics, and that's why she's an alcoholic, and so on). Knowing these things, you have to bind this prayer request to your heart (breastplate), and seek God to reveal His will. You are confronted with two descriptions of the person you are praying for. First, the way she was born into the kingdom, and, second, the will of God for that individual's life. When you come out of intercession with a word from the Lord, God illuminates and perfects what you have brought before Him. In other words, you look on your shoulder and see what she used to be, and then look at the breastplate...giving glory to God for what He has done.

Second Corinthians 4:18 says, "We look not at the things which are seen, but at the things which are not seen: for the things which are seen are temporal; but the things which are not seen are eternal" (KJV). When you put on your ephod in prayer, you can be confident that God is able to do "exceeding abundantly above all that we ask or think," not according to the power of what you see, but according to *His power,* which works within you because of your servanthood humility (Eph. 3:20, KJV).

THE BREASTPLATE

The breastplate was the next piece of clothing Aaron received in Leviticus 8:8: "And Moses put upon Aaron the breastplate; also he put in the breastplate the Urim and the Thummim [articles upon which the high priest put his hand when seeking the divine will concerning the nation]." This garment is vital to becoming an intercessor. Inside the breastplate was a slip of parchment containing the divine name of God, represented by the Urim and Thummim. (See Exodus 28:28–30.)

Urim means "light," and *Thummim* means "completeness." Many believe that God communicated with the high priest by causing individual letters of tribal names to light up in a specific order. When the high priest read the letters in the proper order, he received a complete and true answer from God for the nation of Israel.[2] God's "Ineffable Name" within the breastplate would bring His divine direction to earth.

The breastplate also represents people that you carry to God in prayer, symbolized by the twelve precious stones. This breastplate was worn upon the chest of the high priest, indicating that he carried the people's burdens close to his heart as he served in the tabernacle.

I compare this to a prayer request list. God supernaturally "binds" these people to your chest so that their burdens stay close to your heart. As you pray, light enters the situation and God starts perfecting the thing you have carried to Him in prayer. This is yet another way you know when He has truly "girded" you in intercession. Can you carry a name to the point of victory?

THE MITER

Now we are at the final piece of the garment, the miter, the headpiece. Leviticus 8:9 states: "And he put the turban or miter on his head; on it, in front, Moses put the shining gold plate, the holy diadem, as the Lord commanded him." Moses placed the miter, or turban, on Aaron's head. The miter was like a hat, with one distinguishing feature—the holy crown. This was actually a golden plate that was tied to the front of the miter (Exod. 28:36–38). Its inscription read, "HOLY TO THE LORD" (v. 36). This symbolized that the nation of Israel was completely devoted to God and His service. It also reminded priests never to take holiness for granted as they carried out their duties. At all times they were to conduct their lives worthy of His name.

I believe the miter can be likened to the "helmet of salvation" in Ephesians 6:17. It's an important part of the spiritual armor you use to wage war in prayer: "And take the helmet of salvation, and the sword of the Spirit, which is the word of God: praying always with all supplication in the Spirit, and watching thereunto with all perseverance and supplication for all saints" (vv. 17–18, KJV).

The miter helps you to watch and pray. God fastens it to your head after He has put everything else in place, so that you will never forget to pray and live in a manner that's worthy of your call to be an intercessor. Remember Ephesians 4:1–3:

> I therefore, the prisoner for the Lord, appeal to and beg you to walk (lead a life) worthy of the [divine] calling to which you have been called [with behavior that is a credit to the summons to God's service, living as becomes you] with complete lowliness of mind (humility) and meekness (unselfishness, gentleness, mildness), with patience, bearing with one another and making allowances because you love one another. Be eager and strive earnestly to guard and keep the harmony and oneness of [and produced by] the Spirit in the binding power of peace.

YOU ARE A LIVING TABERNACLE

When you are fully clothed, you have been equipped to stand firmly as a royal priest before God. Having been summoned to serve others in prayer and clothed with the garments of preparation, you are ready to be anointed for your assignment and to enter the holy place. As you move from the brazen altar to the door of the tabernacle you must be holy. In order to move into the realm of that which is holy, there must be a match—a coming together with God in agreement—same life, same mind, same spirit. You are the light of the world, and, as such, you will bear the burden of the Lord in prayer. Now that you have come into divine agreement, you will work in harmony with Him and with others.

The colors and elements you are about to see in the holy place are also in your priestly garments, which creates a match in the Spirit realm. Now everyone should be able to see the "new you," *even the enemy.* Hear me. He will know that his time is short, because you are moving into the realm of intercession. You have washed at the brazen laver and have been purified at the brazen altar—now you have been clothed to go to the next level.

> For we are the temple of the living God; even as God said, I will dwell in and with and among them and will walk in and with and among them, and I will be their God, and they shall be My people.
> —2 CORINTHIANS 6:16

Be careful... if your life doesn't exemplify the characteristics of your priestly clothing, then the priesthood—and the anointing to be an intercessor—won't be upon you. If there's no harmony between the *colors* in your life and those in the holy place, you won't experience the proper flow of the Spirit in prayer—and you won't see results.

Make "your calling and election sure" today, because you are the temple of the Holy Spirit, a living, breathing tabernacle—which gives you entry into His divine presence and gives Him entry into every situation that is brought before Him. You can approach God right now; you don't have to wait until you get to heaven to have a relationship with Him. *Go to Him in your spirit man.* This is the final match, spirit to Spirit, through God's pattern of prayer:

> A time will come... indeed it is already here, when the true (genuine) worshipers will worship the Father in spirit and in truth (reality); for the Father is seeking just such people as these as His worshipers. God is a Spirit (a spiritual Being) and those who worship Him must worship Him in spirit and in truth (reality).
> —JOHN 4:23–24

As you worship God in the realm of the Spirit and in truth, you will move closer to the holy place, holding the fire from your sacrifice on the brazen altar. Suddenly, you will discover that the power of God is really real. Your old prayer life will be gone. *Suddenly*... all things will have "become new" (2 Cor. 5:17, NKJV).

CHAPTER 7

The Tabernacle Door

*I*N THE PROCESS of prophecy and time, God was bringing humanity to the point of receiving Jesus Christ. We see this as Aaron and his sons began serving daily in the tabernacle because their new garments classified them as operating in the authority of God—just as we operate in the authority of Christ. When people saw these men, they knew exactly who they were and what they had been called to do. They recognized that the power of God rested upon God's priests. The priestly wardrobe served as a habitual statute. Any time people saw Aaron or his sons, they knew who they were in God by what they were wearing. When you have come through the outer court, the priestly garments God places on you will be visible to others and will identify the power of God at work in your life.

Jesus was the last and final high priest. After He made the ultimate sacrifice, there was no need for another sacrificial lamb to operate in this role. So when we read about Aaron and his sons operating in the temple, we should understand that by coming into relationship with Christ, we have become the sons of God and are being prepared to assume the priestly role of intercessor. Remember that it takes a high priest and his sons to perform the temple service.

You, as a son or daughter of the kingdom, must have Christ living inside you to be qualified to enter the door to the holy place. Christ was *the way* at the gate to the outer court. When you have washed at the brazen laver and sacrificed at the brazen altar, Jesus has now become *the truth* that lives in your spirit man. You can come boldly before the throne of God, because the High Priest lives in you (Heb. 4:14–16). Jesus has already been adorned with the tunic, the trousers, the sash, the robe, the ephod, the breastplate, the Urim and Thummim, and the turban. So when you "put on" Christ, you have put on the attire of consecration to serve in the holy place. I must repeat this statement—when you accept the work of Christ in the outer court, you have now put on the wardrobe of consecration.

Let me break this down even further. During the Old Testament inauguration service, Moses washed, dressed, and anointed Aaron and his sons to serve in the priesthood. He also anointed the tabernacle and everything in it. (See Leviticus 8.) Then God required them to stay at the entrance of the tabernacle for seven days to complete their inauguration (Lev. 8:31–33). This whole process consecrated them into the priesthood.

Catch the significance of what God is saying to us. Too many believers waste time doing religious things. Too many say things like, "I'm going on a twenty-one-day fast because I want to be consecrated." No! Being clothed properly under the anointing is what consecrates you. When you put on everything that Christ is, knowing beyond any shadow of doubt that Christ dwells in you, making sure that iniquity doesn't strip you of your priestly clothing, you will walk in the consistent power of consecration.

You don't have to go on a fast to become consecrated. You are supposed to walk in the power of consecration every day! You have been given authority in Christ because you are wearing the right clothes. That's why Isaiah 61:10 says, "I will greatly rejoice in the Lord, my soul will exult in my God; for He has clothed me with the garments of salvation, He has covered me with the robe of righteousness, as a bridegroom decks himself with a garland, and as a bride adorns herself with her jewels." Your spiritual garments give you power!

You must always be careful to guard your attitude about God's power within. Once you have come through the outer court, the *religious* part of you can feel that you have been given power in God *by virtue of your own works.* For example, it's easy to become self-righteous when you have completed a twenty-one- or forty-day consecration, because you think that you have earned a deeper place in God.

What I love about God is that He doesn't need our works. He needs our faith in our salvation! That's why any person who is truly saved can cast out a demon or open blinded eyes. You don't have to be an evangelist or a bishop to pray and see somebody get healed of cancer. The only requirement is that you must possess the high priest deep in your spirit. When you guard your garments, you can rebuke the devil and walk in *right now* power of God!

I'm learning every day that staying properly clothed is a decision that must be made through the Word (Truth) and not by my emotions. That's why the enemy works hard to keep us operating in our emotions, because emotions dictate feelings, and feelings dictate response. But when we are robed in righteousness and girded with the belt of truth, we will know that whenever the devil speaks, he's a lying wonder. In other words, you may feel sick in your body, but when you know the truth of the Word, you can walk in the reality that by His stripes you are healed (Isa. 53:5).

As you move into this deeper level of prayer, you cannot walk in your feelings. You must learn how to walk in your new wardrobe.

GUARDING YOUR GARMENTS

You must never forget that the foundation of every garment is the tunic of righteousness. Because of this, it is the responsibility of the Holy Spirit to keep you in check and make sure that your righteousness is authentic. Once while I was praying on the threshing floor (a place of prayer), God said to me, "It is necessary that I expose you to wrongdoing so that I can check your spirit to see if right is really birthed in you." You don't know that your heart is in right standing with God as long as everything is perfectly right around you.

God has to allow real believers to be confronted with real issues—because our walk with Him isn't based on what may be happening externally. This is why it is vital for you to guard your garments. Do you really have righteousness birthed in you, or are you going to church every week (perhaps even speaking in tongues, jumping, shouting, and so on), yet you don't have real salvation? I believe God allows things to happen for you to see how you are going to react. He proves your spirit to birth righteousness in you, because He can only use the righteous to bring His kingdom to the earth through prayer. A true intercessor must consistently display the righteousness of the Lord! That's why Aaron and his sons had to be inaugurated before they could serve in the holy place.

You can go to the door of the tabernacle and not be able to get in. You can go to the place of prayer but still not be able to get an answer from God. You can go to the altar and try to make intercession, but you can't exchange places with someone who is destined to die unless you are righteous.

But if you have truly guarded your garments, when you pray, God's power and wisdom will operate through your prayers, and you will reap a "harvest." James 3:17–18 says, "But the wisdom from above is first of all pure (undefiled); then it is peace-loving, courteous (considerate, gentle). [It is willing to] yield to reason, full of compassion and good fruits; it is wholehearted and straightforward, impartial and unfeigned (free from doubts, wavering, and insincerity). And the harvest of righteousness (of conformity to God's will in thought and deed) is [the fruit of the seed] sown in peace by those who work for and make peace [in themselves and in others, that peace which means concord, agreement, and harmony between individuals, with undisturbedness, in a peaceful mind free from fears and agitating passions and moral conflicts]."

As an intercessor, your job is to get the wisdom from above, because this wisdom is unfeigned; it doesn't carry doubt. There's a huge difference between saying, "Lord, I believe You will do it," and getting the pure wisdom from above that displays every good fruit and yields a harvest. When you are operating in this wisdom according to the righteousness of God, you can pray with peace. You won't see somebody dying of cancer and lose it. The peace of God will be with you, because if death was the route that God chose to heal, then though you are in pain, your spirit is in peace.

This is why I believe it takes this process to come out of outer court prayer and go through the door that leads to intercession in the holy place. As "the righteous," you now reflect the righteousness of God, which means you must be delivered from every form of self-righteousness. Most people perceive that those who walk in true authority are "self-righteous." Not necessarily so! Those who walk in true authority simply recognize the righteousness that's within them. They stay filled with the Word to such an extent that they walk in godly confidence and self-control. These are the kind of believers who can walk into a situation and say, "I can handle this. This isn't a big deal to God," and get the job done for the kingdom.

On the other hand, I believe we must be aware that at this point, a self-righteous attitude can creep in if we do not keep returning to the brazen altar. Self-righteousness is extremely dangerous, because the enemy comes in with deception that tries to keep believers operating in a form of spirituality without personal deliverance. He does this by confronting them only with situations they can handle. This keeps them in a mind-set of believing they are victorious when they are not even involved in warfare! In actuality, they are not confronting the enemy; therefore, he doesn't confront them with anything they can't handle. He never confronts them with things that would cause them to depend upon God.

Too many have been Christians for years and think they are victorious, when that couldn't be further from the truth. That's self-righteousness in its highest form. The enemy also tries to keep these believers away from other believers who could challenge them to go to another level. He knows that if that happened, they would cry out to God. Hear me. If you never have to depend upon the strength of the Lord, then your righteousness doesn't come from God. That's why we absolutely need the white linen tunic underneath all of our other priestly clothing. It covers all of our human nakedness and limitations. By clothing us with the tunic and every other garment, God is demonstrating that He wants our lives to be testimonies to the fact that *He is our keeper.*

As you walk toward the door of the holy place, you have to walk in the strength of the Lord, knowing that if it were up to you, you would have failed every test in the outer court.

THE REAL POWER OF GRACE

It is through the grace of God that we are able to walk in Christ's righteousness. I believe that many believers walk out of context with what the

Word of God teaches about walking in grace. Grace is the strength of the Lord; it is what gives us power to overcome. It also is a never-ending gift of God. "But He gives us more and more grace (power of the Holy Spirit, to meet this evil tendency and all others fully). That is why He says, God sets Himself against the proud and haughty, but gives grace [continually] to the lowly (those who are humble enough to receive it)" (James 4:6).

That's pretty clear, isn't it? *Grace* is the power of the Holy Spirit to help us overcome the evil tendencies of the flesh. Romans 5:20 explains that although we are totally unable to live righteously by following the Law, God's grace can make us victorious over sin:

> But then Law came in, [only] to expand and increase the trespass [making it more apparent and exciting opposition]. But where sin increased and abounded, grace (God's unmerited favor) has surpassed it and increased the more and superabounded.

Sadly, many people say that they *know* the Lord, but they don't really know Him—they only *know of Him*. It may appear as though they are operating from the holy place. Some may even be teaching the Word, yet they are not living in purification. They teach Scripture, based on the elementary level on which they live on a daily basis. They teach a version of the Bible and a limited understanding of God's grace, which causes people to live in the realm of the flesh and feel comfortable.

As sons and daughters in God's kingdom, we should never feel comfortable living in habitual sin, thinking, *Whatever I do is OK, because the Lord is gracious and merciful.* Here is the truth: *Where sin abounds, grace much more abounds.* That means that when an evil opportunity is present, God gives more and more grace (the power of the Holy Spirit) for you to overcome this evil tendency.

In Webster's dictionary, the first definition for *grace* is, "a pleasing or an attractive quality of endowment." To me, this speaks to the fact that God has ascribed and imputed unto me His righteousness. Though I was a sinner, He has endowed me with attractiveness. I have been graced to wear His righteousness as my covering.

The second definition for *grace* is, "mercy or clemency or pardon." Many believers have chosen to live at this level of grace. They carelessly think, *I know God called me to be an intercessor, but I'm going to keep mess-ing up. I'll keep fornicating, lying, and submitting to every evil tendency because God will be merciful. It's OK, because God understands. He knows I'm not perfect.* Do you see the error in this way of thinking? These people put so much emphasis on mercy and grace that the righteousness of God cannot transform their lives!

The third definition of *grace* is, "freely given, unmerited favor of the love of God." While God's grace does give us unmerited favor for salva-tion (and in other areas of our lives), too many have used this as a spiri-tual crutch. They say, "God loves us. He gives grace and mercy. While I'm fornicating, Lord, just keep giving me grace. Whenever I lie, I'll receive Your grace, Lord." Those who live this way aren't even trying to come out of a life of sin! How can God use these people effectively in prayer to deliver others?

Then I came to the fourth definition of *grace*: "the influence of the Spirit of God operating in a human being." Do you see this? When sin abounds, the influence of the Spirit of God within you begins to increase, so that you don't have to fall to the works of the devil! Romans 6:1–5 says:

> What shall we say [to all this]? Are we to remain in sin in order that God's grace (favor and mercy) may multiply and overflow? Certainly not! How can we who died to sin live in it any longer? Are you ignorant of the fact that all of us who have been baptized into Christ Jesus were baptized into His death? We were buried therefore with Him by the baptism into death, so that just as Christ was raised from the dead by the glorious [power] of the Father, so we too might [habitually] live and behave in newness of life. For if we have become one with Him by sharing a death like His, we shall also be [one with Him in sharing] His resurrection [by a new life lived for God].

When we "put on" the Lord Jesus Christ, we can *habitually* live in new-ness of life! Christians have to come out of the mind-set that says, "I'm going to keep messing up because God will forgive me," and embrace the *grace* that says, "When sin comes knocking at my door, the power of God is going to elevate and ignite me from within. God has given me power to stand against this evil tendency!" Do you see this? Every time you are able to say *no* to the devil, you are operating in grace. The mercy of God will keep you from dying in your mess! To have grace means to have power with God through His righteousness! That's how you can boldly enter into the holy place.

With the grace of God at work within you, it will be possible for you to guard your priestly garments. In Ephesians, Paul refers to these garments as the armor of God. He challenges us to "put on God's complete armor, that you may be able to resist and stand your ground on the evil day [of danger], and, having done all [the crisis demands], to stand [firmly in your place]. Stand therefore [hold your ground], having tightened the belt of truth around your loins and having put on the breastplate of integrity and of moral rectitude and right standing with God" (Eph. 6:13–14).

You have to "put on" something to be able to stand. You won't be able to stand merely because you speak in tongues or attend church several times a week. *You will be able to stand when you are dressed for the battle.* The enemy recognizes clothes. I must reiterate the story from Acts 19:14–16, where the sons of Sceva (who didn't have a relationship with Jesus) tried to cast out devils in His name, and the enemy tore off their clothes. They stood before the enemy naked (in the strength of their humanity—not dressed in Christ's righteousness), which gave the enemy the authority to strip them.

Acts 19:15 says, "But [one] evil spirit retorted, Jesus I know, and Paul I know about, but who are you?" The devil exposes you only to who you are. He knows when you're not clothed in righteousness. He knows when you're not operating under the anointing of the Lord. The enemy automatically knows when you're not operating in purification! If you are not ready to let the grace of God live through you, you had better think twice before announcing that you are an intercessor. You have to be fully dressed in prayer, because the devil knows when you are not operating in truth.

Too many Christians are pretending to be intercessors, coming to the altar, speaking in fancy tongues, and so on. When you are an intercessor, you may not make it to the church building to pray. Therefore, you have to walk in the righteousness of the Lord with prayer in your spirit—wherever you may be. Then the devil will know when you wake up in the morning that you are coming to tear his kingdom down. The very fact that you open your eyes each day should be a threat to the devil's kingdom.

Prayer and intercession aren't about coming to the church to pray. It's not about meeting up with your prayer group. Intercession is about having righteousness birthed in you to the point that you no longer operate in the flesh. Instead, you have picked up the burden of the Lord. When you are an intercessor, you might be in the grocery store when God suddenly drops someone into your spirit. When that happens, you won't have time to run to the church. You must have God's power within you, so that whenever you come under the anointing of the Lord you can pray and cast the devil out—whether it be in the grocery store, your living room, on your job—anywhere.

This is why the Lord can't trust a lot of people to pray. When a church announces that it is going to have a musical or that a well-known preacher is coming to minister, the house is packed. But let the church say, "We're going to have a prayer meeting." Only a few people show up, because only the righteous can hear the call to prayer! If you are not among *the righteous*, you can't hear the alarm sounding. You don't truly know that the world is in trouble and that Jesus is the only answer. Only the righteous can pick up the burden of the Lord in prayer!

THE HIGH PRIEST IS CALLING YOU

As a real intercessor, you can never stop praying. You may be driving on the highway when the power of God comes upon you, and you will have to pull over onto the shoulder to pray. When you are a real intercessor, the Holy Spirit can catch you up into the Spirit realm at any time of day or night. An intercessor doesn't just work a regular schedule. He or she often doesn't sleep through the night. An intercessor will say, "Lord, where You lead me, I'll follow." An intercessor will say, "God, whatever You want me to do, wherever You want me to go, whatever You want me to say...I'm willing."

The High Priest leads you into intercession. He keeps leading you to the holy place, because He's the only one who is qualified to bring you to the throne of God. The High Priest pulls you into prayer on behalf of your family. He keeps pulling you to the threshing floor, the floor of prayer, on behalf of your neighborhood.

Every time I think I have prayed something through, the High Priest pulls me into intercession again on behalf of someone else. Then He pulls me into prayer again on behalf of the president or for leaders of other countries. At times He pulls me into prayer for personal needs. The High Priest keeps taking me into the holy place. So I must guard my garments, because Jesus is leading me, and He's fully dressed. I have to remain in agreement with Him.

MAKING A STAND

The biblical story of Shadrach, Meshach, and Abednego gives us a perfect example of the power to stand. (See Daniel 3:19–27.) These three young men refused to bow and worship the golden image. Their refusal angered King Nebuchadnezzar, and he commanded that they be thrown in a furnace that had been heated seven times hotter than usual. The strongest men in his army were commanded to bind Shadrach, Meshach, and Abednego and cast them into the burning fiery furnace (vv. 19–20). "Then these [three] men were bound *in their cloaks, their tunics or undergarments, their turbans, and their other clothing*, and they were cast into the midst of the burning fiery furnace" (v. 21, emphasis added).

The fire was so hot that it killed the men who had thrown them into the furnace. Now look at what happened next:

> Then Nebuchadnezzar the king [saw and] was astounded, and he jumped up and said to his counselors, Did we not cast three men bound into the midst of the fire? They answered, True, O king. He answered, Behold, I see four men loose, walking in the midst of the fire, and they are not hurt! And the form of the fourth is like a son of the gods! Then Nebuchadnezzar came near to the mouth of the burning fiery furnace and said, Shadrach, Meshach, and Abednego, you servants of the Most High God, come out and come here. Then Shadrach, Meshach, and Abednego came out from the midst of the fire. And the satraps, the deputies, the governors, and the king's counselors gathered around together and saw these men—that the

fire had no power upon their bodies, nor was the hair of their head singed; neither were their garments scorched or changed in color or condition, nor had even the smell of smoke clung to them.

—DANIEL 3:24–27

King Nebuchadnezzar commanded the strongest men to bind them up. In the natural realm, a person can still be *bound* by the enemy in the outer court. But Nebuchadnezzar made a fatal mistake—he increased the intensity of the fire by the number seven. Seven is God's number of perfection. Without realizing it, he *perfected* the fire—which means Shadrach, Meshach, and Abednego couldn't be consumed because the perfect fire can only consume what is in God's way. It only consumes carnality, and they were spiritual. Their hearts were in right standing with God.

Instead of going into a consuming fire, they went into a fire that had been transformed into the fire of the Holy Spirit—and that's why Jesus showed up in the furnace! Here's the revelation. Nebuchadnezzar threw three people into the fire. The number *three* symbolizes the Father, the Son, and the Holy Spirit. When Jesus appeared in that fire, He became number *four*, which represents the number of horns on the golden altar—and on the brazen altar as well. On both of these altars the four horns represented spiritual progression, from salvation, strength, and power (the brazen altar) to power, authority, and kingship (the golden altar).

When Shadrach, Meshach, and Abednego stepped into the fire as a group of three, they stepped in representing the Father, Son, and Holy Spirit, but God didn't stop there. He wanted to show forth His power. When Jesus appeared in the midst of the fire as number four, He took control. They were fully dressed, but Jesus stepped in and covered them with His garment. The same thing will happen when you enter the holy place wearing every garment you have been given in the outer court.

Imagine if Nebuchadnezzar had said, "Light up the fire six times hotter." The number *six* would have represented the number of man. If the king had told them to light up the fire two times hotter, it still wouldn't have been the same as saying *seven*, God's perfect number. What I'm saying is this: *when the devil thinks that he's creating a fire to destroy you, he's really orchestrating the victory on your behalf.*

Although the men who threw them into the furnace were killed by the flames, Shadrach, Meshach, and Abednego were not harmed. Not a hair on their head was singed. God had already prepared these three righteous servants for the fire. Their garments had been supernaturally fireproofed! Why? Shadrach, Meshach, and Abednego were already fully dressed when the soldiers came to get them. They knew they had to guard their garments, because they were living in Babylon, the land of their enemies. *This must be your position as a believer and an intercessor.* You must remain on guard at all times, watching, praying, and guarding your relationship with the Lord—because you are living in an evil world that is not your eternal home. Spiritually speaking, this means you must stay fully clothed in your priestly garments.

Remember that the tunic was a top garment for the lower priests and an undergarment for the high priest. When you think of this on a spiritual level, Shadrach, Meshach, and Abednego were stepping into the fire in the office and authority of high priests. That's why sparks from the fire killed the unpurified men who had to thrust them into the furnace! Hear me. Those who aren't properly clothed in intercessory prayer will not be able to stand and worship God through every situation—those who guard their priestly garments will come all the way through in victory!

When you are properly dressed for intercessory prayer, you will be able to stand in any situation. When persecution comes, you can stand and say to those persecuting you, "Be careful; the sparks from God's perfected fire in my life will hurt you. It's a dangerous thing when you touch God's anointed." As a matter of fact, you will have to step away from them and say, "I'm going to step away from you, because you're about to hurt yourself."

The Bible tells us that King Nebuchadnezzar saw "four men loose, walking in the midst of the fire" (Dan. 3:25). Note that as soon as the ropes were exposed to the flames, they burned up. Shadrach's, Meshach's, and Abednego's clothing represented the priestly anointing, and the rope represented the fleshly desires of a foreign king to bind the works of the Lord. *In that perfected fire, only one King could rule!* Nothing that came from an *old king* who ruled from the fleshly realm could take authority over the eternal kingship of Christ. The rope that the enemy used to bind them up was destroyed because it came from the natural realm. But their garments were not even touched! They didn't even smell like smoke. That's definitely a supernatural victory.

When they were in the midst of the fire, anything that hadn't been tried by the divine process—washed at the brazen laver and purified at the brazen altar—was burned up. That which had been tried and proven by God remained. You ought to give God praise for that, because He's doing the same thing today for those who are obedient to His voice. There's great power in being clothed by the High Priest! Nothing shall by any means hurt you!

CHAPTER 8

The Holy Anointing Oil

*N*ow that you are completely dressed for battle, you understand the requirements of how you are to be dressed so that you can be guaranteed of consistent victories in your times of prayer. You now understand that the Lord not only desires for you to know who He is (and how to be qualified to pray), but He also wants you to understand every level and every position that you are in when you're entering into His presence.

God desires that you not be confused about your *posture* in prayer, your *place* in prayer, and your *garments* of prayer. Knowing this, in this chapter we move on to one of the most vital elements in the tabernacle—the holy anointing oil. Since God is a God of detail, He specifically had Moses institute men into the office of becoming apothecaries (perfumers) who were required by the Lord to become the oil makers for the tabernacle. He also required that olive oil would be used as the foundational base of the fragrant holy anointing oil that was used to anoint the tabernacle elements and priests (Exod. 30:24).

The olive oil used to keep the menorah lit continually was made by crushing the olive branch in order to squeeze out the oil. Other components and ingredients were added to this oil to create a holy anointing oil to anoint the tabernacle and its elements, as well as to anoint Aaron and his sons. Each ingredient of this fragrant oil represents a different characteristic of the release of God's power.

This oil represents the illumination of the Lord from His taber-nacle in you—His intercessor. This oil is necessary wherever the Lord requires you to call on His divine presence—whether He sends you to a hospital to pray for a sick person, to pray for someone who has been incarcerated, to go to a mental institution to pray for somebody in need, or if He leads you to have a one-on-one counseling session with an individual who is disturbed. Whenever you feel that unction to pray and bring someone into the holy place (the presence of the Lord where the answer from the Lord is revealed), you will need the holy anointing oil.

As you read this chapter you will understand why the Lord requires that we use the anointing oil. You will learn why these ingredients are important if you are going to be an effectual intercessor and experience quality times of prayer in the divine presence. As we look back to Moses' inauguration of Aaron and his sons, it is important to understand that after Aaron and his sons were washed and received their new priestly garments, Moses anointed them with the holy anointing oil. Then, after their seven-day consecration, fire came down from heaven as they par-ticipated in their first priestly service.

As you submit yourself daily to being a living tabernacle of the Holy Spirit, every element in your tabernacle is anointed. You have passed through the Beautiful Gate (East Gate) by accepting Christ as your per-sonal Savior. You consistently come to receive the Word of the Lord by washing at the brazen laver. You now have the brazen altar within you where you have submitted your will to the Lord. Now...you are ready to move into the next step of the pattern.

As you prepare to enter into the holy place, you can take that fragrant holy oil and anoint yourself. Now you can go in and complete the pat-tern of the Lord in prayer on behalf of somebody else—and that's when (according to Scripture) the fire will come down from heaven upon your sacrifice!

Exodus 28:41 reveals the four-step process:

> And you shall put them [the garments] on Aaron your
> brother and his sons with him, and shall anoint them and

ordain and sanctify them [set them apart for God], that they may serve Me as priests.

God told Moses to *clothe* them, *anoint* them, *ordain* them, and *sanctify* them—and afterwards, *"they would be able to serve Me as priests."* Leviticus 8 tells us that after washing and dressing Aaron for service, Moses anointed the tabernacle and then poured oil over Aaron's head. After this, he clothed Aaron's sons in their garments, sacrificed a bull and a ram, and sprinkled the blood and anointing oil upon them all. (See Leviticus 8:1–30.)

The oil used for anointing Aaron and his sons is very important. There is great significance in every ingredient that went into the holy anointing oil, so Exodus 30:22–30 tells us how the anointing oil was to be put together:

> Moreover, the Lord said to Moses, Take the best spices: of *liquid myrrh* 500 shekels, of *sweet-scented cinnamon* half as much, 250 shekels, of *fragrant calamus* 250 shekels, and of *cassia* 500 shekels, in terms of the sanctuary shekel, and of *olive oil* a hin. And you shall make of these a holy anointing oil, a perfume compounded after the art of the perfumer; it shall be a sacred anointing oil. And you shall anoint the Tent of Meeting with it, and the ark of the Testimony, and the [showbread] table and all its utensils, and the lampstand and its utensils, and the altar of incense, and the altar of burnt offering with all its utensils, and the laver [for cleansing] and its base. You shall sanctify (separate) them, that they may be most holy; whoever and whatever touches them must be holy (set apart to God). And you shall anoint Aaron and his sons and sanctify (separate) them, that they may minister to Me as priests.
>
> —EMPHASIS ADDED

God instructed that the best spices were necessary, because an *impure mixture* would hinder the anointing. Today we see too many *imitations* of the real anointing. Many Christians think that they can do anything, say anything, wear anything, and still say, "I'm anointed." Scripture tells us differently. God has specific ingredients that, when mixed together, are sacred and will release His supernatural power every time.

As an intercessor, I have come to understand there are some things

I can't touch because they will tamper with my anointing. That's one way by which I guard my garments. Hebrews 12:1 says, "Let us strip off and throw aside every encumbrance (unnecessary weight) and that sin which so readily (deftly and cleverly) clings to and entangles us." When you are properly clothed and an *imitation* crosses your path—even a subliminal message, your spirit will say, *Error... I can't digest this. It looks, sounds, and feels like God, but something is missing.* You won't touch what could steal your effectiveness for God in prayer.

500 Shekels of Myrrh

The first ingredient listed in the holy anointing oil was 500 shekels of liquid myrrh. For women in Bible days, myrrh was *a purifier.* It was also used as an embalming fluid. So in using myrrh, God was saying, "Not only do I have to purify your anointing, but I also have to embalm what I put to death so that when you see it again in the realm of the Spirit it won't affect you."

At one time, I needed to have a major surgery that required three separate incisions. During that time, the Lord said to me, "Although you minister in the Word, there will always come a time when you will have to walk in supernatural faith."

When He said this to me, I was preparing to preach at a major event. I remember saying to the Lord, "I don't know if I'm going to be able to preach," because one of the incisions still hadn't closed. It still had a three-inch hole that had not healed. When I went to the doctor, he told me to pack the hole with white, sterilized, purified gauze. Then every twelve hours, I had to take out the gauze, because that would remove any impurities that were attached to it. I will never forget when he said, "There's something foreign in there, so the incision won't close until the foreign thing comes out."

He continued by saying, "You are seeking after beauty, and I'm seeking after purification." That really impacted me. Many believers are seeking the ministry, but they are not seeking after God. They are seeking after preaching and prophesying, all the while saying to themselves, *One day, I'm going to be up there with the rest of the famous people.* The Lord would say to those believers, "You are seeking after beauty, but I am seeking your purification. I can't heal you and prepare you to serve rightly until the foreign thing comes out."

As a part of the holy anointing oil, myrrh is an essential ingredient. It represents our need to be purified for service to God.

250 SHEKELS OF SWEET CINNAMON

The second ingredient was 250 shekels of sweet cinnamon. This speaks of *our attitude and how we treat others.* Have you ever known people who were filled with the Holy Spirit yet were as mean as snakes? They are missing an essential ingredient of the anointing. Let me ask you: how do you handle yourself when people do not treat you right? Because I assure you—you don't have any idea what is inside of you until you are confronted with a problem. For example, let's say you developed a great idea for your church, and somebody else ran and presented it to your pastor as if he or she had come up with the idea. Would the ingredient of sweet cinnamon still be apparent in your life?

Sometimes God will allow people to tell lies about you just to teach you how to shut up! Ministry is for mature believers, those who have been blood washed, purified, sanctified, and broken under the anointing! Otherwise, your ministry would never survive. As an intercessory priest, you must learn how to wrestle with the spirit of a lie, not the person who lies. You have to grab a lie around the neck and confront it, all the while praising God. You have to learn how to embrace people and be kind to them when you know they have been talking about you. That's sweet cinnamon—because you can't grow in prayer unless you learn how to hate the sin and love the people.

Be honest with yourself. There are people in your surroundings right now whom you do not care for or speak to. *You have to realize that the only way you can be anointed with the sacred oil is to be lied about, talked about, and mistreated.* The very person to whom you are not speaking *is your anointing!* So, as I have said from the pulpit on many occasions, you need to send thank you cards to all of your enemies. Tell each one, "Thank you for keeping me on my knees…because you, my enemy, have anointed me!"

One day the Holy Spirit said to me, "Your deliverance rests in the power of your decision to fight the devil instead of struggling with people. You can create the spirit of the anointing so heavy around your enemies that it will cause them to be humbled by your brokenness." The Word tells us, "When a man's ways please the Lord, He makes even his enemies to be at peace with him" (Prov. 16:7). If you can't do that, you don't have real victory! Hear me. You need to find your enemy and love that person to eternal life. Remember, it is the devil that wants to hinder God's purpose in your life.

Oh, yes! Sweet cinnamon is an essential part of the anointing…because it represents your attitude and response to others.

250 SHEKELS OF SWEET CALAMUS

The third ingredient was 250 shekels of sweet calamus. Calamus is also known as "reed-grass." It thrives on the banks of rivers, growing consistently regardless of its age. It represents the *maturity* you must develop to be prepared to be an intercessor. Psalm 1:1–3 likens us to the reed of calamus by saying: "Blessed (happy, fortunate, prosperous, and enviable) is the man who walks and lives not in the counsel of the ungodly [following their advice, their plans and purposes], nor stands [submissive and inactive] in the path where sinners walk, nor sits down [to relax and rest] where the scornful [and the mockers] gather. But his delight and desire are in the law of the Lord, and on His law (the precepts, the instructions, the teachings of God) he habitually meditates (ponders and studies) by day and by night. And he shall be like a tree firmly planted [and tended] by the streams of water, ready to bring forth its fruit in its season; its leaf also shall not fade or wither; and everything he does shall prosper [and come to maturity]."

This is another ingredient that sweetens the anointing oil, because when we come through the outer court and are about to enter the purpose of God in the holy place, the enemy tries to target us like never before. So to help us guard our garments, God gives us a double-portion anointing of sweetness and maturity—far beyond the normal measure that we see and experience in the natural realm. If we want to be effective in intercession, we cannot have a critical spirit, moaning, griping, complaining, and gossiping about whomever or whatever doesn't suit our opinions and desires.

If you aren't stabilized in God it's because you haven't allowed Him to lead you through the process of purification on your way to the threshing floor in prayer and intercession. You haven't guarded your garments in prayer. When you miss a step in God, you become unstable in the anointing. Unless you have been anointed with the sweet calamus of spiritual maturity, God will be unable to plant you in the midst of a mess that needs your intercession! If the sweet calamus of maturity is not a part of your anointing, you will be unable to grow as you encounter each piece of furniture inside the holy place. In fact, you won't even be able to get in the door! If you don't have sweet calamus as part of your intercessory anointing, you will become stagnant in prayer. You won't be able to go to deeper realms in the spirit.

500 SHEKELS OF CASSIA

The final ingredient in the holy anointing oil was 500 shekels of cassia, which they added to the mixture in equal proportion to the amount of myrrh. Cassia is likely to have come from a plant that's related to cinnamon (part of the inner bark of that plant, which is *fragrant and aromatic*). Cassia had to be ground into powder before being blended into the liquid myrrh along with the other ingredients. This spice symbolizes the *completion* of your anointing. It shows that everything you have received from the *river* of the Holy Spirit in prayer has formed the *foundation* for your anointing. Cassia represents the fact that people don't see you anymore: your form, your style of ministry, your personality, and your emotions have all been crushed to be blended into the sweet-smelling savor of the divine presence within you. *When you are anointed with cassia, you have learned to walk in the Spirit—to live, move, and have your being in God.*

When God anoints you with holy anointing oil, it confirms that He has brought you through the necessary channels so the enemy cannot hinder the assignment God has ordained for you to fulfill in the holy place. Because you have been anointed with this special oil, you are not only operating as the temple of the Holy Spirit, but, spiritually speaking, you are also operating in the office of the priest. When you get ready to move into intercession, this oil will anoint you, your Bible, and the place where you are kneeling down.

Finally you are preparing to enter the holy place and approach the altar of incense where true intercession is made. Soon you will enter into the divine presence of God. You are being anointed to approach the altar of incense—representing *power, authority,* and *kingship*—with the right spirit and the right ingredients. You've walked through *salvation, strength,* and *power* into a deeper level of the anointing. You are no longer in the place where you need salvation. You are now in the place where you are getting ready to fight on someone else's behalf. You are taking on power and authority in the Spirit realm where you will be in a position to rule and govern what happens in another person's life—*and all of this happens at the golden altar.*

No one can take this anointing away from you—if man did not anoint you, man cannot take your anointing away from you! People may not like you, but they can never take away the anointing that is on your life! The same holds true for the enemy.

But remember, if you fail to guard your garments, you can give place to the devil. When you have holes in your armor, you become vulnerable to the enemy's devices. Because of your own failure to guard your anointing, it will slip away from you through the holes you allowed in your own armor. So stay properly dressed, and the oil of the anointing will equip you to serve faithfully in the holy place of prayer.

CHAPTER 9

Divine Protection:
The Tabernacle Coverings

*A*s God brings you into the holy place, you must become aware of the tabernacle furniture and how each element relates to you in prayer. This will be the next part of your learning process. But there is a very important thing you must understand is that God will never call you to intercede on behalf of the saints and into battle against the hands of the enemy without protecting and covering you.

The outer court is open to the wind, storms, and other weather conditions that may blow your way as you learn to submit your life to God. However, once you walk into the holy place, you are covered. Do you know what your covering is? Are you aware of the guarantee you have that when you enter into intercession you will not be overtaken by demonic spirits? What assurances do you have that you will not be overcome by the devil?

I have heard too many believers say things like, "When I started praying, I came under an awful attack of Satan." Hear me. Though the enemy may throw darts, Scripture clearly states that "no weapon that is formed against you shall prosper" (Isa. 54:17)! God made this powerfully clear when He designed the priestly clothing and the tabernacle coverings.

As we study about each covering (curtain), you will see a definite connection to the priestly garments. God makes a strong point about garments and coverings. This confirms again that you should never go to battle in intercession without being properly clothed, because your garments identify you as a mighty soldier in the realm of the Spirit. They send a message to Satan on your behalf—even as you approach the door of the holy place.

Let's start by looking more closely at the tabernacle. It had two sections: the holy place and the most holy place. Scripture tells us that the dimensions of the tabernacle were ten cubits by ten cubits for the most holy place, and ten cubits by twenty cubits for the holy place.[1] When you multiply these three numbers together (10 x 10 x 20), the total is 2,000. Prophetically, this confirmed to my heart—as it has to many others in the body of Christ—that when the church entered the year 2000, we entered into a divine season of intercession.

God originally established the tabernacle through Moses so there would be a place for His presence to *rest* among His people (Exod. 25:8). Do you think the enemy could remain anywhere that God has chosen to rest? Absolutely not! The presence of God will cover you as you make intercession—as long as you remain properly dressed. So don't fall back into outer court living! You already know there's no covering there. But the devil cannot follow you into the holy place, and he will have no ground from which to launch an attack against you as long as you guard your garments.

The only way he can come near you is if there is an open door in you—something that you have not dealt with such as fear, shame, offense, and so on. When Jesus prayed in the garden, though Satan came, he could not stay because Jesus was in the process of laying down His will. When He said, " . . . not my will, but thine, be done," whatever Satan had planned was going to be brought to an end. Remember, Satan's visits are only temporary distractions. He cannot stay where there is not a place for him. Satan is a disembodied spirit. He needs a life to live in and to operate in. When his visits are rejected, he has to go! Just lingering in the atmosphere gets him nowhere. He must have a body to operate in. So, right now declare to him: "Not my body, not my mind, and definitely not my spirit! Now go!"

THE FIRST TABERNACLE COVERING: FINE-TWINED LINEN AND WOOL

If you were to stand back just before entering the holy place, and then looked up and around, you would see that the holy place and the most holy place were the parts of the tabernacle structure that required a covering. Exodus 26:1–14 lists the four (layered) tabernacle coverings.

The first tabernacle curtain was woven of white "fine twined linen" and three different colors of wool: turquoise, purple, and scarlet (v. 1). This layer of the covering was classified as "the tabernacle" and was made from the same basic material that was used to weave the priestly ephod in Exodus 28:6. The difference between the two can be seen in the fact that the ephod had a gold strand of thread woven in with each of the other four threads, and the tabernacle curtains did not. The curtains had four, not five, threads that were woven together into an ornate pattern of cherubim, as well as figures of the lion, eagle, and ox, which could be seen on either side of the fabric (we will discuss these figures later).[2]

Here in the design of the curtains we once again see the colors of the finished work of Christ, which laid the foundation for the tabernacle coverings. The first fabric mentioned is the *white linen*, which speaks of the garments of righteousness and salvation that have been given to the saints according to Isaiah 61:1–3, 10. In Revelation 3:5 God's promise for the righteous is revealed:

> Thus shall he who conquers (is victorious) be clad in white garments, and I will not erase or blot out his name from the Book of Life; I will acknowledge him [as Mine] and I will confess his name openly before My Father and before His angels.

When you enter the holy place wearing your tunic of righteousness under your other garments, Jesus will say to you, "You are entering this tabernacle of prayer clothed in righteousness, so I recognize you as being Mine." God is obligated to protect that which belongs to Him (John 10:28–29).

Fully clothed in your priestly garments, you stand at the door of the holy place and immediately look up to see the same colors covering the tabernacle—creating yet another match in the Spirit. Your foundation as an intercessor is the foundational covering of the place where God's presence rests to spread His kingdom to the nations. Knowing this, you can enter into intercession declaring that when "two" touch and agree on anything, God will not only perform His Word, but He will also be in the midst of it! "Again I tell you, if two of you on earth agree (harmonize together, make a symphony together) about whatever [anything and everything] they may ask, it will come to pass and be done for them by My Father in heaven. For wherever two or three are gathered (drawn together as My followers) in (into) My name, there I AM in the midst of them" (Matt. 18:19–20).

DIVINE IMAGES IN THE FIRST TABERNACLE COVERING

The first covering of the tabernacle in Exodus 26:1 displays not only the four workings of Christ through its colors, but also the images of cherubim, the lion, eagle, and ox (bull), according to Ezekiel 1:4–10 and Revelation 4:7.[3] The images of the lion, eagle, and bull correspond to one of the colors in the workings of Christ, and each of these images has significance in prayer. This is why they were intricately woven into the design of this first (foundational) covering. Let me pause here to make note that the image of a human face is mentioned in both Ezekiel and Revelation, yet it is not woven into the curtain…instead, it is symbolized by white, the color that speaks to our righteousness in Christ. (Bear in mind, however, that this first covering can be seen only from inside the tabernacle. In other words, when you move into that deeper place in prayer, you will begin to see the fullness of all that has been made available to you in Christ.)

Cherubim are very different from angels. God commanded that cherubim be woven into the fabric because they are *a manifestation of everything He is.* Angels work on behalf of God in the service of humanity. Cherubim live around the throne of God, exalting Him continually and reflecting His glory. The cherubim embroidered on the tabernacle curtains represent the inwrought work of cherubim who cover you in intercessory prayer and manifest the intricate workings and operation of the Holy Spirit on behalf of the Father and the Son. As you pray, the cherubim remind you of the life, ministry, death, burial, and resurrection of the Lord Jesus Christ.

The image of the *lion* corresponds to purple in the workings of Christ. It speaks of *the righteousness that has been imputed to you as part of the royal priesthood.* The lion reminds you of your royal lineage and lets you know that you are now operating in the authority that transformed you in the outer court. Because of this, you can come boldly to the throne of grace.

The *eagle* corresponds with blue. It reminds you that God enables your spirit to touch Him in the heavenly realm. Blue speaks of *operating in the supernatural.* When you see the eagle, you are assured that God will mount you up on His wings and show you mysteries of heaven so that you can bring His kingdom to the earthly realm.

The image of the *ox* (bull) corresponds to red. Bullocks were sacrificed for the sins of the high priest or the nation. This image represents that you are to remain broken before the Lord so that you can receive and carry His intercessory burdens for the church. A bull charges toward death, so as the Holy Spirit leads you to your final position in prayer at the threshing floor, your spirit will charge toward God knowing that no flesh can see His face and live.

When you walk into the holy place clothed in your priestly garments, a powerful divine match takes place in the heavenlies. Identifying with the colors and images in the first covering identifies you with all of the workings of Jesus Christ—confirming that you legitimately belong there. You are not trespassing illegally in the Spirit realm. You are in divine agreement with the will of God, and no weapon that has been formed against you shall prosper!

Satan has to respect these boundaries. However, if you are in the place of intercession illegally, Satan has a right to take you out, because you are missing a part of the pattern.

If you try to go into intercession illegally, with something about you that represents Satan, then he has a right to control your mind, to attack you, to possess you, and to annihilate you completely. *But when you are in intercession legally, according to the pattern that God has laid out, Satan cannot trespass.*

THE SECOND TABERNACLE COVERING: GOAT'S HAIR

The second layer of covering over the tabernacle was made from black goat's hair (Exod. 26:7). This layer of the curtains, classified as the "tent," was placed on top of the first covering. Goats were used to atone for the sins of individuals, from rulers to common people. (See Leviticus 4:22–5:13.) This means as an intercessor, you will receive the grace to carry the burden of the Lord for anyone, anywhere, at any time—without becoming offended or affected by a person's sin.

How is this possible? You will be able to do this by remembering what Jesus did for everyone. "For our sake He made Christ [virtually] to be sin Who knew no sin, so that in and through Him we might become [endued with, viewed as being in, and examples of] the righteousness of God [what we ought to be, approved and acceptable and in right relationship with Him, by His goodness]" (2 Cor. 5:21). Because Jesus became sin so that we could become the righteousness of God, you can expect this same grace to be available to you as you go into intercession for others. You can believe God to bring total deliverance when you pray!

Since the covering of black goat's hair was laid directly on top of the first tabernacle curtain, it assures you that your sins have been covered; for this reason you should not allow the enemy to remind you constantly of what you used to be. This is one of Satan's common warfare tactics. Satan will try to attack you by saying things like, "You're not really saved." "You are not righteous." "You think that you're something; you think that you're actually hearing God, but I remember when you were..." Satan doesn't have the right to do this! Stay clothed in your priestly garments! Submit to God, resist the devil, and he will have no choice but to flee from you (James 4:7). You can absolutely shut down the voice of the enemy when you get into the realm of the holy place.

THE THIRD TABERNACLE COVERING: RAM'S SKIN

The third layer of the tabernacle covering is given to us in Exodus 26:14. It was made from ram's skins dyed red, and it was one of the final two layers, which were referred to as "covers." The ram was used in guilt offerings (Lev. 5:14–26). In addition, two rams were part of the sacrifices presented when Aaron and his sons were inaugurated into the priesthood (Exod. 29:15–28). After sacrificing the first ram as an elevation offering to God, the second sacrificial ram was called "the ram of perfection."[4] Aaron and his sons received the breast of that ram as their portion (v. 26).

One of the first times the power of the ram is shown in Scripture is when Abraham was preparing to sacrifice his son Isaac (Gen. 22:1–14). In this story, God provided the ram as a substitute for Isaac on Abraham's altar. When Abraham obeyed God, he received the blessing of the nations (vv. 15–19).

Every aspect of the ram is powerful. The ram is a *sacrifice*, a *substitute*, *provision* for our table, and a *symbol of consecration* for divine service. It is no wonder that God commanded for this to be the third covering. It confirms and completes the divine pattern, just as Father, Son, and Holy Spirit are one. This represents that you can have perfect victory in prayer as you depend upon the Lord and upon those things that He has already established in heaven and in the earth. You can stand and withstand in prayer and intercession because, once and for all, Jesus made the perfect sacrifice.

> Therefore He is able also to save to the uttermost (completely, perfectly, finally, and for all time and eternity) those who come to God through Him, since He is always living to make petition to God and intercede with Him and intervene for them. [Here is] the High Priest [perfectly adapted] to our needs, as was fitting—holy, blameless, unstained by sin, separated from sinners, and exalted higher than the heavens. He has no day by day necessity, as [do each of these other] high priests, to offer sacrifice first of all for his own [personal] sins and then for those of the people, because He [met all the requirements] once for all when He brought Himself [as a sacrifice] which He offered up. For the Law sets up men in their weakness [frail, sinful, dying human beings] as high priests, but the word of [God's] oath, which [was spoken later] after the institution of the Law, [chooses and appoints as priest One Whose appointment is complete and permanent], a Son Who has been made perfect forever.
> —HEBREWS 7:25–28

Finally, through this ram's skin covering, God speaks to you from Isaiah 1:18: "Come now, and let us reason together, says the Lord.

Though your sins are like scarlet *[like the color of the ram's skin died red]*, they shall be as white as snow; though they are red like crimson, they shall be like wool." Remember this when you are entering into intercession. Don't ever forget Christ's perfect work for you. Because of the sacrifice of His own blood, you will be able to stand faithfully for others.

THE FOURTH TABERNACLE COVERING: BADGER'S SKIN

The fourth and final tabernacle covering was made of badger's skin (dolphin or porpoise in the Amplified Bible) (Exod. 26:14). This layer was the final *cover* that provided overall protection for each of the other layers. These skins may also have been used to cover the tabernacle elements as the Israelites moved from one location to another. The badger skins were considered strong enough to protect every other layer of the tabernacle against heat, storms, and dirt. Nothing could penetrate that skin.

When the badger's skin was laid over the tabernacle, it didn't matter what the weather was like outside—the glory still remained on the inside. Whether the conditions were hot or cold, temperate or stormy, the glory still remained on the inside. It didn't matter where the tabernacle was taken, the badger skins protected it from any outside intrusion or attack. This is a final confirmation that as you guard your garments and make intercession, you will be protected from any outside onslaught of the devil.

The badger's skin was actually a transitional covering, used not only when the tabernacle was resting in one place, but also while it was being moved to a new location. You must keep this in mind as you discover God in intercessory prayer. You are a living temple of the Lord. While you are learning how to move in the things of God and discovering the realm of the supernatural, you must trust that the badger's skin is there to protect you against the wiles of the enemy—because supernatural experiences can be difficult to comprehend.

Now Let Us Come Boldly

There is one final aspect about the tabernacle coverings that really ministered to me. Specific measurements are given for the first two coverings, the linen-embroidered curtain and the black goat's skin (Exod. 26:1–13). However, when we read about the skins of the ram and badger, there are no measurements. This spoke to my spirit, revealing to me that there were no measurements because Christ's sacrifice cannot be measured. His divine substitution on your behalf cannot be measured. His ability to consecrate you in His presence cannot be measured. And finally, His divine protection against the wiles of Satan is immeasurable.

We should lift our hands and give glory to God because we have accepted Jesus as our personal Savior by accepting His works at the gate and because we now have the Spirit of God living inside of us. John 3:34 says, "For since He Whom God has sent speaks the words of God [proclaims God's own message], God does not give Him His Spirit sparingly or by measure, but boundless is the gift God makes of His Spirit!" This means that the Lord has given His Spirit unto Jesus Christ without measure—and as long as we possess the Spirit of Christ there is no limit to what we can do through prayer in Him.

I am constantly amazed when I think about the amazing faith of Jesus Christ. He went to every length, depth, and height to protect you and to make sure you would be covered in prayer! Knowing this, you can move deeper in intercession toward the threshing floor, and, as you do, you will be able to embrace each piece of tabernacle furniture with confidence.

Come boldly to the throne of God, because the price has already been paid on your behalf. Isaiah 55:1 says, "Wait and listen, everyone who is thirsty! Come to the waters; and he who has no money, come, buy and eat! Yes, come, buy [priceless, spiritual] wine and milk without money and without price [simply for the self-surrender that accepts the blessing]." Believe me, Satan doesn't want you to receive the revelations and mysteries that are contained in this word. He wants you to think that submitting to the call of intercessory prayer in the holy place is too difficult a task—but that is one of his greatest deceptions.

Because of what Christ has done, you can freely come into the presence of the Lord. The price has already been paid for you. The work has already been done. You have come through the gate, which made "the way" for you in the outer court. You are fully clothed. Now that you have walked through the door of the tabernacle, which is "the truth"—you are fully covered to become an effectual intercessor.

Now it is time to go deeper into the tabernacle. It's time to go one step closer to your final position in prayer on the threshing floor.

CHAPTER 10

The Holy Place

*A*S YOU PREPARE to enter the holy place, having been washed, dressed, anointed, and consecrated, you must remember once again that Jesus said, "I am the Way and the Truth and the Life; no one comes to the Father except by (through) Me" (John 14:6). You must remember that you came into the outer court through the gate of His finished work. He became *the way* for you to see your true reflection in the brazen laver and to sacrifice your will on the brazen altar. Now, at the door of the tabernacle, you are about to enter the realm of intercession. You have come into a deeper walk with the Lord under the new anointing He has poured out upon your life.

But, as I said earlier, at this new level you must still approach the Father by way of Jesus Christ. The door has the same four colors that were in the gate: white, blue, purple, and scarlet. But now, they have taken on a deeper meaning.

Let's see how this applies in your daily walk. According to 1 Corinthians 1:30 and Revelation 19:7–8, the *white*, fine-twined linen speaks of the Lord, who has become your righteousness. His righteousness can now be clearly seen in you by others. It is the foundation and assurance of victory for every burden you receive from God in prayer. *Blue* (turquoise), the color of heaven, speaks of Jesus as the second man, the Lord from heaven. He was revealed to you at the gate, and now He's being made manifest in you daily as the living Word. When people see you standing at the door of the tabernacle, they will begin to see the kingdom and will of God being validated in the earth through you.

Purple is the color of kingship, which means you can be clearly identified as an ambassador of the royal family of Jesus Christ. When people see you in the natural, they will see beyond your title, gender, or nationality, all the way to your biblical roots. Principalities and powers in the Spirit realm will also begin to recognize your heritage and bow to your royal lineage. The last color is *scarlet*, which speaks of the sacrificial blood that Jesus shed for you to be saved and come into a deeper relationship with Him. It also signifies that the battle has already been fought and won for you in the Spirit realm. Now as you begin to make intercession, fully clothed in your priestly garments, you will be able to experience the blood of Jesus going before you and setting the captives free.

In the holy place, the realm of total truth, God requires that the grace of His Son be made manifest in you. Why? This door, the first veil of the tabernacle, was not merely an entrance to an enclosed space. This door shut out common (natural) men. Most importantly, it was the only passageway that led to the manifest presence of God on the threshing floor.

ARE YOU READY TO ENTER HIS MARVELOUS LIGHT?

First Peter 2:9 says, "But you are a chosen race, a royal priesthood, a dedicated nation, [God's] own purchased, special people, that you may set forth the wonderful deeds and display the virtues and perfections of Him Who called you out of darkness into His marvelous light."

As God's servant in prayer, you have been called into His marvelous light. Eternal light is your final destination. Now you must walk knowing that you have come out of the outer court where the light is only temporary—because living in temporary light is for carnal believers and the unsaved. As an intercessor, the works of Christ must progressively be revealed in and through you. You can never go back.

As you prepare to enter the holy place, know that you will begin to operate in supernatural light as you learn how to pick up the burden of the Lord. So remember...God hasn't called you into His marvelous light just for you to sit there and gaze or to be afraid on this new level and run back into the *comfort zone* of the outer court. There's a divine purpose for you and grace to meet every need just beyond that door.

There were two reasons why priests entered the holy place. The first was to perform the service of the Lord. In performing the temple service, they made sure to replace the shewbread regularly, which represented the Word of God. They kept the menorah (what we would consider to be the lamp) filled with olive oil, which represented the light of the Lord and the oil of the anointing. They also kept a constant fire burning on the altar of incense, representing the place of worship and total surrender, ensuring that the glory of the Lord was maintained in that whole area.

The second reason they entered was to lay prostrate before God in prayer.[1] Both purposes speak of a higher degree of separation and devotion to God. The golden altar represents a place, time, and position in prayer where you are separated from everybody else. You could be in a room of fifty people, but once you have gone through all the stages of the process—the gate, the outer court, the brazen laver, and the brazen altar—you will be able to experience the oil of the anointing. The Word of the Lord will become alive to you at the golden altar, and true, inexplicable worship will begin to rise out of your spirit.

This is your place of separation. This is also why prayer can be practiced anywhere. You could be in your car and have an undeniable prayer experience. You could be sitting in church, or in a beauty shop or prison cell, and have this experience. Why? *Because God is spiritually positioning your heart for effectual prayer.* This is how we know that we are on our way to the threshing floor, because separation is the heart of the threshing process.

To thresh means "to separate grains or seeds from straw by beating the stems or husks." The divine threshing process actually begins when you enter the gate to the outer court in prayer. Then the process of personal repentance in the outer court separates you from a life of sin into a life of obedience to God. Now that you have moved into the holy place, the separation continues as you begin to live within His purpose. Each piece of tabernacle furniture deepens your intercessory experience.

As we continue studying the prophetic meaning of the tabernacle elements, let's begin by taking another look at the positioning of the tabernacle and all its furniture. In the tabernacle diagram on page 10, you can see that the brazen altar and the brazen laver were positioned between the East Gate into the outer court and the door of the tabernacle. The furniture inside the holy place was positioned with the table of shewbread to the north, the golden candlestick to the south, and the golden altar of incense (and the ark of God in the most holy place) to the west of the outer elements. This reveals the significance of the tabernacle furniture.

As a reminder, looking from the outside, through the East Gate into the holy place, the placement of the furniture completes the shape and image of the cross! Through this imagery, God is signifying again that He wants us never to forget the work that His Son, Jesus Christ, did on the cross at Golgotha. We have already seen His finished work displayed in the gate, the tabernacle door, and coverings. Now we see that even the furniture is positioned by way of the cross. In other words, our pattern of intercessory prayer is made possible only by what Jesus has already done and set in place for us.

This is why I must reiterate that it's impossible for a sinner to be an intercessor. The only prayer that God hears from a sinner is the prayer of repentance! You might be thinking, *I heard a sinner pray, and God did something for that person.* Please understand that as a sinner prays, the will of the Lord is also in motion, because He is sovereign. In the case of a sinner's prayer, God is doing what He has already chosen to do. He doesn't take commands from a sinner. When you see the hand of God moving in this way, His sovereignty is in action—meaning He does only what He has already planned to do.

THE TABLE OF SHEWBREAD

Now let's look at the contents of His holy place. When you enter the holy place, to the right you will find the table of shewbread (Exod. 25:23–30). This table was constructed from shittim (acacia) wood and overlaid with gold. Shittim wood was incorruptible. It was the same wood they used to construct the ark of the covenant. It would stand up against storms, heat, or any severe conditions. The fact that it was overlaid with gold means that it represents *humanity* (wood) *covered by the deity of Jesus*

Christ (gold). Here in this representation, we see once again another level of covering *inside* of the holy place.

The table of shewbread also represents *the Word of God*. It was inlaid with a crown, which symbolized the crown of kingship. Twelve loaves of specially baked bread were on the table at all times. These loaves were baked on Friday and replaced every Sabbath—and they miraculously remained as hot and fresh on the Sabbath day as when they were first baked. At the end of seven days, when the loaves were replaced, they were still fresh enough to be divided among the priests.

The crown spoke of a king's responsibility to provide for the safety and prosperity of the nation. The Israelites believed that they would enjoy prosperity because of the significance of the table of shewbread. As an intercessor, the shewbread represents that you can receive a fresh word from God daily. The people for whom you intercede will prosper as the King of the universe sends heavenly provision through you by way of prayer, making it vital for you to read His Word daily.

In the New Testament, when the people asked Jesus for bread, He said, "For the Bread of God is He Who comes down out of heaven and gives life to the world" (John 6:33). When they asked Jesus to give them a continual supply of this bread, He explained what He meant by saying, "I am the Bread of Life. He who comes to Me will never be hungry, and he who believes in and cleaves to and trusts in and relies on Me will never thirst any more (at any time)" (v. 35). Therefore, he who prays communes with Christ and is lacking nothing!

As an intercessor, you must have an unlimited resource of the Bread of Life from heaven present within you as you perform the service of the Lord at the table of shewbread. When the disciples sat with Christ at the Last Supper, He unveiled the process by which the Bread of Life (the Word of God) becomes the bread of maintenance. "Now as they were eating, Jesus took bread and, praising God, gave thanks and asked Him to bless it to their use, and when He had broken it, He gave it to the disciples and said, Take, eat; this is My body. And He took a cup, and when He had given thanks, He gave it to them, saying, Drink of it, all of you; for this is My blood of the new covenant, which [ratifies the agreement and] is being poured out for many for the forgiveness of sins" (Matt. 26:26–28).

The brazen laver gives you new life as it washes you through the power of the Word. Then when you enter the holy place, the shewbread becomes the bread of maintenance as you begin to eat the Word of God according to John 6:53–57. This is the level of eating the Word that keeps everything God says fresh in your spirit:

> I assure you, most solemnly I tell you, you cannot have any life in you unless you eat the flesh of the Son of Man and drink His blood [unless you appropriate His life and the saving merit of His blood]. He who feeds on My flesh and drinks My blood has (possesses now) eternal life, and I will raise him up [from the dead] on the last day. For My flesh is true and genuine food, and My blood is true and genuine drink. He who feeds on My flesh and drinks My blood dwells continually in Me, and I [in like manner dwell continually] in him. Just as the living Father sent Me and I live by (through, because of) the Father, even so whoever continues to feed on Me [whoever takes Me for his food and is nourished by Me] shall [in his turn] live through and because of Me.

As an intercessor, you must *eat* of Christ to become like Him and be prepared to battle in the heavenly realm. You have to digest the Word regularly to maintain a transformed lifestyle. The shewbread is your strength. After the prophet Elijah defeated the prophets of Baal, he fled from evil Queen Jezebel. (See 1 Kings 19:4–8.) When he stopped, weary from his journey, he fell asleep. While Elijah was sleeping, an angel of the Lord prepared bread and water for him, and woke him up, saying, "Arise and eat" (v. 7). When Elijah ate the second loaf, he went on the strength of that bread for forty days. *See the revelation; it was after the second feeding that he was able to go out for an extended time in the strength of the Lord.*

This is why Psalm 34:8–10 says, "O taste and see that the Lord [our God] is good! Blessed (happy, fortunate, to be envied) is the man who trusts and takes refuge in Him. O fear the Lord, you His saints [revere and worship Him]! For there is no want to those who truly revere and worship Him with godly fear. The young lions lack food and suffer hunger, but they who seek (inquire of and require) the Lord [by right of their need and on the authority of His Word], none of them shall lack any beneficial thing."

Any time you taste (eat) of the Word, it's going to be good, and it's definitely going to be fresh. This is why you need to embrace the table of shewbread before going into intercession at the golden altar of incense. It is here that you will receive the word of the Lord concerning the individuals for whom you are about to intercede. The twelve loaves are continuously on display, because God wants you to know that the word of the Lord about any situation will always be made available to you.

For example, let's say that you go into intercession about a specific matter and end up in prayer for ten days about that particular person or situation. Each day that you go before God in prayer, you have another opportunity to receive a fresh word as the Spirit of the Lord is working and the situation is being turned for His glory. If you ask the Lord, He will even give you insight about how soon deliverance will come.

It is at the table of shewbread where the intercessor (prayer warrior) must embrace and partake of the Word of God, because this is where the Word becomes your sword. Not only do you gain strength at this table, but you also forge (sharpen) your supernatural weapon. This is the place where the Word turns into power as the Lord gives you permission to use the Word on behalf of someone else.

Now that you are in the holy place, you have entered the realm of divine illumination—the place where you are justified and qualified to pray on behalf of others.

THE GOLDEN CANDLESTICK

The golden candlestick or menorah (Exod. 25:31–40) represents *light and illumination,* so it symbolizes *divine understanding of the Word, the next level of insight and revelation where Word and Spirit are one.* At this point, you are becoming able to see and apply the Word whenever and wherever it is needed.

The menorah was made of solid gold. There was no wood in this piece of furniture, and there were also no measurements given for it. Since there was no wood, humanity wasn't represented in the candlestick. The function of the golden candlestick and what it symbolizes has nothing to do with humanity.

Let me explain further. *The Chumash* states that when God instructed

Moses to make a menorah, Moses lamented because the dimensions, details, and curves of the candlestick were impossible for him to envision. So God showed him a menorah of fire and eventually instructed him to throw the stem into the fire, from which the completed menorah emerged.[2]

Moses didn't have the tools to create the menorah according to God's specifications, so God formed it (with all the beaten-in patterns) supernaturally. This leaves us with the understanding that when you embrace the menorah, you have come to the place where God begins to perform everything He reveals to you in prayer. You receive the illumination, and God does the work! This means there are no limitations as you embrace this element. You have access to the mind of the Spirit and are able to discern the deep things of God.

The menorah had a stem (*representing God*) and six branches (*representing the number of man, the church, which was born out from Him*). Jesus confirmed this meaning in the Book of John by saying, "I am the Vine; you are the branches. Whoever lives in Me and I in him bears much (abundant) fruit. However, apart from Me [cut off from vital union with Me] you can do nothing" (John 15:5).

The golden candlestick helps us to see that Jesus Christ is the vine (stem), and we are the branches (six candles) coming out of Him. We can do nothing without the illumination of the candlestick. Though the Word is available to us, we can't do anything with it in our own human understanding. How do I know this? Let's read John 15:6:

> If a person does not dwell in Me, he is thrown out like a [broken-off] branch, and withers; such branches are gathered up and thrown into the fire, and they are burned.

Looking at the revelation of this verse, we find that any intercessor who disconnects from the Vine goes back to the outer court. He or she can't stay in the holy place. If you do not embrace the workings of the golden candlestick, you will be thrown back to square one.

But for the intercessor who abides in the Vine, "If you live in Me [abide vitally united to Me] and My words remain in you and continue to live in your hearts, ask whatever you will, and it shall be done for you" (v. 7).

It is important that I clarify the statement "ask whatever you will." You are able to *ask whatever you will* in that realm because your will was already dealt with at the brazen altar. Once you have entered into the holy place, you came with only *one will—God's will*. Then you continued going deeper in His will by embracing the table of shewbread and, now, the golden candlestick. By illumination of the candlestick, the only thing you are going to ask for in intercession is the will of God—because in this realm, *His will* is the only thing that you desire.

Your *old will* doesn't fit in the holy place, especially at the golden candlestick where there is no human intervention. What you used to think and feel while praying—how you think you should pray or how you want it to work out—is no longer recognized or important.

AN INTRICATE DESIGN

The branches of the candlestick have the same decorations as the stem, a design that was beaten and shaped by fire. This design represents attributes that Jesus gave to His church when we were birthed out from Him.

Jesus gave us His glory, which is why we are called the "light of the world" (Matt. 5:14). Part of being this light to the world is reflecting His image. This is symbolized by the fine gold that was beaten for the candlestick until it was smooth and reflective, in much the same way that metals were beaten into mirrors in Bible times.

This is why we are warned in 2 Timothy 3:5 against taking on the form of God and then denying His power. It's a terrible sacrilege, and it leads the fallen believer toward death. It is extremely dangerous to take on the image of any piece of furniture in the holy place if you don't possess that same power in your spirit man. God cannot allow you to portray an image without power, because the message you will be sending to those who don't know God is that He has no power. Too many believers look like God and try to act like God—quoting scriptures, wearing long skirts, high collars, and so forth—but there's no manifestation of supernatural life. They fail at everyday living.

The word *manifest* means, "readily perceived by the senses, easily understood by the mind." In other words, it is obvious. If the way you carry yourself does not allow people to perceive God readily and to understand who He is, then you are reflecting the wrong image. You have become a stumbling block. This is why Jesus said, "I AM the True Vine, and My Father is the Vinedresser. Any branch in Me that does not bear fruit [that stops bearing] He cuts away (trims off, takes away); and He cleanses and repeatedly prunes every branch that continues to bear fruit, to make it bear more and richer and more excellent fruit" (John 15:1–2). If you are going to take on His image, you must be willing to embrace the workings of His power.

The design on the candlestick was comprised of almonds and flowers, which again was beaten and burned into the menorah by fire. The almond on Aaron's rod was the first branch to bud and blossom, bringing forth fruit to the nation of Israel (Num. 17:8). This speaks to me of *everlasting resurrection*. As you embrace the work of the menorah, God will make sure to burn the image of the almond into your life. Once you may have been spiritually dead, but because of Christ's resurrection, you have been resurrected also to new life. (See John 11:25.) When the image of the almond is in your spirit, it doesn't matter how many tests you endure or how many trials you go through—you have eternal "getting up power"! You have life, and you can speak life into any situation.

The flower (lily) represents *everlasting beauty*. If people cannot see the beauty of Christ when they look at you…if they can't experience the sweet anointing of the Holy Spirit…if there's nothing about your persona or spirit that others desire…then the image of the flower isn't apparent in your life. Remember that by the time you get to the menorah, you have already received a double-portion anointing of sweetness from the cinnamon and calamus in the holy anointing oil. If you lose sight of who you have become in Christ once you are in the holy place, you are headed for disaster, because you can't be hateful and go into the presence of the Lord.

THE NECESSITY OF SACRIFICE

One final, powerful aspect of the golden candlestick that I intentionally left for last is the fact that it was kept lit by the coals from the brazen altar. The fire of God that lit the altar originally came from glory in the third realm, lighting the golden altar of incense and then the brazen altar.

By revelation this means that if there has never been any sacrifice in your life, and if you fail to willingly put yourself on the altar of sacrifice daily, then there will be no fire to light the golden candlestick in your life. There will be no reflection of God's character for others to see.

The fire on the brazen altar will go out unless you continue to put your flesh and your will on the altar of sacrifice. If this sacrificial fire goes out, the fires of illumination on the golden candlestick will subsequently be extinguished. Even worse, the coals of the golden altar of incense will smolder and die. This would be a tragedy, because the fires of illumination provide light in the holy place, and the burning coals on the golden altar keep worship rising to the throne of God continually.

Sacrifice is a vital element. Saying *yes* to God in your mind and in your spirit continually, "God, not my will, but Thy will be done," adds wood to the brazen altar and makes it possible to receive illumination in the holy place—making it easy to worship Him at the altar of incense. This is why many are stuck in dead religion, because they have no relationship.

Most importantly, personal sacrifice safeguards your understanding of what God desires to do in the lives of the people for whom you are praying. When God speaks a word, you are not ignorant or dull of spirit to what He's saying. You are able to understand clearly and to respond to His voice. Therefore, you can be certain of what you are presenting before the throne of grace at the threshing floor. You know what you are going to offer up when you grab the horns of the golden altar of incense—because your heart is supernaturally illuminated.

As a matter of fact, sacrifice lights the way to prayer. If the light goes out on the golden candlestick (the only source of light in the holy place), you will not be able to find the altar of incense, the most vital piece of furniture in the holy place... meaning it will be difficult for you to worship. You have to keep the flames of sacrifice burning! That's how you can guarantee that you will never be in the dark or blindsided concerning any matter of prayer. Sacrifice brings illumination, illumination brings understanding, and understanding carries you into intercession.

The apostle Paul understood the power of illumination, and he demonstrated how to keep the illumination working in one's life when he said: "I will pray with my spirit [by the Holy Spirit that is within

141

me], but I will also pray [intelligently] with my mind and understanding; I will sing with my spirit [by the Holy Spirit that is within me], but I will sing [intelligently] with my mind and understanding also" (1 Cor. 14:15).

This is why we must make sure not to miss the prayer of sacrifice and surrender when we are in the outer court. We will never be able to go to the next level of prayer without it. We will have no revelation of the Word of God, and the fire will go out in our worship. We will sing, and there will be no manifestation of God's glory in the sanctuary. We will pray, and there will be no manifestation of the Lord in our prayer life. No matter what we think we are doing for the Lord, there will be no results, *because we are not praying with an understanding.* We are trying to have illumination without sacrifice—without dying daily to our carnality and to our will.

This takes me back to the properties of gold. Let me explain a little more in detail about the refining process. A little more than twenty years ago, I met a lady at our church who was a jeweler. I expressed to her that I was interested in learning how she made jewelry, so one day she invited me to her house. One of the tools she used was something that looked like a torch, which she used to melt down the gold to make gold pieces. One step of this process was particularly powerful. As she heated up the fire to its highest temperature and began to melt the gold, little black particles rose to the surface. When she saw those particles, she took the gold out of the fire and scraped off the particles.

She said to me, "If you don't get these particles out, then it's not considered to be solid gold." If the particles were not removed, they would begin to corrode the pure gold, leaving cavities on the inside. To get the purest form of gold, she had to keep putting it into the fire, taking it out, scraping off the black particles, and then putting it back into the fire until she had the gold in its most purified state.

When the menorah was created for the first tabernacle, the pounding process the craftsmen used to craft the candlestick would have impacted the gold in such a way that if any impurities remained, they would have caused the fragile, beaten gold to split and break.

In a similar way, we must constantly be placed in the fire of the brazen altar, taken out of the fire, and then put back in so that bad

142

attitudes and ungodly things that are inside are brought to the surface and scraped off by God before He places us back in the fire.

The golden candlestick was crafted of finest solid gold—it was not gold plated. The almond shape represented *resurrection power*, and the image of the flower represented *everlasting beauty*. This means when you go into intercession, and the enemy starts shooting fiery darts at you, your love does not change. Your joy isn't hindered. Your peace keeps flowing like a river, and then longsuffering and temperance kick in as you carry the burden of the Lord. This proves you are not dealing with fool's gold and that your intercessory experience is not merely gold plated, with a bunch of sin and iniquity boiling beneath the surface. When you reach the golden candlestick you will have a *solid-gold encounter* with God, through and through.

It was interesting to me that when the jeweler thought the gold was getting to its purest form, she set the flame at an even hotter temperature. Then one last time she shaped the pure gold into the image of a ring, a cross, or whatever design she was creating for someone who had ordered a particular piece of jewelry.

The bottom line is this: God cannot shape you properly until He gets all the impurities out—so you have to go to the brazen altar! You have to go through tests that reveal the treasure within you. God has to allow people to get in your face the wrong way so that your fighting spirit can surface. Then He will scrape it off and put you back into the fire. Eventually you will get to the point where those impurities are scraped off, and God will be able to shape and mold you into a vessel He can use—a vessel of honor that can be used in intercession.

Think about it. The golden candlestick is able to illuminate the holy place because it was forged in the fire. Eternal stability is built into its design. That's why the candlestick can also symbolize Ephesians 6:13: "Therefore put on God's complete armor, that you may be able to resist and stand your ground on the evil day [of danger], and, having done all [the crisis demands], to stand [firmly in your place]." When you have embraced the power of the golden candlestick, you can stand your ground and hold your priestly position in God.

For example, you wouldn't enter the holy place one day and see the golden candlestick on the south side, and then go back the next day to see it sitting on the north side. You wouldn't walk in and out of the tabernacle only to find the candlestick sitting at the door, and then later see it somewhere else lying on its side. You wouldn't ever see it propped up against the wall, needing somebody to come pick it up and put it back into its place. When the menorah was set into position in the holy place, it wasn't moved. It held its position because it had been forged in the fire. It had been beaten, scraped off, molded, and shaped, because its assignment was to be a light to the world, to be perpetually on fire for God.

PURE OIL OF CRUSHED OLIVES

You may be wondering what kept the menorah lit. How could it shine so brightly to keep the holy place illuminated? God commanded Moses to instruct Aaron and his sons to keep the lampstand filled with pure olive oil: "You shall command the Israelites to provide you with pure oil of crushed olives for the light, to cause it to burn continually [every night]. In the Tent of Meeting [of God with His people], outside the veil which sets apart the Testimony, Aaron and his sons shall keep it burning from evening to morning before the Lord. It shall be a statute to be observed on behalf of the Israelites throughout their generations" (Exod. 27:20–21).

This pure oil of crushed olives symbolizes *the anointing of the Holy Spirit*. When you look at the process they used to make this olive oil, it speaks strongly of the threshing process. Basically, as the olives grow to maturity, the early fruit falls to the ground. Then at harvest time they beat the trees with long sticks to yield the rest of the crop, and then gather all of the olives off the ground. In Bible days, they pressed out the oil either by crushing the olives in the hollow of a stone or by treading upon them by foot.[3]

When the olives were pressed out, two different lots of oil would come forth. Nowadays, the first press of oil is called *extra virgin*, meaning in its purest state. This was the oil that was used to keep the golden candlestick burning. The oil that came out during the second pressing was used in the homes of the people of Israel. Let me confirm to you, there is no anointing without the process of beating and pressing.

When we get to the point of wanting to be used of God, we must receive the anointing of the pure olive oil that illuminates. This goes beyond just having fire or intensity—because the menorah will stay lit continually only if it is filled with the oil of the anointing. You should be shouting *Hallelujah* right now—because this process shows us prophetically that life's tests and trials will bring about a continual oozing of a *new anointing* over our lives—if we stand firm in the place of prayer.

Every morning and evening, the priests would perform the sanctuary service and supply oil in the basins of the golden candlestick. They also had to keep the wick of the candles trimmed. Unless the burnt part of the wick was removed, smoke would be mixed with light in the holy place. Proper lighting was needed to see the table of shewbread and the golden altar of incense. Just so, the burned part of the wick of your spiritual *golden candlestick* has to be removed to enable you to see clearly as you move in the realm of the Spirit.

There should be nothing in the holy place that reminds us of our sins. By the time we reach the holy place in prayer, we should be operating consistently in the newness of God. Old things are passed away, and all things have become new. For this reason, the wicks must be trimmed daily so there will be no residue of what used to be.

TONGUES OF FIRE

One final aspect that I believe is related to the golden candlestick can be found in Acts 2:1–4:

> And when the day of Pentecost had fully come, they were all assembled together in one place, when suddenly there came a sound from heaven like the rushing of a violent tempest blast, and it filled the whole house in which they were sitting. And there appeared to them tongues resembling fire, which were separated and distributed and which settled on each one of them. And they were all filled (diffused throughout their souls) with the Holy Spirit and began to speak in other (different, foreign) languages (tongues), as the Spirit kept giving them clear and loud expression [in each tongue in appropriate words].

As an intercessor, you need the oil of the Holy Spirit on a daily basis. This means that it is an absolute necessity for you to be filled with the Spirit as the disciples were on the Day of Pentecost. Without that infilling, there will be no supernatural utterance from heaven in your prayer closet. Since oil symbolizes the Holy Spirit, and oil had to be *refilled* in the candlestick twice daily to keep the holy place illuminated, there is a strong emphasis on the vital role this experience holds in an intercessor's life.

I believe this is also why the fires on the candlestick were lit from the coals of the brazen altar, which had been kindled by the divine fire from God. Be careful that people do not talk you into falsely manifesting the Holy Spirit. Don't allow someone to blow on you and say that now you have the Holy Spirit. Be careful that people don't just lay hands on you and say, "Oh, that's it..." or declare you have it as soon as they think they hear you speaking in another tongue. Listen to me. Take your time to make sure you are properly baptized in the Holy Spirit—because this particular fire must come divinely from God.

Finally, when you are sure that you have been filled with the Holy Spirit, allow your filling to be clearly evident before you start interceding for others. Everything about the ministry God has given you must remain well lit. If the Spirit is clearly recognizable in your life and ministry, people will not look at you strangely because they don't understand where you are coming from. They will be able to see how God is using you in their lives.

Anything mystical is cast with a shadow of darkness. When you operate in the things of God, your actions should not appear to be mystical. You are not operating in the shadow of darkness. The wick has been trimmed, so there should be clear confirmation in the hearts and lives of those for whom you are interceding. There should be a crystal-clear understanding of what, why, and for whom you are making intercession, as well as of the Spirit who is working through you. Oh, yes. Pure olive oil is necessary.

THE GOLDEN ALTAR OF INCENSE

This third and central piece of furniture in the holy place is the only element capable of ushering you into the divine presence of God. Now you are ready to experience the power of intercession. Let's pause briefly from the tabernacle furniture and study the definition of the word *intercession*. The prefix *inter-* means, "between, among, mutually, reciprocally, as in interdepartmental, intermarry, interweave."[4] The word *cession* is defined as, "the act of ceding as by treaty, official legal document...something that is ceded as territory, justification, realms of authority." To *cede* means, "to yield or formally surrender to another, to cede territory [as an intercessor], to grant or transfer as by will [meaning the will of God]." When you become an *intercessor*, you "stand between and among, you intermarry, you interweave on behalf of another person."

You actually stand between what a person needs and his or her answer from God. While you are standing there, you act as the point of contact that causes Satan to yield or surrender to the will of God. You act as one who grants or transfers according to God's will. When you become an intercessor, you stand in the gap for somebody else, and you don't come out of that place until the enemy has fully surrendered that ground and given up that territory to you.

The word *intercession* is defined as, "an act or instance of interceding, an interposing or pleading on behalf of another person, a prayer to God on behalf of another." Another meaning for intercession is to *impinge,* which means, "to encroach, infringe, to impinge on another's rights, to strike, collide, light, impinging on the lens to make an impression, have an effect, ideas that impinge upon the imagination, ideas that affect the imagination." Your prayers infringe upon the enemy; they strike and begin to collide with the enemy. This makes an eternal impression and a powerful effect against the workings of Satan.

Another root word, *encroach*, means, "to advance beyond established or proper limits, making gradual inroads to trespass upon the property, domain or rights of another, especially gradually or stealthily." This means that when I begin to intercede and pray on someone's behalf, I advance beyond the established *proper* limits. The enemy thinks that it is *proper* (perfectly understandable and something he expects us to do) for believers to pray from the outer court. To do so simply tells him that we *accept* what he is trying to do. For example, we pray, "Lord, my sister is so sick..." By beginning our prayer in that way, we have acknowledged that we accept the illness Satan has caused. But when we *encroach* upon him in prayer, we go beyond the outer court into the holy place and then behind the veil to our final position in the presence of the Lord. In that position, Satan's works are no longer *acceptable* to us.

Another root word is *importunity*, which means, "an importunate solicitation or demand." According to Isaiah 45:11 (KJV), when you go before God to solicit in intercession on someone else's behalf, you can "command" Him regarding the work of His hands. "Thus saith the LORD, the Holy One of Israel, and his Maker, Ask me of things to come concerning my sons, and concerning the work of my hands command ye me."

To be *importune* means, "to urge or press with excessive persistence, to trouble, annoy, to make urgent or persistent solicitations." When you are a true intercessor, you never stop praying. When you are a true intercessor, you pray without ceasing—at all times... morning, noon, and night. Jesus said, "Men ought always to pray, and not to faint" (Luke 18:1, KJV). As an intercessor, I am importune. I encroach; I impinge; I enter in. I intermarry with the person for whom I'm interceding, causing God to answer my prayer and the enemy to give up his ground.

THE DIVINE ATTRIBUTES OF THE INCENSE ALTAR

Now you are ready to pray from the third realm. As you stand at the golden altar of incense, you are just one step away from a threshing floor experience.

In Exodus 30:1–11, God gave Moses instructions concerning the golden altar of incense. There was a significant difference between the construction of the golden altar of incense and the brazen altar. The brazen altar was made from bronze and wood, but the golden altar was made from shittim wood overlaid with gold. One of the most notable qualities about the golden altar was that it was positioned in the center, so it sat in the heart of the holy place. This correlates to intercession being the heart of God. Whatever comes from the golden altar must come from your heart. That understanding is one of the reasons that God provoked me to write the book *Matters of the Heart.*

The condition of your heart can also hinder you from having an intimate relationship with God.

The purpose of the golden altar was threefold: *prayer, intercession,* and *worship*. The fire on the golden altar was never supposed to go out. After both altars were lit supernaturally, the priests kept the fires burning continually, taking coals off the brazen altar daily and using them to keep the fire kindled at the golden altar. This represents that the fire in our worship, intercession, and prayer—though it is rekindled by our ongoing sacrifice—must come directly from God.

It also represents who Jesus Christ is for us—and who we must become for others. Always remember that in order to be like Jesus Christ, in prayer you must do the same things that He had to do. He offered Himself up to the Father on wood as a sacrifice, and therefore we must offer ourselves up to Him. And because Jesus "ever liveth to make intercession" for us, we must ever live to make intercession for others (Heb. 7:25, kjv).

Like the table of shewbread, the golden altar was also made of shittim wood overlaid with gold. Here again we see a blending of humanity with the deity of God. The brazen altar, which was structured of shittim wood overlaid with bronze, had limitations because the covering wasn't pure gold. If you spiritually embrace only the brazen altar, you will be limited to that level of an experience with God, one based on the limitations of humanity. But if you embrace the golden altar, which was constructed of wood overlaid with gold (symbolizing the deity of God), your prayers, intercession, and worship will be strengthened by the supernatural deity of God. You will be able to handle the weight of intercession at the golden altar because, although you are in a human body, you have embraced the deity of God, the supernatural power of His work through you.

The golden altar was constructed to be three feet in height, which corresponded to the height of the ark of the covenant. Actually, the ark was two and one-half feet high, but when adding the height of the two cherubim on its cover, it measured exactly three feet. In practice, this means that when you worship at the golden altar, that piece of furniture brings you to a level where you can commune with God according to His divine pattern—creating yet another match in the Spirit. It also helps you to understand that unless you are on God's level, you will not be able to pray and intercede on behalf of others. Your worship, praise, and intercession must be the same height as the glory of God—or you won't be able to comprehend what God will ultimately speak.

THE INCENSE INGREDIENTS: SWEET, PURE, AND HOLY

The holy incense that burned continually upon the coals of the golden altar was made up of several ingredients. This divine mixture of "pure and holy" ingredients symbolizes our prayers, intercession, and worship—ignited by our sacrifice—giving us entrance into the third realm, the divine presence and revelation of God, behind the veil from the mercy seat.

As we study the four ingredients of the holy incense, you will recognize that these same ingredients are found in Jesus Christ. His intercession went up to God even while He was being crucified. Luke 23:33–34 tells us:

> And when they came to the place which is called The Skull [Latin: Calvary; Hebrew: Golgotha], there they crucified Him, and [along with] the criminals, one on the right and one on the left. And Jesus prayed, Father, forgive them, for they know not what they do. And they divided His garments and distributed them by casting lots for them.

As His physical body was dying, Jesus began to offer up prayers for those who were putting Him to death. This means that His eternal ministry of intercession started on the cross (Heb. 7:25). When Jesus breathed His last breath, the veil that had separated the most holy place in the tabernacle was torn evenly from top to bottom, and He was immediately translated into the third realm. In other words, He went immediately into the presence of the Father. It is because of this that He was able to appear before the disciples in the upper room, even though they were behind a door that was tightly shut and locked (John 20:26). There was no longer *anything* in the natural realm that could hinder Jesus from moving into *any area* to help those who were crying out for His aid.

When someone is crying for help today, and the four ingredients of intercession are present in your prayer life, you cannot be rejected from entering into the supernatural realm to receive help and answers from the Lord on behalf of others.

With God, everything in the Spirit realm relates to measurements and ingredients. He keeps emphasizing these things because He doesn't want our prayer life to be one of chance, trickery, and luck. He doesn't want us to hit and miss in prayer. God wants to make sure that we are following the correct pattern and that we possess all the right ingredients—because if the pattern remains intact, we'll hit a bull's-eye in prayer every time.

There were four ingredients used to create the holy incense. "Then the Lord said to Moses, Take sweet spices—stacte, onycha, and galbanum, sweet spices with pure frankincense, an equal amount of each—and make of them incense, a perfume after the perfumer's art, seasoned with salt and mixed, pure and sacred" (Exod. 30:34–35).

The first spice in the holy incense was *stacte*, a resin that would ooze spontaneously out of the storax tree.[5] By revelation I believe this means that our *prayers, worship, and intercession must not be programmed.* They must emerge spontaneously at the direction of the Spirit of God. This is why so many churches and people today are stagnated in the things of the Spirit. So many are always trying to come up with a *program* for weekly services—fifteen minutes are allowed for worship, five minutes for prayer time, and maybe two minutes for intercession. There's no spontaneity, no responsiveness to the Spirit of the Lord in such a program. When we place limits on God at the golden altar, which was designed for deity and humanity to flow together, we limit ourselves from allowing God sovereignly to direct our spirit *any time, anywhere,* and *in any way* that He desires to use us in intercession.

The Book of Ezekiel speaks strongly about receiving the burden of the Lord. In preparing to do so, we must be sensitive to the heartbeat of God at any given moment. Remember that the golden altar sat in the heart of the holy place, directly in front of the ark of the covenant. Since prayers, intercession, and worship are literally the heartbeat of God, when we become intercessors at this place called the golden altar of incense, we receive the ability to pick up His heartbeat in order to receive His burden.

The Spirit of the Lord may move upon you in the grocery store. He could reveal a situation to you that is happening in someone's life in another state or country. If He does this, He doesn't have time for you to wait until you get to church on Sunday to make intercession for two minutes. In fact, He doesn't even want to wait until you get home from the store. Therefore, *stacte* must be part of your prayers, intercession, and worship—because God needs for you to be instantly obedient to His voice and promptings. If He needs you to pull your car off of the highway to go into spontaneous intercession, that's what stacte will prepare you to do.

The second spice that was part of the holy incense was *onycha*, which was extracted from a shellfish that lived in the depths of the Red Sea. The revelation of this means *you must have depth in your worship*. You can't be satisfied with merely singing the same songs you hear everybody else singing. You must avoid limiting yourself to singing only worship songs that were written by someone else, and learn to sing from your spirit.

Your level of prayers, intercession, and worship unto God must come from a depth in the Spirit. You must be able to leave the *surface* of what has already been done to tap into a realm of new experiences that flow from the heartbeat of God.

The *onycha* anointing also means that God will require you to think more deeply about the prayers you pray than to constantly repeat Jesus' model prayer in Matthew 6:9–13. He will require more from you than a mere recital of a common bedtime prayer or some other repetitious prayer you have prayed for years. When you are in front of the golden altar of incense, the deep things of the Spirit of God will call forth *the deep* that is within you. Scripture says, "Deep calleth unto deep..." (Ps. 42:7, KJV).

The third spice was *galbanum*, a pungent resin that could only be acquired by breaking or splitting the branch of a tree. The word *pungent* means, "affecting the organs of taste or smell with a sharp acrid sensation." In other words, it was a bitter ingredient, not at all pleasing to the senses. As an intercessor, there will be times when you go through *galbanum* experiences. Yet during *difficult seasons and manifestations*, you must come to a place where you can declare, "Though I'm having a bitter experience, I'm still going to stay in the posture of prayer, intercession, and worship.

As you serve at the golden altar of incense, God will begin to train you in order to help you understand that everything in your life is not always going to run smoothly. You are going to have some rocky days and situations where it may feel as if you are being *split*. There will be times when bitterness seems to ooze out of you because of situations in your family, at church, or in the workplace—situations that hurt you. There will be times when you are physically wounded or your emotions are shaken. But in the midst of these *galbanum* experiences, you must learn how to keep offering up prayers, intercession, and worship unto God from a deep place in your spirit.

The fourth and final spice that was added to the holy incense was *frankincense*, a resin that was collected early in the morning from the Boswellia tree. This reminds me of Psalm 63:1–2 (KJV):

> O God, thou art my God; early will I seek thee: my soul thirsteth for thee, my flesh longeth for thee in a dry and thirsty land, where no water is; to see thy power and thy glory, so as I have seen thee in the sanctuary.

When you seek the Lord from the ingredient of *frankincense*, you are *seeking Him early*—which doesn't necessarily mean a time of day. This precious resin is collected early in the morning *because it readily flows out at that time*. What is God saying here? You must seek God early in the morning of your trial—before you reach the afternoon and evening of that trial. Determine to seek Him at the beginning of your trial, before trouble comes, before there's an accident or misunderstanding, before there's trouble on the line. In the holy place, it becomes your way of life to seek Him early. When you do this, there will always be a ready flow of His Spirit. You will have a consistent flow of His anointing.

After blending together the four ingredients of the holy incense, one final element was used to *temper* them all together: "And make of them incense, a perfume after the perfumer's art, seasoned with salt and mixed, pure and sacred" (Exod. 30:35).

You are the "salt of the earth" (Matt. 5:13)—especially as you function in your priestly role as an intercessor. You are the key element that brings it all together at the golden altar. You have to make prayer, intercession, and worship a personal priority. You have to invest yourself into this divine process completely. You can't rely on other people to do this for you. There will come a time in your walk of prayer when you will have to turn off the tape recorder, take the CD (with somebody else's praise and worship on it) out of the player, and become the *salt* God has created you to be for His glory. If you don't, you won't be good for anything except to be "thrown out and trodden underfoot by men" (Matt. 5:13).

When you arrive at the golden altar of the holy incense, *stacte, onycha, galbanum*, and *frankincense* have become vital ingredients of your intercessory service unto God. At that point you are just a heartbeat away from a threshing floor experience *behind the veil*. You are in the posture where revelation is awaiting you at the mercy seat, deliverance is imminent, and total victory is guaranteed, because you have learned to carry the burden of the Lord in prayer.

CHAPTER 11

The Power of Intercession:
Entering the Most Holy Place

*Y*OU ARE ABOUT to enter into the most sacred part of the tabernacle, so I must take time to make sure that you are ready. This most holy place is where you become absolutely sure that God hears your prayers, and it is the place where you are finally ready to receive the answers. Let's go through our checklist from the previous steps of prayer:

1. Did you enter through the Beautiful Gate? Did you accept Jesus Christ as your Savior and Lord by receiving His finished works as represented by the four colors: blue, purple, scarlet, and white?

2. Have you passed through the outer court of your initial conversion experience? Have you moved beyond religion (talking to God at church once or twice a week) into a closer relationship with Christ? Are you becoming less focused on what you need in prayer and more focused on becoming who you are in Christ?

3. Did you go to the brazen laver? Have you allowed the Holy Spirit to begin building God's character in you by washing at the laver of the Word of God? Are you now a "doer of the

155

Word" and not just a "hearer"? Do you truly understand that you have now been cleansed through the Word?

4. Did you embrace the brazen altar? Have you offered every part of yourself to Him, including areas that could prove to be hindrances or weights in your walk with God? Do you place yourself on this altar daily for God to purify you and your motives? Have you freely offered yourself as a living sacrifice?

5. Are you wearing your tunic of righteousness? Do you understand that you have been made the "righteousness of God in Christ Jesus"? Are you disciplining yourself to walk in righteousness, declaring the victory daily?

6. Have you put on the priestly garments of completion: the sash, the robe of blue, the ephod, the breastplate with Urim and Thummim, and the miter? Are you walking in your priestly anointing as a "living tabernacle" so that you can enter His divine presence in prayer and intercession?

7. As you prepared to approach the tabernacle door, did you experience a deeper revelation of the works of Christ? Have you regularly gone to the place of prayer with the understanding of His works being made manifest in you?

8. Have the ingredients of God's holy anointing oil—liquid myrrh, sweet-scented cinnamon, fragrant calamus, and cassia— become part of your life? Have you begun to walk consistently in purity before the Lord, keeping the right attitude with God and others? Are you coming into spiritual maturity and experiencing "completeness" in your intercessory anointing during prayer?

9. Are you experiencing the power of divine protection through the spiritual coverings of your tabernacle: fine-twined linen and wool, goat's hair, ram's skin, and badger's skin? At this deeper place in prayer, are you learning how to relax and trust in His supernatural provision, protection, and direction?

10. Have you embraced the tabernacle content in the holy place: the table of shewbread, the golden candlestick, and finally, the golden altar of incense? Is the power of each of these elements literally beginning to work within you and through you as you pray for others?

Let me say this even more plainly. Before God will allow you to operate in the faith that brings results through effectual prayer and intercession, there are foundational requirements for every intercessor that you must satisfy in your life. There are increasingly deeper levels of your walk with Christ that take you to higher dimensions in your prayer closet. *Keep this in mind, because you are about to enter the most holy place—the supernatural realm where you have eternal communion with God.*

Now let's look straight ahead at the divine entrance through the veil. There you will see the golden altar of incense. Because the golden altar of incense was centered in the tabernacle structure, it was the nearest piece of furniture to the divine presence of God behind the veil. It represented the heart of tabernacle service. Anyone could come into the outer court and wash at the brazen laver before sacrificing at the brazen altar. But only the lower priests and the high priest were allowed to serve in the holy place amidst the table of shewbread, the golden candlestick, and the golden altar. And only the high priest could enter into the most holy place.

As you have learned, God administers a tremendous warning in Scripture to those who are not spiritually qualified to minister in intercession and prayer. We must carefully guard against mixing the wrong ingredients into our worship. The sacred ingredients of the holy incense were carefully measured in the right quantity and blended together according to the instruction of the Lord before they were beaten into a fine powder. When this holy mixture was sprinkled onto the hot coals in the golden altar, it released a sweet fragrance into the atmosphere that permeated the entire holy place. Remember, the aroma of burnt flesh arose from the brazen altar—but the sweet aroma of holy incense arises only from the golden altar.

When you are a true intercessor—a believer who prays, intercedes, and worships at home, at work, in church, or wherever you may be—anyone who comes into your presence should be able to feel the presence of God upon you. There should be a sweet odor of prayer and worship wherever you go. People should be able to attend your church and say, "The people pray in this church. I can feel God's presence. I can smell the aroma." The same should happen in your home. The essence of prayer, intercession, and worship should permeate the atmosphere around you.

If this isn't the case in your life, does it mean that you are not praying? No. It simply means that you are not praying correctly according to the proper pattern. You are not praying to the depth and with the correct ingredients that God has set forth as His prerequisites for effective intercession. Remember that those who haven't come by way of the brazen laver and the brazen altar cannot enter or serve in the holy place—and they definitely cannot approach the golden altar of incense. Let me take you to a few stories in the Bible that illustrate this point.

KING UZZIAH'S STRENGTH

In 2 Chronicles 26 we find the story of King Uzziah. As an intercessor, it is important that you understand the nature of this king, for he defied the law of God concerning the altar of incense. Although he was only sixteen years old when he began his reign, we learn that he "did right in the Lord's sight, to the extent of all that his father Amaziah had done. He set himself to seek God in the days of Zechariah, who instructed him in the things of God" (vv. 4–5).

So we see that in the early years of his reign, King Uzziah had a relationship with God. He began his reign correctly under the spiritual covering of the prophet Zechariah. In his early years, King Uzziah yearned for and sought after the Lord, and God prospered him. Then his situation started to turn. We must never forget that *starting out* in right standing with God does not automatically qualify us to minister in the holy place—especially if we go off kilter after we begin.

Uzziah was able to defeat many of the cities of Israel's enemy the Philistines. God helped him to be successful, "and his fame spread abroad even to the border of Egypt, for he became very strong" (v. 8). He developed an extremely strong and capable combat army of more than three hundred thousand men, "who could fight with mighty power to help the king against the enemy" (v. 13). He became famous throughout the land and known for his strong army, which was well prepared with weapons and machines of war that Uzziah provided to his army.

But by reading the twenty-sixth chapter of 2 Chronicles, you will notice that King Uzziah went from being classified as a person who *sought after and yearned for the Lord* to becoming *a famous man known for his great success*. As his fame became widespread, he began to trust in the strength of his own abilities. This same thing happens today. For example, let's say you are a great preacher or singer, and your fame spreads everywhere. If you are not careful, your posture to seek after God will cease. That's why we must be careful to keep washing at the brazen laver and sacrificing at the brazen altar. If we become strong in ourselves, we may end up like Uzziah, saying, "I don't need the Lord anymore. I can handle this on my own." This attitude is extremely dangerous, which we can see in the life of Uzziah. Take note of verse 16: "But when [King Uzziah] was strong, he became proud to his destruction; and he trespassed against the Lord his God, for he went into the temple of the Lord to burn incense on the altar of incense."

When pride and arrogance take over, a haughty spirit follows close behind—which means this person won't receive correction. Listen closely. If you are being used in the service of the Lord, yet you are walking in pride and haughtiness and aren't submitted to the correction of spiritual authority, then you are headed for shipwreck.

King Uzziah stormed by the brazen laver, ignored the brazen altar, and went straight into the holy place. He ignored the table of shewbread and the golden candlestick, which means that he gave no recognition to the Word of God or to the Holy Spirit. His life was no longer *beaten and pressed out*. Pride had entered in, and the workings of the flesh were fully manifested in him. Disregarding his degraded spiritual condition, he went inside the holy place, straight to the golden altar of incense! Look what started to play out in verses 17–18:

> And Azariah the priest went in after him and with him eighty priests of the Lord, men of courage. They opposed King Uzziah and said to him, It is not for you, Uzziah, to burn incense to the Lord, but for the priests, the sons of Aaron, who are set apart to burn incense.

> Withdraw from the sanctuary; you have trespassed, and that will
> not be to your credit and honor before the Lord God.

Do you see this? It doesn't matter what you have accomplished—you
are not going to get any credit in heaven by entering into the presence
of God illegally. Some try to say, "I get up every morning at 6:00 a.m.
and pray." It doesn't matter what time you get up if you are not praying
according to God's pattern, because your prayers are in pride.

Others say, "I volunteer at the church several days a week, and every
Sunday morning they ask me to lead in prayer...because God has an
anointing on my life." If this is you, pride is taking over. You have walked
past the brazen laver, and you have avoided sacrificing at the brazen altar.
You have ignored the shewbread and the golden candlestick. Now you
want to stand before God in pride and offer up prayers? You won't get
any credit for it in glory! You might be praised by the people in your
church. You might be honored by all your buddies who pump your spirit
into deeper levels of pride—*but you will get no credit from God.*

Verses 19 and 20 tell us what happened to King Uzziah:

> Then Uzziah was enraged, and he had a censer in his hand to burn
> incense. And while he was enraged with the priests, leprosy broke
> out on his forehead before the priests in the house of the Lord,
> beside the incense altar. And as Azariah the chief priest and all the
> priests looked upon him, behold, he was leprous on his forehead!
> So they forced him out of there; and he also made haste to get out,
> because the Lord had smitten him.

Let me draw a parallel for you. The true sign of a person who has
ignored the prerequisites God established for a true intercessor is this:
when correction comes, that person becomes angry—and that's a dangerous place to be with God.

An intercessor starts out by seeking God and going forth in Him. That
happens long before anyone recognizes the anointing on that person's
life. Before anyone recognizes your talents or giftings, you begin on your
face, seeking after God. You yearn after God, panting after Him like a
deer that "pants and longs for the water brooks" (Ps. 42:1).

But something happens when the *fame* of becoming an intercessor gets out, and people see the anointing of God on your life. They begin to seek you out. When that happens, you must be careful not to step over into pride and lose credit with God. Look what happened to King Uzziah. He began to trust in his own strength, and, as a result, he ended up a leper for the rest of his life (2 Chron. 26:21–23).

As an intercessor, it is essential that you understand the power of the golden altar of incense. It must not be disregarded or mishandled. We must spend quality time at the golden altar to achieve the right mixture of prayers, intercession, and worship before God. We cannot rush into the holy place and expect an *instant* anointing to be given to us on our terms! Each ingredient in the holy incense undergoes a specific process before it is ready to be added to the incense mixture in a specific amount. For the anointing to be authentic, it must be God's mixture.

Our prayers and worship are to be given to God—and to Him alone. With the instructions for making the incense, God gave this warning to Moses: "And the incense which you shall make according to its composition you shall not make for yourselves; it shall be to you holy to the Lord. Whoever makes any like it for perfume shall be cut off from his people" (Exod. 30:37–38). When we come into the holy place, our praise, worship, and everything we are must be given to God for His glory only.

Presumption in the Priesthood

Why would anyone who came up with a false mixture of the holy incense would be cut off from Israel (Exod. 30:37–38)? When you create a false mixture of the anointing, you are drawing to yourself the worship and praise that belong to God alone.

Aaron's sons Nadab and Abihu died when they offered up "strange fire" before the Lord (Lev. 10:1–3). This took place immediately after the priesthood was established, and it speaks to what can happen early in a believer's walk with the Lord. King Uzziah represents a deeper level of deception, which can happen after an individual is called into position and begins seeking the Lord. Uzziah was filled with pride after being raised up and set in office.

In another biblical illustration, three men—Korah, Dathan, and Abiram—desired to fill the position that only a priest was allowed to fill. They gathered a group of 250 leaders and men of distinction to stand against Moses and Aaron and challenge their leadership. (See Numbers 16:1–4.)

It is a very dangerous thing to desire the office of the priesthood when you haven't been purified to that level.

God alone can call you to stand in the midst of the congregation and minister the Word of God (which is the shewbread) or to be a part of the moving of the Spirit (which is the candlestick). You must wait upon the Lord to be called to minister by way of intercession.

Korah, Dathan, and Abiram tried to discredit what Moses had done in obedience to the Lord. They challenged how he was leading the children of Israel. "Why can't we be priests, too?" they asked.

Moses responded with this warning: "In the morning the Lord will show who are His and who is holy, and will cause him to come near to Him; him whom He has chosen will He cause to come near to Him" (Num. 16:5). In other words, he was telling those men, "You are not challenging me; *you are challenging God.*"

Here's where the Bible reveals that although the enemy may lie to you, truth will be revealed at the golden altar. When Korah and 250 of his men took their censers and filled them with coals of fire, they withstood Moses and Aaron at the entrance of the holy place and assembled the whole congregation against them. As a result, God sent judgment. The earth opened and swallowed up the tents (families) of Korah, Dathan, and Abiram, and fire consumed the 250 men with censers. All of them died before the Lord (vv. 23–35).

Some people start out wonderfully in God, going to the brazen laver and the brazen altar. Then as soon as God elevates them to the office of the priesthood, and they become an intercessor or start preaching the gospel and moving in the things of the Spirit, they get lifted up in pride. Before you know it, you don't hear about them anymore. They used to preach, prophesy, lay hands on the sick, and interpret tongues, but they have disappeared, because they broke His pattern. They failed to wait before the Lord to be processed to the level of purification for the priesthood. Instead of responding in obedience to the Lord's process of purification, they desired to gain the office of their own accord. They had not laid down a great enough sacrifice to be able to enter into that realm in God, and for that reason they were swallowed up in their own destruction.

So I say to you, *wait on the Lord*. Make your calling and election sure (2 Pet. 1:10). Every believer has been called to pray according to what Jesus taught in Luke 18:1–8. We ought always to pray and not faint. However, you must come to another level of maturity in God before you can enter the realm of intercessory prayer. Think about Moses' walk with the Lord and how God prepared his spirit to lead a nation. In Numbers 12:7–8, God told Miriam and Aaron: "*[Moses] is entrusted and faithful in all My house. With him I speak mouth to mouth [directly], clearly and not in dark speeches; and he beholds the form of the Lord.*"

Continual sacrifice and brokenness are required to reach that depth of relationship and communication with God where God speaks to you face-to-face, directly and clearly, and where you will be able to behold the form of the Lord. Though God desires for everybody to have this level of relationship, you have to wait until He qualifies you to be there, or you will be swallowed up and utterly destroyed by the workings of the flesh.

The workings of your flesh will destroy the sweet mixture of the holy incense. Only a pure mixture of the "sweet spices"—stacte, onycha, and galbanum, with pure frankincense—will remain *sweet, pure,* and *holy* unto the Lord. "Dead flies cause the ointment of the perfumer to putrefy [and] send forth a vile odor; so does a little folly [in him who is valued for wisdom] outweigh wisdom and honor" (Eccles. 10:1).

When God calls you into the office of the priesthood or that of an intercessor, there cannot be anything in your life that could be considered as being *folly*. It would be like dropping a dead fly into the oil of the apothecary, which would send a stinking smell throughout the temple.

Some believers create all kinds of things of their own design and mix them together, calling it *God*. But these people are worshiping illegally. Dead flies have gotten into the oil of the anointing upon their lives. Because they haven't surrendered to God or followed His pattern, they don't possess the pure oil of olive or have the right ingredients for the incense. As a result, God cannot use them to change people's lives. I would remind such believers of Proverbs 14:12: "There is a way which seems right to a man and appears straight before him, but at the end of it is the way of death."

We must be careful that we do not mishandle the golden altar of incense, because it stands directly in front of the ark of the covenant. Unlike the brazen altar, which deals with your flesh, the golden altar deals with your faith. It's our passageway behind the veil into the holy of holies.

THERE'S POWER IN FOLLOWING THE PATTERN

After judgment fell upon Korah, Dathan, and Abiram, the children of Israel rebelled against Moses. Their rebellion so angered the Lord that He said to Aaron and Moses, "Get away from among this congregation, that I may consume them in a moment" (Num. 16:45). Immediately, Moses and Aaron fell on their faces.

Because of God's wrath, a plague began to sweep over the disobedient congregation. In fear, Moses told Aaron to run and get a censer, put fire in it from the altar, and begin to make atonement for the people. "So Aaron took the burning censer as Moses commanded, and ran into the midst of the congregation; and behold, the plague was begun among the people; and he put on the incense and made atonement for the people. And he stood between the dead and the living, and the plague was stayed" (vv. 47–48).

When you embrace the golden altar of incense properly, you will have the power to take God's anointing off that altar and run and stand between the living and the dead to declare life. When you transport the power of the Lord from your prayer closet, you become the golden censer. The prayers, worship, and intercession on those coals of fire remain ignited from your continual sacrifice on the brazen altar. The ingredients of the holy incense are within you, and wherever YOU go—whether it's to the beauty shop, the hospital, the bank, the grocery store, a prison cell, or in your own house or church—*you* become the censer with coals of fire and fragrant incense continually going up to God. According to the Word of God, *you* are capable of stopping the plague in the earth. *You* can stop sin, sickness, and disease. God has given *you* the authority to come out of the holy place and stand between the living and the dead. *YOU* can declare life!

Do you see this? You must understand and embrace the power of the golden altar of incense. Like Aaron, you must learn to guard your garments and minister at the golden altar every morning and every night—because you must stand in the gap for those who need an answer from the Lord.

LET'S REVIEW

When the high priest was adorned in all of his priestly garments to enter the holy place, he was wearing his tunic and breeches, which represented *righteousness*. He was girded with the long sash, which represented the *strength of the Lord*. He was also wearing the blue robe, which represented *authority*, and the ephod, which symbolized that he had been *proven* for his priestly role. Finally, he was wearing the breastplate that contained the Urim and Thummim, which represented *light* and *completeness* for him to receive the word of the Lord for Israel. He was also wearing the miter with a holy crown, which symbolized being completely *devoted* to God and His service.

When properly clothed, Aaron and his sons (who wore only tunics and sashes) could enter the holy place to perform the service of the Lord. But only the high priest could enter the most holy place.

Once a year on the Day of Atonement, Aaron was required to undergo the process of purification a second time, including taking off all his normal priestly garments and putting on the "most holy" linen tunic and undergarments, before he could enter behind the veil. As high priest, if Aaron hadn't faithfully maintained all of his garments with righteousness as his foundation, he would have disqualified himself from entering the divine presence. *As an intercessor, what does this mean to you?* In the divine presence of the Lord, there is no interference; nothing is tainted. There is nothing standing between you and God. In other words, *there is no veil*. When the high priest went into that divine place, there was no separation between him and God. Righteousness was his foundation.

What does this say to us today? Even though there are certain requirements (clothing) for us to be able to operate in ministry, when we are preparing to enter the divine presence of God, the thing that is required above everything else is that we are wearing the *tunic of righteousness.* Aaron dethroned himself of his usual priestly garments, the miter, the breastplate, the ephod, the blue robe, the sash, the tunic, and the breeches, and he went into the most holy place wearing his *most holy* garments. Why? Because he had already walked these things out. If we want to enter behind the veil, we must dethrone ourselves of everything we do in the service of the Lord (our reasonable service)—because nothing except the righteousness imputed to us by Christ can take us there.

As Aaron passed through the veil, He saw the same colors that were in the Beautiful Gate to the outer court and in the door to the holy place. He also saw the cherubim, the lion, the eagle, and the ox as he walked through the veil to minister at the ark of the covenant. We must remember as we go into the divine presence of the Lord—though we may have sacrificed and served God for many years—that we can only enter this place through the finished works of Jesus Christ. Nothing we have done in service to the Lord qualifies us to enter behind the veil—only what Christ has done on our behalf.

When Jesus shed His blood and died on the cross, that veil was torn from top to bottom. Now we can stand before the most holy place as priests unto God, offering up the *sweet, pure,* and *holy* incense of our worship. Why? Because when we get to the altar of incense, that is not the place where we war—that is the place of worship. We no longer have to wait to enter through the veil, because the veil has already been opened. The blood of Jesus has made atonement on our behalf. That's why He is able to do "exceeding abundantly above all that we ask or think, according to the power that worketh in us" (Eph. 3:20, KJV). That power is the very image, character, and nature of Christ—represented by all of the colors and images that are operating in our lives. That is what we see and experience on our way to the mercy seat.

When Jesus died on the cross, He took on the sins of the world and became sin, and the Father had to turn His back on His own Son. Christ had taken on everything that was unrighteousness, and His Father had to separate Himself from His only begotten Son while He was dying. If you are not living right, you will not be able to pray effectively, because God has to turn His back on you. The only way God can see you and not send judgment is to look at you through the blood of His Son.

Before the high priest could approach the golden altar of incense on the Day of Atonement, he first had to make sacrifices for his own sins and for the sins of the children of Israel (Lev. 16:5–13). Without the blood sacrifice of Jesus at salvation, you cannot be saved. Without applying that same blood as an intercessor—by maintaining the operation of His blood through your walk with Him—then God can't talk to you from the mercy seat. He has to turn His back on you.

But when He looks at you through the blood of Jesus, He not only sees you through the blood that has been applied to your life, *but He also sees Christ in you.* God will not destroy His own Son because Jesus has already conquered death, hell, and the grave. Jesus cannot and will not ever die!

Let me say it another way. When the Father looks at you, and you are living right according to the finished works of His Son, it is like He is looking at Jesus. You should have been cut off long before because of sin and iniquity, but the blood covers you so that you can give prayers, intercession, and worship to God according to His pattern. The Son sits *in you,* so that when you go behind the veil, you can apply that blood to the mercy seat where Christ forever lives to make intercession for us. As long as Christ lives in you, whatever the devil sends your direction cannot wipe you out—because you have come to the point that Christ is "ever living" in your heart and making intercession (standing in the gap) for you. He's praying for you that your faith will not fail.

Bless God for Jesus! He is the reason you are saved. He is the reason you can walk in obedience to God. Jesus is your righteousness! That's why none of your troubles have been able to break you or silence your praise! You can keep praising God, because Christ lives in you! This is why you can never ignore the priceless sacrifice that clothes you in righteousness. Because of what Jesus has done, when your flesh is weak, *you are strong* (2 Cor. 12:9).

When your flesh tells you to stop, you can keep pressing forward in God! Don't stop coming to God in times of weakness. During those times when you feel heavy-laden in your emotions, you can lift your hands in praise to God anyway... *because Christ lives in you* (2 Cor. 5:17).

Look carefully at 2 Corinthians 5:17–6:2. These are your benefits:

Therefore if any person is [ingrafted] in Christ (the Messiah) he is a new creation (a new creature altogether); the old [previous moral and spiritual condition] has passed away. Behold, the fresh and new has come! But all things are from God, Who through Jesus Christ reconciled us to Himself [received us into favor, brought us into harmony with Himself] and gave to us the ministry of reconciliation [that by word and deed we might aim to bring others into harmony with Him]. It was God [personally present] in Christ, reconciling and restoring the world to favor with Himself, not counting up and holding against [men] their trespasses [but cancelling them], and committing to us the message of reconciliation (of the restoration to favor). So we are Christ's ambassadors, God making His appeal as it were through us. We [as Christ's personal representatives] beg you for His sake to lay hold of the divine favor [now offered you] and be reconciled to God. For our sake He made Christ [virtually] to be sin Who knew no sin, so that in and through Him we might become [endued with, viewed as being in, and examples of] the righteousness of God [what we ought to be, approved and acceptable and in right relationship with Him, by His goodness]. Laboring together [as God's fellow workers] with Him then, we beg of you not to receive the grace of God in vain [that merciful kindness by which God exerts His holy influence on souls and turns them to Christ, keeping and strengthening them—do not receive it to no purpose]. For He says, In the time of favor (of an assured welcome) I have listened to and heeded your call, and I have helped you on the day of deliverance (the day of salvation). Behold, now is truly the time for a gracious welcome and acceptance [of you from God]; behold, now is the day of salvation!

Jesus gave His life so that you could live and restore others to a right relationship with God. That's why you have to come through His completed works at every step of the pattern of prayer. You can do all things through Christ, but without Him you can do nothing.

He wants you to be able to walk with the testimony: "I almost died, but Jesus said, 'Not so!' I almost lost my mind for good, but the *blood of Jesus* healed and restored me!" *What can wash away your sin?* Nothing but the blood of Jesus! *What can make you whole again?* Nothing but the blood of Jesus! Only the precious flow of His redeeming blood can make you whiter than snow. Stop right now and thank the Lord, because when the enemy comes in like a flood, the Spirit of the Lord lifts up a standard against him! Thanks be to God for giving us the victory and causing us to triumph!

When you have come all the way through the outer court and into the holy place to minister at the golden altar of incense, you can declare the victory! As you prepare to go into the most holy place behind the veil, you know He's alive! When you lie at His feet in prayer and intercession, whether it's day, night, summer, spring, or winter, you know He's the only one who can keep you. In trials and tribulations, He is Lord. When the devil tries to wipe you out and tell you that you're not going to make it, Jesus is "exceeding abundantly" able to keep you alive and take you to your next level!

When you have entered the holy place, *you are covered*. You need not fight your battles—they have already been fought on your behalf, and the victory has already been won!

THE ANCHOR OF YOUR SOUL...

Hebrews 6:17–20 says:

> Accordingly God also, in His desire to show more convincingly and beyond doubt to those who were to inherit the promise the unchangeableness of His purpose and plan, intervened (mediated) with an oath. This was so that, by two unchangeable things [His promise and His oath] in which it is impossible for God ever to prove false or deceive us, we who have fled [to Him] for refuge might have mighty indwelling strength and strong encouragement to grasp and hold fast the hope appointed for us and set before [us]. [Now] we have this [hope] as a sure and steadfast anchor of the soul [it cannot slip and it cannot break down under whoever steps out upon it—a hope] that reaches farther and enters into [the very certainty of the Presence] within the veil, where Jesus has entered in for us [in advance], a Forerunner having become a High Priest forever after the order (with the rank) of Melchizedek.

What a mighty scripture! When God saves you and gives you a promise from His Word, you don't have to hope in anything fleshly. Our hope goes far beyond the outer court and the holy place into the divine presence of God! This hope is steadfast and sure, and it will anchor our soul (our mind, emotions, and will). Only Jesus is able to hold our emotions in place, because the Bible says this hope can never slip or break down...no matter what may come!

When your soul has been anchored by this oath and promise from God, it cannot break down under the devil's attacks, *because that promise is anchored in the divine presence of the Lord.* This is why as a priest and intercessor you can go into His presence, already knowing what God is able to do. You go in already knowing that He is the ultimate answer for those who are locked in the outer court and can't find their way into the divine presence. You go in to liberate those who are held in shackles and chains by the hands of the enemy. You go into the divine presence knowing that you will receive an answer from God and come out with the victory for someone in need.

Now you can wage an effective warfare against the enemy in prayer because your soul is anchored, and your feet won't slip. You can declare right now, "I will not be shaken, I will not be moved, but having done all...I will stand." You are ready to enter the most holy place, the divine presence of God.

CHAPTER 12

Eternal Communion:
The Ark of the Covenant

*L*ET'S LOOK MORE closely at the ark. Instead of focusing on its construction, I would like to make mention more about what it symbolizes in being a third-dimension intercessor. Why? I believe the ark represents the human heart—the deepest, most intimate part of who you are, and the place where the glory of God can take up residence and transform everything around you. *When the church begins to live within the third dimension of prayer, joining our hearts with the heart of God in the most holy place within us, then life as we know it will be forever changed.* Believers will no longer be content simply "playing church." Religion will no longer satisfy. Then we'll see His glory released in the earth like never before.

As with all the other elements of the tabernacle and its furniture, God gave specific instructions to Moses for the construction of the ark of the covenant. Exodus 25:10–16 says:

> They shall make an ark of acacia wood: two and a half cubits long, a cubit and a half wide, and a cubit and a half high. You shall overlay the ark with pure gold, inside and out, and make a gold crown, a rim or border, around its top. You shall cast four golden rings and attach them to the four lower corners of it, two rings on either side. You shall make poles of acacia wood and overlay them with gold. And put

the poles through the rings on the ark's sides, by which to carry it. The poles shall remain in the rings of the ark; they shall not be removed from it [that the ark be not touched]. And you shall put inside the ark the Testimony [the Ten Commandments] which I will give you.

Foreknowing that a believer's body would ultimately house the Holy Spirit, God demonstrated that He didn't need to create something big to house an enormous seat of power. If you read my book *Matters of the Heart*, you will remember that the human heart is so powerful that it forms, develops, and starts beating in a fetus before the brain develops.[1] It's the only organ in your body that doesn't have to obey the brain. In fact, the heart keeps beating long after the brain is dead. Not only this, but I have also learned that the measurements between the cherubim on the mercy seat (on top of the ark) are similar to the measurements of the human chest cavity. Your heart—the head of your temple—can hold tremendous power, which is imparted directly from heaven in third-dimensional, threshing floor prayer.

The ark was overlaid with solid gold on the inside and outside, which represents *the perfected union of God and man*. Let's look quickly at the three elements that were placed within the ark:

1. The *testimonial tablets* (Exod. 24:12), which represent *the perfected Word* manifested in your life

2. *Aaron's rod,* which budded as a *symbol against rebellion to God-given authority* (Num. 17:8–10)

3. An *omer of manna,* which represents *supernatural provision and freedom from bondage* (Exod. 16:32–34)

When these three elements were maintained inside the ark, it housed the glory of God. Without them present, the ark became just another empty gold box. When the testimonial tablets were missing (during the era of the second temple), the "empty" ark could not be kept in the tabernacle.[2] Do you see what God is saying? We must also come to understand that in order for us to walk in the perfected power of God, these same elements must be present and remain:

1. *There must be a manifestation of the Word, not just sitting in my heart, but operative in my everyday lifestyle.* My life must come to a place where I am no longer failing every test and being defeated on every hand. I must have testimonies. My life must declare to others, "I was tested and tried on every hand, but yet I lived right to tell the story. Yes, I kept my spirit right. Therefore, sitting within my heart are my testimonial tablets."

2. *Just like Aaron's rod budding, I must be able to not just stand against that which rebels against God, but in everything I am, I must come to a place that whatever decision God makes for me, my answer is, "Yes, Lord, Thy will be done."* I must become willing and obedient to His every command, and Aaron's budding rod is there to remind me that if I choose at any given time to walk in rebellion, I will end up walking out a penalty.

3. *My omer of manna represents the fact that I have come to trust the Lord, and not man, for everything I need . . .* therefore freeing me from the bondage of worry and fear. My experience during my time in the wilderness has brought me to a place where I know without a shadow of a doubt that my God shall supply all of my needs according to His riches in glory, therefore freeing me from leaning on the arms of flesh.

If your heart has not been perfected through the process of these elements, you will not be able to come into the most holy place of His glory! This sad condition is true of too many Christians. And this is why many believers have not entered the realm of effective, fervent prayer. You see, it is not enough to just pray. *We need to receive answers to prayer.*

You need to stop right now and declare, "From this day forward, I'm going to crucify my flesh. I'm going to put my desires on the altar, enter the place of prayer, and seek God until He searches out the true intents of my heart, bringing it into full submission to His will." If you say this and really mean it, your life will never be the same—because God is faithful. He will lead you all the way through each step of the process until you come into His glory—because His ultimate goal is that you not only see His glory, but that He gets glory out of your life.

When you are in the beginning stages of your prayer ministry, God has many things that He wants to tell you in secret. But He has a time-table and a schedule to bring each of them to fruition. When the Lord gets ready to launch your prayer ministry, it doesn't mean that He's finished dealing with you in every area of your life.

A lot of believers don't understand this process. If you were to order videocassettes of my ministry from 1996 until now, you could literally see and hear the transformation of the Lord. The more I died to self...the more I gave up to God and told Him *yes*...the more I learned to endure hardship as a good soldier—the greater the anointing became in my life. It wasn't about what was being done to me from *without*. It wasn't whether or not I wore white, black, or green—that wasn't important. The important thing was that God was perfecting me *from within*. He was bringing me from a place of merely *knowing* of Him to the place of *intimate communion with Him* where my heart would commune with His heart in the most holy place.

Hear this. After you enter in through the gate of Christ's righteousness, you need to give yourself some time and space for the process of dying to self. When you come into the presence of the Lord on the threshing floor, the flesh must already be dead. You may have to die to yourself in many areas before you can walk into the deepest part of the tabernacle. You can't just stroll behind the veil with an *empty* heart (one that hasn't gone through the process), just merely trying to praise God, expecting to experience His glory. You can't enter the third-dimensional realm of prayer simply because you have a spiritual title by which you are known. You have to die to all of the personal issues that separate you from His presence in order to enter His glory. Don't misunderstand me: *God still loves you.* You are His child. But to become His intercessor—a vessel of honor that is fit for His use—you must be purified.

When I started my journey to go behind the veil (the most intimate level of prayer), God used to knock me out in the Spirit a lot in church. I would be minding my own business while the praise team was singing, "We exalt Thee," and, *bam*—I would be out cold on the floor! At times when the moving of the Spirit in our church service would go to a higher level, I'd be sitting in the back, but the next thing I knew, God was throwing me all the way up to the front of the church on the altar. The beginning of my journey wasn't pretty. That's when I suddenly realized that I had been in church all of my life, but I had not experienced the divine Spirit of God for myself. This was the point when I began to realize there was a level in God that went beyond a religious experience. I was bored with listening to the choir. I was bored with hearing the praise team. I just couldn't take it any more. I knew there had to be another, higher experience in God. If everything I had known was all I could experience in God, then I knew that I was in trouble.

Does this sound familiar? *Please hear this: if your entire Christian walk is comprised only of where and when you go to church, you are already in trouble.* You are an accident waiting to happen. Your Christian experience must be about your relationship with the Lord. As a result of learning to stay in His presence, you will also experience change through your time spent with the Lord, such as moments when you can feel the chastisement of the Lord rebuking your spirit, bringing about the needed correction to ensure effective results in prayer.

Remember from chapter seven that God wants you to grow through every level of the manifestation of His grace. After coming through the first two levels of grace—knowing to do good and still messing up, and experiencing His pardon when you still habitually fall into sin—you reach the third level of grace, where you must submit to the divine empowerment of God as He transforms you into His image. When God began revealing this to me, He said, "The third level of grace is for the people who have learned how to be steadfast and unmovable in their walk with God. These are the people who have moved beyond bleeps and blunders. This level is for those who have made up their minds that yielding to temptation means, *I will annihilate something that I am praying and believing God for. I choose to see victory in the lives of others, rather than to enjoy the pleasures of my flesh for a fleeting moment.* These are the people who truly live behind the veil." I understand this clearly now. An *empty heart* cannot dwell in a sacred place. But those who have been purified through the process of prayer can enter boldly. Hebrews 4:14–16 says:

> Inasmuch as we have a great High Priest Who has [already] ascended and passed through the heavens, Jesus the Son of God, *let us hold fast our confession [of faith in Him]*. For we do not have a High Priest

Who is unable to understand and sympathize and have a shared feeling with our weaknesses and infirmities and liability to the assaults of temptation, but One Who has been tempted in every respect as we are, yet without sinning. Let us then fearlessly and confidently and boldly draw near to the throne of grace (the throne of God's unmerited favor to us sinners), that we may receive mercy [for our failures] and find grace to help in good time for every need [appropriate help and well-timed help, coming just when we need it].

—EMPHASIS ADDED

God will always love us, yet He desires for us to "hold fast" to our confession of faith in Him and grow beyond an elementary understanding of grace to dwell with Him in His presence. So if you are not able to contain what God imparts into your heart, then you don't really have His power. Hear me. The working of your flesh will ultimately fail you. You must constantly keep in mind that the ark of the covenant was perfected *within* and *without,* so it held the manifest glory of God—despite its small dimensions. The more of the impartation of God's grace (the power of the Word working in you), the more your *outer man* will reflect His glory—and that's when His power will be released through you in prayer.

One of the problems in Christendom is this: too many believers talk about living behind the veil without even knowing what it means. Many have mistaken *behind-the-veil* experiences as being those times when they were touched deeply during a high point in a service or when they were *slain in the Spirit* during worship. Although that is part of the experience, it does not constitute the total meaning of a spiritual encounter with God. Why? Going behind the veil is not a one-time event or experience. *It is a lifestyle.*

Allow me to ask you this question: *Who would dare to go behind the veil into the most holy place, and then come right back out?* Once you enter the "lifestyle" of the third dimension of prayer, you are to live in that place. It's not a fluke experience. It's an everyday reality. We cannot minimize the true meaning of living behind the veil by relegating it to a mere song that is sung, or to whether or not everything in the order of service has gone according to plan. Again, living behind the veil is a supernatural lifestyle. This means that whatever occurs in your life from that point on is the result of decisions you have made that have originated from the heart of God. Let me make it simple. If your fleshly nature is in control, *God isn't*.

When you have entered the third dimension (when your heart begins to hold the precious things God imparts unto you in prayer), you will experience a mighty manifestation of His power! This is the level where you must be convinced of His ability to bring you through any situation. So no matter what you are going through, declare to yourself right now: "*I am going behind the veil to the third dimension.*" Serve your worries, fears, trials, and family circumstances notice that the grace of God is taking you deeper in prayer. Let all who have embraced you understand that you are becoming a behind-the-veil, threshing floor intercessor!

WILL YOU CARRY THE MANTLE OF PRAYER?

Who will be able to receive the mysteries of God's Word if our bellies cannot handle spiritual meat? To whom is our Father in heaven going to be able to talk? Can you trust God enough to obey Him at every level, so that you can meet Him in the most holy place and carry the mantle of prayer to this generation?

In Mark 1:17–20, Jesus called some ordinary men:

> Come after Me and be My disciples, and I will make you to become fishers of men. And at once they left their nets and [yielding up all claim to them] followed [with] Him [joining Him as disciples and siding with His party]. He went on a little farther and saw James the son of Zebedee, and John his brother, who were in [their] boat putting their nets in order. And immediately He called out to them, and [abandoning all mutual claims] they left their father Zebedee in the boat with the hired men and went off after Him [to be His disciples, side with His party, and follow Him].

Jesus is saying the same thing today: "Come after Me and be My disciples, and I will make *you* fishers of men. Come after Me so that I can get rid of everything I see in you that doesn't match the principles of My kingdom." Jesus did not save you so that you could go to church, sit in a pew, shout, jump, and sing in the choir. He didn't bring you into God's kingdom to merely have a "Christian" experience. He brought you into this heavenly realm to become a *fisher of men*.

The Lord did not deliver you from addictions and spirits of depression and oppression to enable you to sit in a cozy building wearing a nice suit wondering when you are finally going to get a front-row seat. He didn't fill you with His power for you to sit idly by, wondering, *When are they going to ordain me to be an elder?* God drew you into His house to disciple you so that, in turn, you will make disciples.

The place of prayer is where you will receive your spiritual assignment—and the power to walk it out.

When Jesus called the disciples, they left their nets immediately. They immediately walked away from their own abilities and put their faith in Jesus, the living Word (testimonial tablets). They submitted to His authority (the rod of Aaron that blossomed) and trusted Him to deliver them from bondage and provide for all of their needs (the omer of manna). From that day forward, they walked in a third-dimensional reality of true intimacy with the Lord. Today, there are a lot of people who pray, but there are not a lot of third-dimensional intercessors who meet God on the threshing floor.

When Jesus calls you to *salvation*, it speaks of the outer court. When He calls you to *discipleship*, it relates to the holy place, the place of maintenance. But when He calls you to your divine assignment as a *fisher of men* (the intercessor), you can only fulfill this commission through the workings of the Holy Spirit. That is where you develop spiritual disciplines—maintaining the anointing, keeping oil in the menorah, putting fresh bread on the table of shewbread, and refreshing the coals on the altar of incense. You have come to realize that without these elements you cannot enter the knowledge of the Spirit of God. *Without possessing these elements, you will not be able to hear what He hears, see what He sees, and know what only He knows.*

You cannot become a *fisher of men* and complete your divine assignment as a third-realm intercessor until you yield all to Jesus and *drop your net!* You cannot come into this level by thinking, *I have a title; I am not supposed to lie on the floor,* because this level requires a prostrating of your body (most of the time) and a prostrating of your heart at all times. Now, *drop your net!* Drop what you think ministry is supposed to be, and give it all to Jesus. Drop what you think God has called you to do, because without a life of prayer you will never be able to finish what you have started. You cannot enter the third realm with God until you lay it all down and say, "God, I'm willing to be transformed into an intercessor who knows what You *see, feel,* and *desire* to be accomplished. Show me the assignment You have ordained me to fulfill for Your kingdom."

The twentieth verse of Mark 1 states that the disciples *abandoned all mutual claims.* When you meet the Lord behind the veil, you can abandon your religious claims because you have received the highest call in God's kingdom—the call to *effectual, fervent* prayer. In other words, you won't glory in simply being a deacon when you have answered the call to prayer. You won't care if you don't sing in the choir when God meets with you in the third dimension of prayer. All things of the religious realm will begin to take a lesser seat and take on a lesser meaning. You will abandon all claims, titles, and rights.

As you are reading this book right now, I believe the Spirit of the Lord is girding you with the mantle of intercessory prayer! Anyone can pray, but not everyone is equipped to make effective intercession. Going to church is easy—anyone can do it. But can you stand in the gap for someone's life? Can you command HIV to let someone go? Can you command a crack cocaine addiction to be broken off someone's life? Hear me. *God is aching.* He's in travail today because of prayer-less preachers, evangelists, prophets, teachers, and choir members. The gifts and callings of God are given without repentance—but what we do in God's kingdom isn't about gifts. It's about saving souls from destruction. It is about snatching others from the fire of destruction, for Jude 23 says:

> [Strive to] save others, snatching [them] out of [the] fire; on others take pity [but] with fear, loathing even the garment spotted by the flesh and polluted by their sensuality.

When God calls you to Himself, He empowers you to come through not only the outer court, but also the holy place and the most holy place. In this three-step process, you will also encounter the power of the three altars (as they are represented in the Bible). First, there is an *altar of stone*—the place where you must come to repentance. Then there is the *altar of brass,* where your flesh struggles against submission to the Word and is ultimately laid on the fires of purification.

Then we come to the *altar of gold,* which is the place where you enter into worship. It's where you lay yourself down and let God pick up the work. Let me explain. At this altar, the Lord is working with you and teaching you how to lay down the earthly ministry and pick up His ministry, which is the ministry of prayer. Your flesh has ceased from the battle against the Word as you learn to *let go* and *let Go*d. The altar is where we die and Christ begins to live through us.

Remember... at this level God doesn't have to stand over you with a whip, convincing you to not yield to temptation. When your heart has reached the third dimension, you can stand and praise God in the midst of darkness. Listen. *The only way that the power of God can be made manifest through you is for you to sit in the midst of degradation.* By being confronted with wrong, you can discover the "right" that has been birthed within you. Righteousness isn't *what you do*—it's *who you are*. Because you live in His presence where you are being transformed daily by the glory of the Lord, you can stand in the midst of wrong and still do right.

My mind goes back to a day when I was shopping; I had picked out a few items and took them to the register. Then I realized that I had not brought enough money. So I told the cashier, "Put this back... and that... because I didn't bring enough cash." She put it all back. At the same time, a young girl who was bagging up my purchases recognized me. When I got home, I emptied the bag and noticed that she had put in a jacket I had told the cashier to put back. Immediately I looked at my receipt and saw that the jacket was not itemized.

I took that receipt, stuck a hole in it, put it on a hanger with the jacket, and hung that jacket in my closet to be returned to the store. Why? I am an intercessor. Anything that I allow to get in my spirit can compromise my position. If that happens, I won't be able to stand in the gap for anyone. I do not intend to lose my intercessory position over a jacket. It took me too long to get to this level in God. I've fasted too many days and stayed up too many nights praying and purifying—and I'm not going to lose it all for a jacket.

When this is your lifestyle, you can come boldly before the throne on behalf of someone that is on his or her way to hell, someone who may not even know that you are praying. You see, when you come to this place you don't spend time praying for yourself. You have come to realize that God has your back. His glory (His manifested presence from the ark) is your rearguard. That's why I dare to let God purge, wash, and cleanse me! When I live behind the veil, I know that He is forever making intercession for me as I pray for others. I don't have to be afraid of the enemy's devices. Jesus is interceding *for me* because I have submitted to the call of being an intercessor *for Him*. He prays for me throughout the day. When I'm in trouble, I only have to call upon Him, and He immediately takes up intercession for me—because I have submitted to the call of becoming an intercessor.

What about you? Have you ever been going through a test or trial, and suddenly you lifted your hands to God and started speaking in your prayer language? Then afterward you thought to yourself, *My God, where did that come from?* Remember—Christ is forever living to make intercession for you. That was Jesus telling you, "I've got it. Since you are on assignment, keep praying for those whom I have given you—I've got your back." When you have submitted to the process of prayer—the call to the threshing floor—when you have been washed, cleansed, purified, and purged, the Holy Spirit begins to cover every area of your life.

First- and second-realm people think they are going to get the same benefits. They carelessly confront the enemy and say, "I command you, Satan." Let me warn you. If you know that you haven't entered the realm of purification, don't presumptuously try to engage the enemy. You are not yet able to command in the realm of the Spirit until God is able to see a reflection of Himself in you from spending time in His glory. Jesus is the Living Word, so when He gave His life in total submission to the Father, He was able to command a cancellation of judgment and the release of mercy and grace. He was able to command the Father not to kill humanity in our mess by covering us with His blood.

If you are not living a submitted life, God isn't going to listen to your *empty* commands. If His Word is not operating in you, you won't be able to bring God into remembrance of His Word and receive His promise to move in a situation. God doesn't hear the flesh. When your life is not clean, you cannot travail for anybody. God does not hear you. Isaiah 1:11–15 says:

> To what purpose is the multitude of your sacrifices to Me [unless they are the offering of the heart]? says the Lord. I have had enough of the burnt offerings of rams and the fat of fed beasts [without obedience]; and I do not delight in the blood of bulls or of lambs or of he-goats [without righteousness]. When you come to appear before Me, who requires of you that your [unholy feet] trample My courts? Bring no more offerings of vanity (emptiness, falsity, vainglory, and futility); [your hollow offering of] incense is an abomination to Me....And when you spread forth your hands [in prayer, imploring help], I will hide My eyes from you; even though you make many prayers, I will not hear. Your hands are full of blood!

REVELATION IN THE THIRD REALM

Let's review. The work of the sacrifices is done in the outer court, and the holy place contains the workings of the sanctuary. But when you pass through the veil into the most holy place, the work of the flesh ceases and the work of the heart of God begins. It is there that you will begin to *see* what God is *doing*, over and above *hearing* His voice. When you are in His manifest presence, God will say, "I want to show you My glory! I want to show you what I am going to do for you and where I am taking you. I want to show you that you have victory and power. I don't want to just *speak* to you. *I want to reveal Myself to your inner man so that I may speak through you.*"

Every time God is preparing to do something that is going to change the course of your life and surroundings, He will show it to you beforehand. This is why some things cannot be spoken, because the devil would try to take them. Satan will come along and give you another "word" to confuse your sense of direction—but on this level it becomes a little more difficult for him to confuse your vision. He can't tell you what you didn't see in the depths of your spirit man.

How can you discern when God is showing you something? One of the best ways to recognize a true vision from God is that it should not make any sense to your natural mind. It should look like something you couldn't possibly do. It's too big for your mind to handle. It costs too much...it would be impossible to accomplish. It's not your level or your grade in the Spirit. If a vision doesn't scare your flesh to death, then it most likely didn't come from God. It should be so awesome that it should look as if you don't have what it takes to walk out this vision; nevertheless, your spirit says, "I'm going to do it anyway."

THE POSTURE OF THE THIRD REALM FROM THE THRESHING FLOOR

Have you ever seen people praising God and then just fall to the floor without anyone touching them? When you tap into the third realm, your body automatically yields into a prostrate position under the weight of His glory. Something inside is helping you to understand and recognize that you are in the presence of a Spirit whom you are not worthy to see.

When King Solomon brought the ark of the covenant into the new temple, the glory of the Lord filled that place until the priests could not remain standing to minister. (See 1 Kings 8:5–11.) Let me say this again. When you enter the glory of this realm, the flesh profits nothing. Your spirit can only commune with the Spirit of the Lord as you lie prostrate at His feet.

Remember that according to the custom of Moses, the high priest wore all of his priestly garments—the tunic of righteousness and sash, the robe of blue, the ephod, the breastplate, and the miter—in the outer court and in the holy place where the works of sacrifice and priestly service were performed. But when it was time for him to go behind the veil once a year, he took off his *works* and entered the most holy place wearing only the white garment that represented imputed righteousness. In establishing this pattern, the Lord was saying to them: "You are working too hard. You don't need all of these workings in the third realm. You just need to stay pure before Me." So hear me. You don't have to have a title. You only have to maintain your relationship and right standing with God.

When you get to this level of intercession, God will begin to show you things about your kids that they didn't think you knew. He will take you into the lives of family members and other people with whom you interact on a regular basis. He will take you to the other side of office doors where people are meeting to try and cut you out of a deal. When you get on your face and tap into this realm, God will make sure that nothing blindsides you. You might be asking, "What do you mean, Prophetess, by this statement, 'On my face'?"

Although the terminology *on your face* seems to be used throughout Christendom, once again, many who use it really don't have the knowledge (or may I say the *biblical* knowledge) as to how much power and authority it really brings to their lives. When you look at the biblical revelation, you will see that Revelation 7:9–12 illustrates the pattern:

> After this I looked and a vast host appeared which no one could count, [gathered out] of every nation, from all tribes and peoples and languages. These stood before the throne and before the Lamb; they were attired in white robes, with palm branches in their hands. In loud voice they cried, saying, [Our] salvation is due to our God, Who is seated on the throne, and to the Lamb [to Them we owe our deliverance]! And all the angels were standing round the throne and round the elders [of the heavenly Sanhedrin] and the four living creatures, *and they fell prostrate before the throne* and worshiped God. Amen! (So be it!) they cried, Blessing and glory and majesty and splendor and wisdom and thanks and honor and power and might [be ascribed] to our God to the ages and ages (forever and ever, throughout the eternities of the eternities)! Amen! (So be it!)
>
> —EMPHASIS ADDED

When praise rang out in the heavens, the angels began to sing, and all of the elders and every existing celestial being began to prostrate themselves before the King of kings. This was the prostration of worship. Everything in them recognized that they were in the divine presence of God. Nothing in them or around them had the desire to remain standing, because they were all consumed by Him. This was a time when they were being called into true purpose. For the angels, it was not time to be messengers. For the elders, it was not time to sit in eternal counsel. For the cherubim, it was not time to be the manifestation of His works. *For all* it was time to worship God. This indeed is one of the facets of what it means to prostrate before Him...I fall on my face in worship to a Presence I am not worthy to behold. I fall on my face to show Him that I respect the fact that I do not consider myself to be equal to His glory. So I lower myself to the floor and put my face into position on the floor, because when His presence is being revealed, it only becomes important what He looks like, the part of Himself that He desires to reveal to us.

Now, let's take a look at the same terminology as it relates to the intercessor. We must understand that not only are there positions of prayer—such as kneeling, standing, walking, and lying down—but there is also a place of prayer, and of all of the "places" I have experienced, none have compared to the floor (the threshing floor).

THE THRESHING FLOOR

Though you have received a definition of the threshing floor process, you might be wondering, *What is the purpose and meaning of the threshing floor? What does the threshing floor really represent?* There are several examples in the Old Testament, two of which are the settings of powerful breakthroughs—for King David and for Ruth. In 2 Samuel 24:18, David purchased a threshing floor from Araunah the Jebusite and made sacrifices of repentance that stopped a plague that had killed 70,000 Israelites. His son Solomon later constructed his temple in that place. (See 2 Chronicles 3:1.) This helps us to see the threshing floor as the place where God intervenes when good is separated from evil. This is confirmed by the meaning of the word *thresh*, "to separate grains or seeds from straw by beating the stems or husks." When the threshing process was complete, only the pure wheat of the harvest remained. This is what God desires to achieve through you as an intercessor.

In my next book, as we begin to deal further with being in the manifest presence of God on the threshing floor, you will learn about the story of Ruth (symbolizing the church) and Boaz (typifying Christ). When Ruth went in to the threshing floor (the intimate place of Boaz) to seek his favor, she came to his feet first. In turn, he covered her with his mantle (prayer shawl/tallit). This was a powerful exchange that we will go into in much greater depth in my next book.

The point that I would like to bring out is this. Before Ruth entered the threshing floor, her mother-in-law had given these instructions: "Wash, change your clothes, and anoint yourself." Please make note that every time we see instructions being given to individuals to enter the presence of the Lord (or a typology of His presence), they are instructed to *wash* something, to *remove* something, or to *anoint* themselves. Ruth washed herself (brazen laver), changed her clothes (holy garments), and anointed herself (altar of incense) before going in to Boaz on the threshing floor. Do you see the comparison? Moses was required to remove his shoes when God spoke to him from the burning bush. Whenever there is the sanctifying of holy ground for a holy purpose, you will always be required to remove something that represents the old you and your own direction.

Now that the pattern for operating on the threshing floor has clearly been established, you should be able to see the revelation of the threshing floor being made manifest through the story of Ruth, including the things Ruth had to go through *before going* to the threshing floor, the things that she accomplished *while on* the threshing floor, and what she was able to *carry away* from the threshing floor. This can be compared to the same pattern we follow by coming into prayer at the East Gate (which represents the feet of Jesus at the tabernacle), stopping at the brazen laver to be washed, and going all the way to the altar of incense to be anointed to come into the Divine Presence. (Remember that Ruth came into the threshing floor at Boaz's feet. See Ruth 3:1–7.) To get a better picture of this, refer back to the diagram of the tabernacle on page 10. When we go before God on our threshing floor, we do not only come out with victory for ourselves; we come out with victory for those who are assigned to our lives. Though the threshing floor in the Old Testament may have been in an open field on the far side of the country, God is still establishing the fact that wherever you make *your* threshing floor, and wherever God sanctifies that spot, *you are guaranteed* to come out with the same result—because this is truly a biblical pattern that is being established; it is not an opinion. It is a fact that always leads to victory.

Even as the prophet Ezekiel foresaw the fall of Babylon, God said to me, "Whatever you are up against that you can't see, it won't come down until you lie down." Although there are situations in which the Lord requires that we stand, yet there will come a time in His presence when He will require us to prostrate ourselves before Him! Believe me when I tell you that you can't see all of your deliverance while standing in your own power, because as you stand, you are standing face-to-face with your situation. And as soon as you get past one predicament, another one is staring you in the face. This is why you stay discouraged and often find yourself overwhelmed. When you are lying down, you don't see all of that. You see only what God is revealing to you. You can see what governs and dictates events in the natural realm.

This is how the intercessor learns to operate. He or she understands that "the impossible" is simply an assignment designed to reveal how great God truly is! When you take the posture of intercessory prayer, you will begin to see that nothing can pierce God's power and bring you down. God uses "light afflictions" to further empower and anoint you. In this, He demonstrates to you that the greater your warfare, the greater your anointing will be.

First- and second-realm believers say, "Satan, the Lord rebukes you. I bind you, devil. Come on out, Satan." Third-realm intercessors enter the threshing floor and lie before the mercy seat saying, "God, I worship You. I give Your name the praise," because they know that before they come to God, they must believe that He is, and that He is a rewarder of them who diligently seek Him (Heb. 11:6). Third-level people don't tell God the problem. They lie down in His glory and praise God for the answer: "God, I thank You because You are more than enough. I thank You because You are Jehovah Jireh, my Provider. I thank You because Your blood covers and washes me. God, I thank You because You are already making a way out of no way." (They begin to decree and declare a word.)

There's no failure from this posture on the threshing floor. There is nothing in this realm that can interfere with the will of God. His will cannot be tampered with; it cannot be hindered or touched by Satan. His will is revealed and carried out. From here you get results. The Word tells us that when you decree a thing, it shall come to pass. So remember, you may have been feeling like the enemy is all around you, but God has been waiting to bless you. This is true because He can only prepare the table of blessing when the enemy is present. So rejoice, I say. And again I say, rejoice!

This realm is a posture in God; it's not about just getting stuff. I know some people who lived in the third realm and never dreamed of possessing earthly riches. A powerful woman of God, Mother Estella Boyd, was eighty-five years old when she left this life. She didn't own a Mercedes or live in a mansion, but her spirit was wealthy with something that many empty believers do not possess.

Many of us are rich in our pockets, but we are bankrupt in our spirits. God forbid. When you are truly wealthy in the Spirit, you can tap into a level in God where demon spirits are afraid of you. You will be able to walk into a beauty shop or gas station where no one knows you are saved and watch as everyone starts whispering and lowering their voices because of the anointing. You'll rejoice when people curse and then say, "Excuse me…" when they see you—because you won't have to wear a Jesus button. The glory of God will literally be pouring out of you to a lost and dying world.

Let's just pause for a moment and read Matthew 26:36–39. This will really bless you if you are called to be an intercessor.

> Then Jesus went with them to a place called Gethsemane, and He told His disciples, Sit down here while I go over yonder and pray. And taking with Him Peter and the two sons of Zebedee, He began to show grief and distress of mind and was deeply depressed. Then He said to them, My soul is very sad and deeply grieved, so that I am almost dying of sorrow. Stay here and keep awake and keep watch with Me. And going a little farther, *He threw Himself upon the ground on His face and prayed saying,* My Father, if it is possible, let this cup pass away from Me; nevertheless, not what I will [not what I desire], but as You will and desire.
>
> —EMPHASIS ADDED

What an example of a threshing floor experience!

Think about Jesus. He had to do the very same thing He is requiring us to do. When He was in the Garden of Gethsemane He had to prostrate His will to the Father. Luke 22:41–44 also tells us that He agonized until sweat rolled from Him as "clots of blood" (v. 44), and when He (figuratively) came to the altar of incense, He broke through and said, "Father…not My will, but [always] Yours be done" (v. 42). It was then that the Word said in verse 43, "And there appeared to Him an angel from heaven, strengthening Him in spirit," so that He could have the power to go to the crucifixion—not to go home and escape the crucifixion. The angel's strengthening Him was only for the purpose of gaining the testimony that He now has the keys to death, hell, and the grave, and forever lives to make intercession for us continually.

Jesus is eternally empowered to make intercession for all of humanity, because He walked in obedience, purity, and holiness. He went to the cross and yielded up everything that pertained to the flesh, and the Father imparted all power unto Him. *Jesus Christ is the pure* gold *that covers the* wood *of your* humanity *and makes your* heart *a place where the glory of God can be revealed*—just as His glory has shone forth from the ark of the covenant.

Now that you have come through the process of reading this book, let's take a brief final exam to see if you are authentically ready to become an effective, third-realm intercessor. *Have you embraced every element in the pattern of prayer?* Use the following checklist (which complements the detailed questions at the beginning of chapter eleven and adds a few points from this chapter) to be absolutely sure:

❑ Have you entered through the Beautiful Gate by accepting Jesus Christ as your Savior and Lord?

❑ Have you passed through the outer court of your initial conversion experience into a closer relationship with Christ?

❑ Have you allowed the Holy Spirit to begin building God's character in you by washing at the laver of the Word of God?

❑ Have you embraced the brazen altar and become a living sacrifice? Do you place yourself on this altar daily for God to purify you and your motives?

❑ Have you disciplined yourself to wear your tunic of righteousness every day by walking in righteousness and declaring the victory in Christ?

❑ Have you put on the priestly garments of completion: the sash, the robe of blue, the ephod, the breastplate with Urim and

Thummim, and the miter? Are you walking in your priestly anointing as a "living tabernacle" so that you can enter His divine presence in prayer and intercession?

❏ Have you regularly gone to the place of prayer and experienced a deeper revelation of the works of Christ as reflected in the tabernacle door?

❏ Have the ingredients of God's holy anointing oil—liquid myrrh, sweet-scented cinnamon, fragrant calamus, and cassia— become part of your life? Have you begun to walk in consistent purity before the Lord, always maintaining the right attitude with God and others?

❏ Have you received and activated the power of divine protection available to you through the spiritual coverings of your tabernacle: fine-twined linen and wool, goat's hair, ram's skin, and badger's skin?

❏ Have you embraced the tabernacle content in the holy place: the table of shewbread, the golden candlestick, and finally, the golden altar of incense? Is the power of each of these elements literally beginning to work both *within you* and *through you* as you pray?

❏ Have you died to self and submitted to the full process of purification that is required to go behind the veil into the most intimate level of prayer at the ark of the covenant? Have you abandoned all personal claims to become a "fisher of men"? Is your lifestyle of prayer empowering your prayer time, so that you no longer have to engage in warfare during prayer? Does it now feel normal for you to prostrate yourself before the Lord, worshiping Him and thanking Him by faith for every answer?

Once you have checked every item and are fully confident in your spirit that you have walked out this divine pattern, *you are ready to become a true intercessor.* This means that when you come into His divine presence, you will hear:

Well done, you upright (honorable, admirable) and faithful servant!
You have been faithful and trustworthy over a little; I will put you
in charge of much. Enter into and share the joy (the delight, the
blessedness) which your master enjoys.

—MATTHEW 25:21

Also know and be eternally encouraged by this: *when your intercession
is empowered and directed from His divine presence, it will shatter the gates
of hell.* Remember, James 5:16 (KJV) says that it is only the "effectual
fervent prayer of a righteous man" that "availeth much."

The more you come to God with a pure heart, the more He will take
you to new levels and fresh, exciting experiences through your walk of
prayer. If you are ready to find God beyond religion, denominationalism, or anything you have ever seen or experienced—*He is calling for
you.* Let God lead you through His pattern of prayer all the way into His
presence behind the veil...because that's where the impossible is not
only possible—*it becomes reality.*

Six Kinds of Prayer

1. *Intercession.* Intercession is standing in the gap to reconcile a supplier with the needy. It is learning to bear up people, places, or situations in prayer.

   > And he saw that there was no man, and wondered that there was no intercessor: therefore his arm brought salvation unto him; and his righteousness, it sustained him.
   >
   > —Isaiah 59:16

2. *Faith.* The prayer of faith is asking God to intervene in a situation. It is urgent, and therefore comes up when an immediate result is desired.

   > And the prayer of faith shall save the sick, and the Lord shall raise him up; and if he has committed sins, they shall be forgiven him.
   >
   > —James 5:15

3. *Consecration.* The prayer of consecration is offered when the believer needs to know or do the will of God. At such times, the expressions "if it be thy will" or "let thy will be done" become appropriate.

   > And he went a little farther, and fell on his face, and prayed, saying, O my Father, if it be possible, let this cup pass from me: nevertheless not as I will, but as thou wilt.
   >
   > —Matthew 26:39

4. *Petition (supplication).* The prayer of petition is often called supplication in Scripture. It gives the believer the opportunity to petition God until the answer comes. While the prayer of faith is prayed once and requires immediate response, the prayer of petition may be presented several times, either as an oral or written request.

   > I exhort therefore that, first of all, supplications, prayers, intercessions and giving of thanks, be made for all men; for kings and for all that are in authority; that we may lead a quiet and peaceable life in all godliness and honesty. For this is good and acceptable in the

sight of God our Saviour; who will have all men to be saved and to come unto the knowledge of the truth.

—1 TIMOTHY 2:1–4

5. *Praise.* Praise is a form of prayer. It is praising the supplier without focusing on the need.

Ah, Lord GOD! behold, thou hast made the heaven and the earth by thy great power and stretched out arm, and there is nothing too hard for thee.

—JEREMIAH 32:17

6. *Agreement.* When at least two or three people band together in the name of Jesus to request a thing from God, God promises to grant it. The power of this prayer is in the quality of agreement and the strength of unity among those who are praying.

Again I say unto you, That if two of you shall agree on earth as touching any thing that they shall ask, it shall be done for them of my Father which is in heaven. For where two or three are gathered together in my name, there am I in the midst of them.

—MATTHEW 18:19–20

SIX WAYS TO PRAY

1. *Aspirations.* A strong aspiration and desire to pray will create the proper climate for effective intercession.

And not by his coming only, but by the consolation wherewith he was comforted in you, when he told us your earnest desire, your mourning, your fervent mind toward me; so that I rejoiced the more.

—2 CORINTHIANS 7:7

Blessed are they which do hunger and thirst after righteousness: for they will be filled.

—MATTHEW 5:6

2. *Fervency.* Fervency changed Elijah's situation, suspended natural laws, and brought about supernatural miracles through prayer.

Confess to one another therefore your faults [your slips, your false steps, your offences, your sins] and pray [also] for one another, that you may be healed and restored [to a spiritual tone of mind and heart]. The earnest [heartfelt, continued] prayer of a righteous man makes tremendous power available [dynamic in its working]. Elijah was a human being with a nature such as we have [with feelings, affections, and a constitution like ours]; and he prayed earnestly for it not to rain, and no rain fell on the earth for three years and six months.

—JAMES 5:16–18, AMP

3. *Perseverance.* On some items, there will be instant results as we pray, while answers for other requests might take time. However, Scripture talks about persevering and enduring until the answer comes, learning to add patience to our faith.

And pray in the Spirit on all occasions with all kinds of prayers and requests. With this in mind, be alert and always keep on praying for all the saints.

—EPHESIANS 6:18, NIV

... That ye be not slothful, but followers of them who through faith and patience inherit the promises.

—HEBREWS 6:12

4. *Intercession.* This book is intended to achieve two things. First, it is intended to help address your needs; and second, it is intended to assist you in interceding for others. Prayer denigrates and belittles God if the only thing we do is give Him our shopping list for approval. True pray-ers know the importance of standing in the gap between God and others until the result comes.

5. *Praying in tongues.*

But you, beloved, build yourselves up [founded] on your most holy faith [make progress, rise like an edifice higher and higher], praying in the Holy Spirit.

—JUDE 20, AMP

Pray at all times [on every occasion, in every season] in the Spirit, with all [manner of] prayer and entreaty. To that end keep alert and watch with strong purpose and perseverance, interceding on behalf of all the saints [God's consecrated people].

—EPHESIANS 6:18, AMP

6. *Choose a comfortable posture:*

- Kneeling
- Sitting
- Standing
- Prostrating

Practical Power Prayer Tools

Listed on the following pages are Prayer Topics from Pastor Matthew Ashimolowo's *The Power of Positive Prayer Bible*. They address almost every area of life and will be a powerful help for your time on the threshing floor. Remember, as you pray you must bring God in remembrance of His Word, so use this topical concordance as the Holy Spirit leads you in intercessory prayer. Write down what God reveals to your heart at the mercy seat in your prayer journal.

Abundance
Gen. 15:1
Gen. 16:10
Gen. 17:6
Gen. 30:43
Exod. 1:7
Num. 14:7
1 Kings 10:7, 23
2 Sam. 12:2
1 Chron. 22:5
2 Chron. 9:6
2 Chron. 32:27
Ps. 21:6
Prov. 3:9, 10, 28
Prov. 10:5, 22
Prov. 10:24
Prov. 11:25, 28
Prov. 12:11
Prov. 13:4, 22
Prov. 15:16
Prov. 16:7
Prov. 18:20
Prov. 19:15
Prov. 20:13
Prov. 21:5, 13
Prov. 22:1, 4
Prov. 22:7, 9
Prov. 22:16, 26
Prov. 23:21
Prov. 24:32–34
Prov. 26:13, 15
Prov. 27:11
Prov. 28:8

Prov. 30:8–9
Jer. 31:14
Ezek. 37:10
Mal. 3:4, 5
Mal. 3:11, 12
Phil. 4:19
Rom. 12:3, 17
Eph. 1:19
Eph. 3:20

Accomplishment
Lev. 22:21
1 Kings 5:9
1 Kings 6:9
1 Kings 6:14
1 Chron. 28:20
2 Chron. 24:14
Ezra 6:14
Neh. 6:15
Ezra 5:8
Prov. 13:19
Prov. 17:18
Dan. 1:8
Zech. 4:9
Matt. 7:17
Luke 14:29–30
Luke 18:31
Luke 22:37
John 4:34
John 19:30
Acts 20:24
Acts 21:5
Rom. 9:28

2 Cor. 4:17
2 Cor. 8:6
Gal. 6:9
Col. 3:17
Col. 3:23
2 Tim. 4:7
Heb. 4:3
Matt. 21:42
1 Kings 6:14
Rev. 10:7
John 17:4

Affection
1 Chron. 29:3
Rom. 12:8
Rom. 12:10
Prov. 27:5
2 Cor. 7:15
1 Thess. 2:8-9
Col. 3:2
3 John 1–3

Anointing
Exod. 30:30
1 Sam. 10:6
1 Sam. 10:7
1 Sam. 10:9–10
Ps. 45:7
Ps. 89:20–21
Ps. 92:10–11
Eccles. 8:4
Isa. 10:27
Isa. 45:1

Isa. 61:1
Isa. 61:3
Nah. 2:1
Acts 7:55
Acts 10:38
Ps. 23:5
1 Sam. 10:1
Heb. 1:9
1 John 2:27
1 John 3:8

Anxiety
Ps. 142:4
Dan. 3:16
Jer. 17:8
Isa. 26:3
Matt. 6:24–25
Matt. 6:34
Matt. 6:21
Matt. 22:16
Luke 8:14
Luke 10:41
Rom. 8:28
1 Cor. 7:32
Phil. 3:12
Phil. 4:6
Phil. 4:10
Mark 4:38
1 Pet. 5:6–7

Attainment
Lev. 22:21
Job 14:6

Prov. 1:5
Deut. 8:17–18
John 14:14
Job 31:25
Rom. 9:30–31
Phil. 3:11, 12
Phil. 3:16
Col. 3:23
1 Tim. 4:6
1 Pet. 5:9
3 John 2

Attitude
Deut. 30:19
Judg. 20:20
1 Sam. 30:6
Prov. 10:4–5
Prov. 12:11
Prov. 12:24
Prov. 13:11
Prov. 19:15
Prov. 20:13
Prov. 22:29
Dan. 1:8
Matt. 5:16
John 14:15
Rom. 12:11
Rom. 12:16
Phil. 2:5
Col. 3:22–23
1 Thess. 4:11, 12
2 Thess. 3:10
2 Tim. 1:6–7

Barrenness
Gen. 11:30
Gen. 25:21
Exod. 23:26
Deut. 7:14
1 Sam. 2:20
Ps. 113:9
Prov. 30:15–16
Isa. 54:1
Gal. 4:27

**Believers increase
in spiritual gifts**
2 Chron. 15:7

Prov. 8:14
Prov. 18:16
Isa. 35:3
Isa. 41:10
Hab. 3:19
1 Cor. 12:8
1 Cor. 14:1
2 Cor. 2:12
2 Cor. 2:14
2 Cor. 2:17
Deut. 6:3
Job 8:7
2 Cor. 4:8
2 Cor. 6:3
2 Cor. 6:4
2 Cor. 9:8
2 Cor. 12:9
Eph. 3:20
1 Tim. 4:14
2 Tim. 1:6

Blessing
Gen. 12:2–3
Gen. 22:17–18
Gen. 28:3
Gen. 32:28
Gen. 49:26
Exod. 23:25
Lev. 25:21
Num. 6:24–25
Deut. 11:26
Deut. 23:5
Deut. 24:19
Deut. 26:15
Deut. 28:8
Deut. 33:11
Josh. 17:14
Josh. 17:16–18
Josh. 24:13
Ruth 2:4
1 Sam. 2:20
2 Sam. 6-11
1 Kings 18:41
1 Chron. 4:10
2 Chron. 2:3
Ps. 1:1
Ps. 3:8
Ps. 5:12

Ps. 16:7
Ps. 29:11
Ps. 32:1
Ps. 41:1
Ps. 84:5
Ps. 89:15
Ps. 128:5
Ps. 132:15
Prov. 8:32
Prov. 10:6
Prov. 10:22
Prov. 11:11
Prov. 11:26
Prov. 20:7
Prov. 28:20
Isa. 44:3
Isa. 65:8
Ezek. 44:30
Dan. 2:6
Zech. 8:13
Mal. 3:10
Eph. 1:3
1 Pet. 3:9

**Breaking cultic
and occultic
power**
Obad. 1:17
Joel 2:32
Ps. 18:50
Mal. 3:5
Isa. 47:13
Deut. 23:14
Judg. 10:11
1 Sam. 7:3
Job 6:23
Job 22:30
Job 33:28
Isa. 46:4
Isa. 10:27
Luke 10:19
Isa. 52:2
Isa. 10:17

**Breaking the
curse**
Gen. 8:21
Gen. 12:3

Gen. 27:12
Gen. 27:29
Exod. 21:17
Exod. 22:28
Lev. 19:14
Num. 22:6
Num. 23:8
Deut. 11:26
Deut. 23:4
Deut. 27:16–26
Judg. 9:27
Judg. 9:57
2 Sam. 19:21
Neh. 13:2
Ps. 62:4
Ps. 119:21
Prov. 11:26
Prov. 24:24
Prov. 28:27
Jer. 17:5
Jer. 48:10
Zech. 8:13
Mal. 2:2
Matt. 5:44
Acts 23:12

**Breaking the
stronghold of fear**
Exod. 15:16
Prov. 4:23
Isa. 54:14
Matt. 10:28
Matt. 17:7
Mark 5:36
Mark 6:50
Phil. 1:14
Heb. 13:6
1 John 4:18
Rev. 1:17

**Breaking ungodly
relationships**
Matt. 5:14–16
Prov. 11:30
Prov. 4:19
Rom. 16:17
Ps. 119:63
Prov. 13:20

197

Prov. 28:7
Eph. 5:11
Rom. 13:2
Eph. 5:8
1 Thess. 5:5
Job 34:22
Job 37:19
Isa. 50:10
Luke 11:34

Career

Deut. 28:13
Deut. 31:6
Deut. 31:8
Josh. 1:8
1 Sam. 22:29
2 Chron. 20:15
2 Chron. 20:20
Jer. 17:7
Jer. 29:11
Ps. 32:8
Ps. 90:12
Prov. 20:5
Prov. 29:25
Isa. 30:21
Isa. 42:16
Isa. 48:17
Isa. 58:10
Matt. 6:26
Mark 9:23
Mark 11:22
Mark 11:23
Luke 14:28–30
John 14:7
2 Cor. 9:8
Phil. 4:6
Heb. 10:35

Change

1 Chron. 4:10
Job 14:14
Ps. 102:26
Mal. 3:6
Matt. 18:3
1 Cor. 15:51
1 Cor. 15:52
2 Cor. 3:18
Phil. 3:21

Heb. 1:12
Heb. 7:12

Cheerfulness

Neh. 12:43
Ps. 9:2
Ps. 16:11
Ps. 19:8
Prov. 15:13
Isa. 55:12
Acts 27:22
Acts 27:36
2 Cor. 9:7
James 5:13
1 Pet. 1:8

Church growth

Acts 2:42–47
Acts 5:11
Acts 14:23
Acts 16:5
Acts 20:28
1 Cor. 14:12
1 Cor. 16:1
1 Cor. 12:28
Eph. 3:10, 21
Eph. 5:23, 27
2 Tim. 2:2
Heb. 10:25
James 5:14

Church unity

Josh. 9:2
Lam. 4:16
Ps. 133:1
Acts 1:14
Acts 2:1
Acts 5:12
Acts 8:6
Acts 14:4
1 Cor. 1:13
1 Cor. 12:3
Eph. 4:3, 13
Phil. 2:2
Col. 3:14

Comfort

Gen. 24:67

Gen. 37:35
Gen. 38:12
2 Sam. 14:17
Ruth 2:13
Job 2:11
Job 6:10
Job 16:2
Ps. 69:20
Ps. 77:2
Ps. 94:19
Ps. 119:50
Ps. 119.52
Ps. 119:76
Eccles. 4:1
Isa. 52:9
Isa. 54:11
Isa. 57:18
Isa. 61:2
Isa. 66:13
Jer. 8:18
Zech. 1:17
Matt. 5:4
Matt. 9:22
John 14:18
John 14:26
Acts 9:31
Acts 20:12
Rom. 1:12
Rom. 15:4
1 Cor. 14:3
1 Cor. 14:31
2 Cor. 1:3–4
2 Cor. 1:6
2 Cor. 7:4, 7
2 Cor. 13:11
Eph. 6:22
Phil. 2:1–2
Phil. 2:20
Col. 2:2
Col. 4:8, 11
1 Thess. 2:11
1 Thess. 3:2
1 Thess. 3:7
1 Thess. 4:18
1 Thess. 5:14
2 Thess. 2:16
2 Thess. 2:17
1 Pet. 3:8

Commitment

Job 14:14
Prov. 3:5
Matt. 7:7
Matt. 10:22
Luke 9:23
Luke 9:24
Luke 9:25
1 Cor. 9:27
1 Tim. 6:20
2 Tim. 1:12
Acts 21:12–14
2 Tim. 4-6
Titus 1:3

Concentration

Matt. 7:7–8
John 9:4
Rom. 15:19–20
1 Cor. 9:24
Phil. 3:14
Phil. 4:8
Heb. 10:23
Heb. 12:12

Confidence

Ps. 27:3
Ps. 118:8–9
Matt. 10:32
Heb. 3:6
Eph. 3:12
Prov. 3:26
Prov. 14:26
2 Cor. 5:26
2 Cor. 5:8
Eph. 6:14–18
Phil. 1:6
Phil. 1:14
Phil. 4:13
Mic. 7:5

**Conquering your
thought life**

Ps. 103:1
2 Cor. 10:3–5
1 Pet. 1:13
Rom. 12:2
Rom. 8:7, 27

1 Cor. 6:20
Col. 3:2
Rom. 12:3
Prov. 23:7
1 Cor. 13:5b
Phil. 4:8
Gal. 6:3
2 Tim. 1:7
1 Cor. 2:16
Prov. 24:9
Heb. 8:10
Eph. 4:23
1 Cor. 13:7
Matt. 6:25
Phil. 2:2
Phil. 2:3
Phil. 2:4
Phil. 2:5

Consecration
Exod. 29:37
1 Chron. 29:5
2 Chron. 29:5
Ps. 15:1
Ps. 15:2
Isa. 29:23
Rom. 12:1
Rom. 12:2
2 Cor. 7:1
2 Tim. 1:9
1 Pet. 2.9
2 Pet. 3:11
1 John 1:7
1 John 1:9

Courage
Num. 13:20
Deut. 31:6
Josh. 1:7
Josh. 2:1
Josh. 23:6
1 Chron. 28:20
2 Chron. 15:8
2 Chron. 19:11
2 Chron. 32:7
Ps. 27:14
Ps. 31:24
Isa. 41:6

Acts 28:15
1 Cor. 16:13

Dedication of a house
Ps. 119.38
2 Chron. 2:4
Mark 7:9–13
Heb. 9:18
Deut. 20:5
2 Kings 12:17–18
1 Chron. 28:12
1 Kings 7:51
Ezek. 44:29
Lev. 27:28
2 Chron. 5:1
2 Kings 12:4–5
1 Chron. 26:27
2 Sam. 8:11
2 Chron. 31:12
1 Chron. 18:11

Deliverance
Ps. 32:8
Ps. 36:9
Ps. 18:30
Ps. 27:11
Ps. 43:3
Ps. 119:125
Ps. 119:130
Ps. 119:169
Prov. 3:5–6
Prov. 3:13
Prov. 4:18
Prov. 8:14
Prov. 25:8–9
Jer. 33:3
Isa. 30:21
Luke 24:45
Eph. 5:17
2 Tim. 2:7
1 John 2:20
Gen. 45:7
Num. 31:5
Judg. 15:18
2 Kings 13:17
Ezra 9:13
Ps. 18:50

Ps. 22:5
Ps. 32:7
Ps. 44:4
Prov. 11:8–9
Prov. 11:21
Isa. 54:14–17
Isa. 49:25
Joel 2:32
Obad. 17

Deliverance from all afflictions
2 Kings 19:16
Ps. 4:6
Ps. 85:4–6
John 9:1–3
John 15:2
Neh. 9:32
Ps. 119:76
Jer. 31:8
Lam. 5:1
Neh. 1:8–9
Ps. 9:13
Ps. 39:12
Mark 9:24
1 Pet. 5:10
Job 36:8
Job 36:9
Ps. 10:1
Jer. 17:14
Isa. 54:7
Isa. 29:6
Heb. 12:10
Ps. 102:2
Isa. 64:9
John 16:20
Deut. 4:30
Ezek. 20:37
Ezra 9:13

Destroying the root of rejection
Eph. 1:4–6
Ps. 94:14
1 Pet. 3:12–17
1 John 3:1
Isa. 53:3–5
1 Pet. 1:6

Heb. 4:15
2 Cor. 4:18
1 Pet. 1:7
Heb. 4:16
Isa. 51:7
Prov. 18:24
Isa. 51:8

Difficult people
Exod. 7:14
Neh. 2:10
2 Sam. 7:17
Neh. 6:1–19
Dan. 6:4–5
Dan. 6:24
Acts 13:6–10
Acts 19:13–17
Eph. 1:22
Rev. 12:11

Diligence
Prov. 4:23
Prov. 10:4
Prov. 12:24
Prov. 12:27
Prov. 13:4
Prov. 15:19
Prov. 19:15
Prov. 21:5
Prov. 21:25
Prov. 22:13
Prov. 22:29
Prov. 27:23
Eccles. 10:18
Acts 18:25
Rom. 12:8
Rom. 12:11
1 Cor. 9:27
2 Cor. 8:7
1 Tim. 2:8
2 Tim. 4:9
2 Pet. 1:10

Divine acceleration
Gen. 15:1
Gen. 16:10
Gen. 17:2

Gen. 17:6
Gen. 30:43
Exod. 1:7
Num. 14:7, 8
1 Sam. 20:41
1 Kings 4:29
1 Kings 10:7
1 Kings 10:23
1 Chron. 22:5
2 Chron. 9:6
2 Chron. 32:27
Ps. 21:6
Ezek. 37:10
2 Cor. 4:17
Eph. 1:19
Eph. 3:20

Divine direction
Deut. 31:8
Deut. 32:11
Deut. 32:13
Num. 32:11
Num. 32:12
Job 32:8
Ps. 5:8
Ps. 16:7
Ps. 16:11
Ps. 25:4, 9
Ps. 27:13–14
Ps. 32:8
Ps. 43:3
Ps. 73:24
Ps. 119:133
Prov. 3:5–6
Prov. 4:18
Prov. 16:3, 9
Prov. 16:22–23
Prov. 24:3–4
Prov. 29:18
Eccles. 10:10
Isa. 42:16
Isa. 58:11
Isa. 61:8
Jer. 33:3
Hab. 2:2–3
Luke 1:79
Rom. 8:14
Eph. 1:11

Rev. 7:17

Divine elevation
Exod. 11:3
1 Sam. 2:1
1 Sam. 2:10
Neh. 1:11
Neh. 9:5
Job 5:11
Ps. 37:34
Ps. 75:10
Ps. 89:17
1 Pet. 5:6
Ps. 92:10
Ps. 112:9
Prov. 11:11
Isa. 30:18
Isa. 33:10
Dan. 1:8–9
Matt. 23:12
Luke 18:14
Acts 13:17
2 Cor. 10:5
Phil. 2:9
James 1:9

Divine favour
Gen. 18:3
Gen. 29:17
Gen. 39:6
Gen. 39:21
Exod. 3:21
Exod. 11:3
Exod. 12:36
Num. 11:14–15
Deut. 33:23
Judg. 21:22
Ruth 2:13
1 Sam. 16:22
1 Sam. 25:8
2 Sam. 15:25
2 Sam. 20:11
Esther 2:17
Esther 5:2
Job 10:12
Job 33:26
Ps. 5:12
Ps. 30:5

Ps. 30:7
Ps. 41:11
Ps. 44:3
Ps. 45:12
Ps. 77:7
Ps. 85:1
Ps. 89:17
Ps. 102:13
Ps. 104:6
Ps. 112:5
Prov. 3:4
Prov. 8:35
Prov. 11:27
Prov. 12:2
Prov. 13:15
Prov. 14:9
Prov. 14:35
Prov. 15:16
Prov. 18:22
Prov. 22:1
Prov. 28:23
Song of Sol. 8:10
Isa. 45:1–3
Isa. 60:10
Dan. 1:4
Dan. 1:9
Luke 1:28
Luke 2:52
Acts 2:47
Acts 7:9–10

**Divine
vindication**
Gen. 49:19
Deut. 25:1
1 Kings 8:32
2 Chron. 6:23
Job 11:2
Job 13:18
Ps. 51:4
Ps. 98:1
Isa. 43:9
Isa. 50:8
Isa. 54:17
Matt. 11:19
Matt. 12:37
Titus 3:7
James 2:25

1 John 2:13

Dominion
Dan. 4:3
Dan. 4:2
Dan. 6:26
Dan. 7:14
Dan. 7:26
Dan. 11:5
1 Pet. 4:2–6
Dan. 11:5
1 Pet. 4:11

Encouragement
Deut. 1:38
Deut. 3:28
Judg. 20:22
1 Sam. 23:16–17
1 Sam. 30:6
2 Sam. 11:25
2 Chron. 31:4
2 Chron. 35:2
Isa. 41:6–7
Col. 3:16
1 Pet. 5:10

Endurance
Job 14:14
Matt. 24:13
Mark 13:13
1 Cor. 4:12
2 Cor. 4:8
2 Cor. 4:9
2 Tim. 2:12
Heb. 10:32
Heb. 10:33
Heb. 10:34
Heb. 11:27
Heb. 12:2

Example
Matt. 20:26
Matt. 20:27
Matt. 20:28
John 13:15
Rom. 10:17
1 Cor. 10:6
2 Cor. 3:18

1 Tim. 4:12
James 5:10
1 Pet. 2:21

**Facing the
challenges of
singleness**
Gen. 24
Gen. 2:18–25
Job 29:13
Prov. 14:1
Prov. 18:22
Prov. 5:20
Prov. 20:20
Prov. 21:9, 19
Prov. 2:14
Prov. 2:16
Isa. 54:17
1 Cor. 5:9
1 Cor. 6:9
2 Cor. 6:14
2 Cor. 6:18
Eph. 5:3
1 Thess. 4:3
Heb. 12:16

Faith
Prov. 20:6
Prov. 28:20
Matt. 9:29
Matt. 17:20
Rom. 10:17
Rom. 12:3
2 Cor. 5:7
Gal. 3:11
Heb. 11:3
Heb. 11:39
Heb. 10:23
1 Pet. 1:7
1 Pet. 5:9
1 John 5:4
Jude 3
Jude 20

**Faithfulness of
God**
Ps. 36:5
Ps. 40:10

Ps. 89:1–2
Ps. 89:5
Ps. 89:8
Ps. 89:24
Ps. 89:33
Ps. 92:2
Ps. 119:90
Isa. 25:1
Lam. 3:22
Lam. 3:23
Rev. 2:10

Families
Gen. 12:3
Gen. 18:19
Gen. 47:12
Deut. 12:7
Deut. 14:26
Deut. 15:20
Deut. 33:11
Prov. 20:7
Ps. 68:6
Ps. 113:9
Deut. 28:11
Prov. 2:16
Prov. 4:1–10
Ps. 127:1–5
Ps. 128:3–4, 6
Prov. 5:15
Prov. 8:33–34
Prov. 9:13
Prov. 10:1, 4
Prov. 10:5
Prov. 11:11
Prov. 11:16, 29
Prov. 12:4
Prov. 4:1
Prov. 15:5
Prov. 15:20
Prov. 17:25
Prov. 18:22
Prov. 19:13
Prov. 19:14
Prov. 21:9
Matt. 10:36
Luke 19:9
Acts 16:31
Acts 18:8

1 Cor. 16:19
Gal. 6:10
Eph. 2:19
Eph. 3:15
1 Tim. 3:4–5
1 Tim. 3:12
1 Tim. 3:15
1 Tim. 5:14
2 Tim. 1:16
2 Tim. 4:19
Heb. 3:4–5

Favour
Gen. 39:6
Num. 6:25
Num. 6:26
Deut. 28:13
Deut. 33:23
Ps. 5:12
Ps. 8:5
Ps. 30:5
Ps. 102:13
Prov. 8:35
Prov. 11:27
Prov. 12:2
Dan. 1:9, 17
Matt. 6:33
Luke 2:40, 52
Luke 6:38
Eph. 2:10
Eph. 3:19–20
2 Pet. 1:4

**Finances in
general**
Gen. 26:12
Deut. 6:3
Deut. 16:17
Job 42:12
Ps. 23:5–6
Ps. 34:10
Ps. 35:27
Ps. 37:25
Ps. 66:12
Ps. 68:19
Ps. 84:11
Ps. 112:1–3, 5
Prov. 3:9–10

Prov. 11:16
Prov. 12:24
Prov. 13:4, 22
Isa. 48:17
Mark 4:8
Luke 12:34
Rom. 13:8
Gal. 6:6–9
Eph. 3:20
Phil. 4:17
Phil. 4:19
2 Pet. 1:3
3 John 2
Deut. 8:18
Deut. 28:1–6
Josh. 1:8
1 Kings 17:15–16
Ps. 50:14
Isa. 1:19
Prov. 8:12
Prov. 10:4
Prov. 10:22
Prov. 24:3–4
Mal. 3:10
Matt. 6:33
Matt. 25:22–23
Mark 11:23–25
Luke 5:6–7
Luke 6:38
Luke 12:31–32
Luke 12:42–44
Luke 16:11
1 Cor. 9:7–10
2 Cor. 9:7
Eph. 3:20
Eph. 4:28
James 4:3

Focus
Josh. 1:5–8
Ps. 112:7
Isa. 50:7
Luke 9:62
2 Cor. 4:18
Phil. 3:14
Phil. 4:8
Heb. 12:2

Freedom from bondage

Gen. 45:7
Num. 31:5
Deut. 28:1–14
Judg. 3:9
Judg. 15:18
2 Sam. 22:2
2 Kings 5:1
2 Kings 13:17
1 Chron. 4:10
1 Chron. 11:14
2 Chron. 12:7
Ezra 9:13
Esther 4:14
Ps. 18:50
Ps. 22:4
Ps. 32:7
Ps. 44:4
Ps. 70:5
Ps. 144:2
Prov. 11:8–9
Prov. 11:21
Prov. 28:26
Isa. 49:24–25
Joel 2:32
Obad. 17
Matt. 11:28
Luke 4:18
Rom. 11:26

Fruitfulness

Gen. 17:6
Gen. 17:20
Gen. 28:3
Gen. 41:52
Gen. 43:11
Gen. 49:22
Exod. 1:7
Ps. 1:3
Ps. 89:20–21
Ps. 92:14
Ps. 107:34
Ps. 107:37
Ps. 127:3
Ps. 128:3
Ps. 132:1
Prov. 8:19

Prov. 11:30
Prov. 12:14
Prov. 13:2
Prov. 18:20–21
Prov. 27:18
Prov. 31:16
Prov. 31:31
Isa. 29:17
Isa. 32:15–16
Isa. 57:19
Jer. 23:3
Ezek. 17:5
Ezek. 36:11
Hab. 3:17–19
Matt. 13:23
Mark 4:20
Mark 4:28
Luke 8:15
Acts 14:17
Rom. 7:4
Col. 1:6

Fruit of the Spirit

Ps. 37:7–9
Ps. 119:165
Prov. 16:32
Eccles. 7:8–9
Mal. 2:5
Rom. 5:3
Rom. 6:6
Rom. 13:14
Rom. 14:17
Gal. 5:16, 24
Gal. 6:9
Phil. 3:19
Phil. 4:5–7
Eph 4:1–2
1 Tim. 6:11
2 Tim. 1:7
Heb. 6:15
1 Pet. 2:11
1 Pet. 4:1–2
2 Pet. 1:5–6

Future

Ps. 1:6
Ps. 128:6
Isa. 34:14

Matt. 6:30
Matt. 6:34
Rom. 8:28
2 Cor. 10:4–5
Phil. 1:6
Phil. 3:14
Heb. 12:2
Heb. 13:5

Glory

Exod. 16:7
Exod. 16:10
Exod. 24:16
Exod. 33:18
Exod. 40:34
Deut. 5:24
Deut. 33:17
1 Kings 8:11
1 Chron. 16:27–28
Ps. 8:1
Ps. 8:5
Ps. 24:7–10
Ps. 45:3
Ps. 104:31
Ps. 111:3
Ps. 148:13
Isa. 60:13
Dan. 2:37
Dan. 4:36
Dan. 5:18
Dan. 7:14
2 Cor. 4:17
1 Thess. 2:12
1 Pet. 1:8

Growth

Gen. 21:8
Gen. 47:27
Ps. 92:12
Isa. 11:1
Jer. 12:2
Ezek. 47:12
Hos. 14:5
Hos. 14:7
Zech. 6:12
Mal. 4:2
Mark 4:27, 32
Acts 12:24

Acts 19:20
Eph. 2:21
Eph. 4:15
2 Thess. 1:3
1 Pet. 2:2
2 Pet. 3:18

Guidance

Exod. 15:13
2 Chron. 32:22
Ps. 25:9
Ps. 31:3
Ps. 32:8
Ps. 48:14
Ps. 73:24
Ps. 78:52
Ps. 78:72
Ps. 112:5
Prov. 6:6–8
Isa. 45:1–2
Isa. 58:11
Mic. 7:5
Matt. 3:16
John 16:13
Acts 18:31
Rom. 2:19

Handling personal mistakes

2 Chron. 7:14
Rom. 8:35–37
Rom. 8:31–32
2 Sam. 24:10
1 John 5:4
Matt. 17:20
Job 22:23
2 Cor. 4:9
Matt. 19:26
Job 34:32
Ps. 60:12
Mark 10:27
Ps. 51:17
1 Cor. 15:57
Rev. 21:7
Joel 2:25
Ps. 92:4
Deut. 4:29
1 John 1:8

2 Cor. 2:14
Deut. 4:31

Handling tough problems
2 Chron. 32:7
1 Kings 2:2
Ps. 34:6
Ps. 34:19
Ps. 75:6
Ps. 108:13
Ps. 126:1, 4
Joel 3:10
Obad. 13
Rom. 4:20
Rom. 5:3
Rom. 8:35
Rom. 12:12
2 Cor. 8:2
2 Cor. 1:14
2 Tim. 4:5
1 Pet. 1:7
1 Pet. 4:12

Healing
2 Kings 2:21
2 Kings 20:5
2 Kings 20:8
2 Chron. 7:14
2 Chron. 30:20
Ps. 6:2
Ps. 30:2
Ps. 41:4
Ps. 103:3
Ps. 107:20
Ps. 147:3
Prov. 4:22
Prov. 12:18
Prov. 13:17
Prov. 16:24
Eccles. 3:3
Isa. 19:22
Isa. 30:26
Isa. 57:18–19
Isa. 58:8
Jer. 3:22
Jer. 17:14
Jer. 30:17

Jer. 33:16
Ezek. 47:8
Hos. 5:13
Hos. 6:1
Hos. 11:3
Hos. 14:4
Mal. 4:2
Matt. 4:23
Luke 7:3
Luke 9:11
Acts 4:30

Healing and divine health
Exod. 15:26
Exod. 23:25–26
Ps. 91:16
Ps. 103:2–3
Ps. 107:20
Isa. 53:4–5
Isa. 54:1–4
Isa. 55:11
Matt. 8:2–3
Matt. 8:16–17
Mark 11:23–24
Acts 10:38
Gal. 3:13
2 Tim. 1:7
James 1:17
James 5:14–15
1 John 4:4
3 John 2

Healing of the memory
Rom. 12:2
2 Cor. 5:17
Rom. 3:25
Phil. 3:13
Eph. 147:3
Isa. 43:19
Eph. 2:2–3
Isa. 42:9
Eph. 5:26

Honour
Exod. 14:18
Exod. 29:12

Lev. 19:15
Lev. 19:32
Job 22:8
Prov. 3:16
Prov. 8:18
Prov. 13:18
Prov. 18:12
Prov. 21:21
Prov. 22:4
Prov. 25:2
Prov. 27:18
Prov. 29:23
Jer. 33:9
Isa. 29:23
Dan. 4:34
Mark 6:4
1 Pet. 2:9

Hunger and thirst for righteousness
Ps. 1:1–3
Ps. 15:1–5
Isa. 29:19
Matt. 5:6
Matt. 6:20
Matt. 6:33
Matt. 13:44–46
Luke 9:23
Rom. 12:1
Rom. 14:19
Phil. 3:9
Phil. 4:8
1 Pet. 3:14
James 3:8
Gen. 30:33
1 Chron. 16:29
Ps. 27:4, 8–9
Ps. 34:9
Ps. 42:1–2
Ps. 51
Ps. 52:3
Ps. 73:23–28
Ps. 106:3
Isa. 41:2
Isa. 54:14
Isa. 58:8
Matt. 5:6
Matt. 6:33

2 Cor. 5:17
2 Cor. 7:1
Eph. 5:9
Phil. 3:10
Col. 3:1–4
Heb. 12:14
Luke 1:75
Rom. 6:3, 6
Rom. 6:14
Rom. 14:17
2 Cor. 9:10
Eph. 6:14
Phil. 3:9
Phil. 3:10
Col. 3:1–4
1 Tim. 6:11
Heb. 1:9
2 Pet. 2:2
2 Pet. 2:22

Impossibility
Matt. 19:26
Matt. 17:20
Mark 10:27
Luke 1:37
Luke 18:27
Heb. 6:18
Heb. 11:6

Increase
Gen. 7:18
Gen. 30:43
Lev. 19:25
Deut. 7:13
Job 1:10
Job 8:7
Ps. 49:16
Ps. 62:10
Ps. 67:6
Ps. 85:12
Prov. 9:9
Prov. 9:11
Prov. 11:24
Isa. 29:19
Ezek. 16:7
Dan. 12:4
Amos 4:9
Luke 2:52

John 3:30
Acts 6:7
2 Cor. 9:10
2 Cor. 10:15
Col. 1:10
3 John 2
Lev. 26:4
Deut. 28:11
Deut. 33:19
1 Kings 18:41
1 Chron. 27:23
Job 8:7
Job 36:31
Ps. 36:8–9
Ps. 67:6
Ps. 116:7
Prov. 1:5
Prov. 3:10
Prov. 28:19
Isa. 30:23
Isa. 54:3
Joel 2:26
Eph. 3:20
Col. 1:10

Joy
1 Kings 1:40
Ps. 42:4
Ps. 43:4
Prov. 23:24
Eccles. 9:7
Isa. 61:3
Isa. 29:19
Isa. 55:12
Neh. 8:10
Jer. 15:16
Jer. 31:13
Jer. 33:11
Deut. 28:47b
Ps. 98:8
Ps. 113:9
Eccles. 9:9

Keeping on
Job 14:14
Ps. 30:5
Ps. 72:7
Ps. 89:36

2 Thess. 1:4
2 Tim. 2:10
Heb. 6:15
Heb. 10:32
Heb. 10:34
Heb. 11:27
Heb. 12:2
James 1:12
1 Pet. 5:10

Knowledge
Exod. 31:3
Deut. 1:13
1 Sam. 2:3
Job 15:2
Job 34:2
Job 35:16
Job 38:2
Job 42:3
Job 36:3
Ps. 19:2
Prov. 1:7
Prov. 2:3–6
Prov. 2:10–11
Prov. 3:20
Prov. 5:2
Prov. 8:10
Prov. 12:1
Prov. 13:16
Prov. 14:6
Prov. 15:2
Prov. 15:7
Prov. 17:27
Prov. 22:20
Eccles. 1:18
Eccles. 2:21
Isa. 5:13
Isa. 11:2
Isa. 11:9
Isa. 53:11
Dan. 2:21
Dan. 5:12
Dan. 12:4
Hos. 4:6
Hos. 6:6
Mal. 2:7
1 Cor. 1:5
1 Cor. 12:8

1 Cor. 15:34
James 3:13
Col. 2:3
1 Pet. 3:7
2 Pet. 1:5
1 John 2:27

Labour
Exod. 23:16
Deut. 26:7
Deut. 28:33
Josh. 24:13
Ps. 104:23
Ps. 127:1
Ps. 128:2
Prov. 14:23
Prov. 16:26
Prov. 21:25
Prov. 23:4
Eccles. 2:10
Eccles. 2:21
Eccles. 2:24
Eccles. 3:13
Eccles. 4:9
Eccles. 5:12
Eccles. 5:19
Eccles. 10:15
Isa. 55:2
Isa. 65:23
Hab. 3:17–18
John 4:38
John 6:27
Acts 20:35
Rom. 16:12
1 Cor. 3:9
1 Cor. 15:58
2 Cor. 5:9
Eph. 4:28
Col. 1:29
1 Thess. 2:9
Heb. 6:12

Media
Deut. 32:3
Neh. 8:15
Esther 1:20
Esther 3:14
Hab. 2:3

Ps. 26:7
Ps. 68:11
Prov. 15:3
Prov. 25:25
Isa. 52:7
Jer. 5:20
Jon. 3:7
Nah. 1:15
Hab. 2:2
Mark 1:45
Mark 13:10
Acts 10:37
Phil. 4:8

Missionaries
1 Chron. 15:2
1 Chron. 23:13
2 Chron. 15:7
Ps. 2:8
Ps. 23:1
Ps. 27:1, 5
Ps. 146:7
Prov. 8:14
Isa. 35:3
Isa. 40:11
Isa. 41:10
Isa. 54:17
Isa. 55:11–12
Jer. 23:4
Ezek. 34:5
Hab. 3:19
Matt. 18:18
Mark 16:15
Acts 8:4–8
Acts 8:14–17
Acts 11:19–24
1 Cor. 12:8
2 Cor. 4:8
2 Cor. 6:3–4
2 Cor. 9:8
2 Cor. 12:9
2 Cor. 2:12, 14, 17
2 Cor. 3:2–3, 17
Eph. 6:19
2 Thess. 3:3
1 Pet. 4:11

Nations that need the gospel
Deut. 14:2
Josh. 23:4
Ruth 2:11
2 Chron. 7:14
2 Chron. 20:6
Rom. 10:15
Ps. 2:1
Ps. 2:8
Ps. 79:10
Isa. 11:9
Ezek. 34:28
Ezek. 39:21
Zech. 14:4
Matt. 28:19
Rom. 10:14
Gal. 1:16
1 John 4:4

Oppression
Exod. 3:8
Lev. 25:14
Deut. 23:16
Isa. 49:26
Jer. 30:20
Judg. 2:18
Judg. 6:9
Ps. 9:9
Ps. 10:18
Ps. 74:21
Ps. 103:6
Isa. 1:17
Isa. 38:14
Isa. 58:6
Deut. 26:7
Job 36:15
Ps. 42:9
Ps. 44:24
Ps. 107:2
Eccles. 5:8
Ps. 55:3
Isa. 35:15–16
Isa. 54:14
Zech. 7:10
1 Sam. 12:4
Job 27:13
Ps. 54:3

Ps. 72:4
Ps. 119:121

Overcoming addictions and compulsions
Luke 4:18
Ps. 107:20
Ps. 34:14
Ps. 55:18
Prov. 28:26
Prov. 28:13
Ps. 81:6
2 Chron. 7:14
Isa. 55:6–7
Ps. 107:6
1 John 1:9

Overcoming bad habits
1 John 1:9
Prov. 28:26
Luke 4:18
2 Chron. 7:14
Ps. 55:18
Ps. 81:6
Ps. 34:14
Ps. 107:6
Ps. 107:20
Prov. 28:13
Isa. 55:6–7

Overcoming betrayal
Ps. 27:11–12
Ps. 34:7–8
Prov. 14:5
Eph. 4:31
Ps. 27:14
Ps. 41:9–11
Isa. 50:7–9
2 Tim. 4:17
Ps. 31:13
Ps. 55:12–14
Mic. 7:8
1 Pet. 3:16
Ps. 31:15
Ps. 91:4–5

Matt. 26:14–16
Ps. 35:1–15
Ps. 31:16
Ps. 45:22
Ps. 35:19
Ps. 35:20

Overcoming bitterness
Isa. 38:17
Col. 3:13
Prov. 10:12
Heb. 12:15
Prov. 10:18
James 3:11–12
Eph. 4:31
James 3:13–16

Overcoming discouragement
Josh. 1:9
Ps. 41:10
2 Thess. 2:16–17
Ps. 37:3
Ps. 37:4
Ps. 37:5
2 Cor. 2:14
Isa. 43:2
Jer. 29:11
Ps. 66:8–9
Phil. 1:6
Isa. 51:3
Heb. 6:10–11
Heb. 6:12
Ps. 69:30
Ps. 138:3
Isa. 51:12
Ps. 103:17
Ps. 69:32
Ps. 138:7–8
Deut. 31:6
Ps. 73:23
Zech. 4:6
Prov. 4:18

Overcoming emotional damage
Deut. 15:10
Judg. 6:9
1 Chron. 4:9
Esther 9:22
Job 41:22
Ps. 9:9
Ps. 72:4
Ps. 74:21
Ps. 78:53
Ps. 91
Ps. 119:134
Ps. 127:2
Prov. 10:22
Prov. 28:3
Isa. 9:4
Isa. 35:10
Isa. 49:26
Isa. 53:4
Isa. 54:6
Isa. 61:1–3
Jer. 22:3
Jer. 30:11, 20
Jer. 31:13
Ezek. 26:21
Matt. 10:26
Matt. 10:28
Matt. 20:31
Mark 6:20
John 16:20
Acts 10:38
Phil. 1:28
1 Pet. 3:14–15
Rev. 21:4

Overcoming false accusation
Ps. 27:11–12
Ps. 34:7–8
Ps. 101:7
Eph. 4:31
Ps. 27:14
Ps. 35:19–26
Prov. 14:5
2 Tim. 4:17
Ps. 31:13–14

205

Ps. 41:9–11
Isa. 50:7–9
1 Pet. 3:16
Ps. 31:15–16
Ps. 91:4–5
Mic. 7:8

Overcoming family problems
Gen. 12:3
Deut. 28:11
Ps. 127:1, 3
Ps. 128:3
Prov. 4:1, 10
Prov. 5:15
Prov. 6:24, 32
Prov. 10:1, 4–5
Prov. 11:16, 29
Prov. 12:4
Prov. 14:1
Prov. 15:5
Prov. 15:17, 20
Prov. 17:25
Prov. 18:22
Prov. 19:13–14
Prov. 19:20
Prov. 21:9, 19
Prov. 31:10, 30
Isa. 54:3–4
Jer. 31:3
1 Cor. 7:14
1 Cor. 7:15
Eph. 5:29, 32

Overcoming financial crises
Gal. 6:9
Isa. 48:17
Prov. 10:22
2 Pet. 1:3
Josh. 1:8
Ps. 34:10
2 Cor. 8:9
Gen. 14:18–20
2 Thess. 3:10
Deut. 8:18
Rom. 8:32
2 Cor. 9:9–10

1 Tim. 5:8
3 John 3:2
Gal. 3:13–14
Prov. 13:22
Deut. 14:28
Phil. 4:15–17
Phil. 4:19
Isa. 45:2–3
Prov. 28:20
Deut. 24:19
Gal. 6:6–9
Deut. 28:12
Isa. 1:19
Eph. 3:20
Deut. 28:1–2

Overcoming frustration
Zech. 4:6
Prov. 4:18
Rom. 14:19
Isa. 30:15
Rom. 8:31
John 14:27
Prov. 16:3
Col. 3:15
Isa. 41:13
Rom. 8:26
Heb. 4:9–12
Ps. 27:13–14
John 8:31–32
2 Cor. 7:6
Rom. 8:37
Heb. 4:16
Ps. 73:26–28
Phil. 4:13
Gal. 5:10
1 John 5:4
Ps. 32:6–11
Isa. 26:3–4
Prov. 3:26
Phil. 3:3
2 Cor. 5:21
Prov. 14:26
1 John 5:14
Prov. 28:1
Heb. 13:6

Overcoming guilt
2 Sam. 24:10
Prov. 28:13
2 Sam. 12:13
Isa. 43:25
Isa. 55:7
2 Chron. 7:14
Isa. 1:18
Ps. 32:1
Rom. 8:1
2 Chron. 30:9
Ps. 51:17
1 John 1:9
Ps. 51:9
Ps. 103:12
Heb. 8:12
Ps. 130:4
1 John 1:7
Isa. 61:1
Matt. 1:21
2 Cor. 5:17
Jer. 31:34
Jer. 33:8

Overcoming indebtedness
1 Sam. 22:2
Prov. 22:26
2 Kings 4:1–7
Prov. 13:22
Prov. 22:7
Mal. 3:10
Matt. 6:12
Matt. 12:29
Matt. 18:27, 32
Mark 11:23
Rom. 8:12
Rom. 13:8
Eph. 6:8
Phil. 18–19

Overcoming impossible situations
Ps. 3:2
Ps. 4:8
Ps. 5:10
Ps. 18:19, 34

Ps. 21:2
Ps. 33:18–19
Ps. 35:7–9
Ps. 37:15
Ps. 38:16–20
Ps. 41:9–11
Ps. 55:21–23
Ps. 56:3–4
Ps. 56:8–9, 13
Ps. 57:4–11
Ps. 58:6–7
Ps. 91
Isa. 40:4
Isa. 42:16
Isa. 45:2
Jer. 32:17
Matt. 17:20
Matt. 29:26
Acts 12:1–11
Rom. 8:32
Eph. 3:20

Overcoming insecurity
Ps. 27:3
Ps. 56:11
Ps. 118:8
Ps. 118:9
Prov. 3:26
Prov. 14:16
Isa. 30:15
Ezck. 28:26
Mic. 7:5
Rom. 2:19
2 Cor. 5:6
2 Cor. 6:8
2 Cor. 9:4
Phil. 1:6
Phil. 1:14
Phil. 3:13

Overcoming jealousy
Deut. 5:21
Prov. 24:1
James 3:14
Ps. 10:3
Prov. 3:31

Prov. 23:17
Prov. 23:18
1 Cor. 10:24
Ps. 37:7
Prov. 14:30
Gal. 5:26
Ps. 51:7
Prov. 27:4
James 3:16
2 Cor. 10:5
Ps. 51:10
Eccles. 4:4
James 4:5
Phil. 4:8

**Overcoming
loneliness**
John 8:16
John 10:27
John 8:29
Exod. 33:14
Heb. 13:5
John 16:32
Lev. 16:12
Josh. 1:5
Matt. 18:20
Matt. 28:20
Prov. 18:24
Prov. 17:17

**Overcoming
marital problems**
Gen. 2:23
Luke 11:4
James 1:5
Matt. 5:7
Luke 6:37
James 5:16
Gen. 2:24
Matt. 5:31
Rom. 12:21
Ps. 27:1
Ps. 6:2
Mark 10:8
Eph. 5:28
Ps. 27:3
Prov. 19:11
Matt. 5:32

Eph. 5:33
Ps. 27:14
Luke 6:36
Heb. 13:4
Ps. 31:3
Ps. 31:4

**Overcoming
mental and
physical fatigue**
1 Sam. 2:9
Ps. 18:1–2
Isa. 40:29
2 Chron. 20:15b
Ps. 27:3
Ps. 116
Isa. 40:31
Ps. 3:3
Ps. 27:5
Ps. 127:2
Isa. 41:10
Ps. 5:3
Ps. 73:26
Prov. 3:24
John 14:1
Ps. 9:9
Phil. 4:6
Phil. 4:7
John 14:27

**Overcoming
offences**
Lev. 19:18
Ps. 91:15
Matt. 5:22
1 Cor. 13:4
Ps. 7:1
Ps. 94:14
Matt. 6:14
Col. 3:8
Prov. 12:16
Luke 17:4
2 Tim. 2:24
Prov. 20:22
Rom. 12:17
2 Tim. 4:17–18

**Overcoming
opposition**
Ps. 27:11
Ps. 31:13, 15–16
Ps. 34:7–8
Ps. 35:11, 15
Ps. 35:19–20
Ps. 41:9–11
Ps. 55:12–14
Ps. 91:4–5
Ps. 119:133
Prov. 3:30
Prov. 13:10
Prov. 14:5
Prov. 22:10
Isa. 40:31
Isa. 41:10
Isa. 44:25
Isa. 44:11
Mic. 7:8
Matt. 26:14–16
Matt. 26:45
Rom. 12:18
Rom. 14:19
Eph. 4:31
2 Tim. 4:17
1 Pet. 3:16
James 3:16

**Overcoming
personal hurts**
1 Cor. 13:4
Phil. 4:8
Prov. 16:32
James 3:13
Eccles. 7:9
2 Cor. 10:4
Matt. 5:9
Eph. 4:31
Ps. 37:8
1 Cor. 13:4–5
Eph. 6:10
Prov. 14:17
Gal. 5:22–23

**Overcoming
pride**
Prov. 6:16–17

Rom. 12:3
James 4:6–7
Prov. 11:2
Prov. 21:4
Matt. 23:11
Isa. 57:15
1 Pet. 5:5
1 Pet. 5:6
Prov. 22:4

**Overcoming
sexual abuse**
Luke 13:11–12
Phil. 3:14
1 John 1:7
2 Cor. 5:17
James 1:21
John 8:32
Rom. 6:4
Matt. 5:44
Phil. 1:6
1 John 3:1
Rom. 8:2
1 John 3:2
Phil. 3:13
John 10:10

**Overcoming
sexual
temptations**
Matt. 5:28
1 Cor. 6:18
James 1:13
James 1:14
James 1:15
Mark 10:19
1 Cor. 10:8
Col. 3:5
2 Pet. 2:9
1 John 2:16
1 Cor. 6:13
Acts 15:20
1 Tim. 4:1
Matt. 26:41
1 Cor. 6:15
1 Cor. 6:16
Prov. 2:16
Eph. 4:22

1 Thess. 4:3
1 Thess. 4:4
Prov. 4:14
Prov. 1:10
1 Cor. 10:13
Prov. 2:11
1 Pet. 2:11
Prov. 6:32
Prov. 6:33
Prov. 6:23
Prov. 6:24
Prov. 6:25

Overcoming spiritual assassins
Heb. 4:16
Gal. 1:4
Matt. 12:29
2 Tim. 2:26
Ezek. 22:30
Mark 16:17
Rev. 12:11
Heb. 1:4
1 John 3:8
Rom. 8:26
Col. 1:13
2 Cor. 2:11
Isa. 58:6
James 4:7
2 Cor. 4:18
Eph. 6:12
Eph. 6:16
Luke 10:19
1 Cor. 6:12
Col. 2:15
Eph. 4:27

Overcoming spiritual problems
2 Chron. 34:27
Ps. 34:14
Prov. 2:11, 16
Prov. 10:12
Prov. 11:13
Prov. 14:7, 29
Prov. 16:17–18, 32

Prov. 22:24–25
Prov. 25:28
Prov. 28:26
Isa. 38:17
Matt. 5:22, 28
Matt. 18:4
Matt. 26:41
Acts 24:16
Rom. 6:11–13
Rom. 8:35–37
2 Cor. 7:1
Gal. 2:20
Gal. 5:16, 18
Gal. 5:22–25
Eph. 4:2, 26
Col. 3:5, 13
Col. 3:17
James 1:19–20
James 3:11–16
James 4:10
Heb. 12:15
1 John 1:9
1 John 2:16
1 John 5:4

Overcoming spiritual weakness
1 Cor. 15:57
Eph. 3:16–17
Ps. 37:39
Rom. 3:4
Eph. 6:10
Heb. 11:34
1 John 5:4
Matt. 26:41
2 Chron. 15:7
Joel 3:10
Rom. 4:19–21

Overcoming temptations
James 1:13
Matt. 4:6–7
James 1:2–4
Matt. 4:9–10
James 1:4
1 Chron. 21:1

Josh. 7:21
Prov. 28:20
Job 1:9–12
Job 1:10
Job 1:11
Job 1:12
1 Cor. 10:13
Matt. 4:1
Matt. 16:1
1 Tim. 6:9
John 13:2
2 Pet. 2:9
Rev. 3:10
Gal. 4:14
1 Pet. 1:6

Overcoming the feeling of being used and abused
Heb. 10:32–35
Ps. 3:1–3
Ps. 42:9
Jer. 31:13
Isa. 60:10
Isa. 62:2

Overcoming weariness
Ps. 20:6
Ps. 27:1
Ps. 29:1
Ps. 39:13
Ps. 46:1
Ps. 68:35
Ps. 73:26
Eccles. 10:18
Jer. 30:10
Rom. 12:11
Heb. 6:12
Jer. 31:25

Parents
Deut. 4:9
Gen. 33:5
Gen. 44:20, 30
Gen. 17:18
Deut. 11:19
1 Sam. 1:27

Gen. 48:13–20
1 Tim. 3:4, 12
Ps. 127:3
Exod. 2:2–3
Heb. 11:20
Joel 1:3
Titus 2:4
Judg. 13:8
Col. 3:21
Matt. 19:13
2 Sam. 18:5, 33
1 Chron. 29:19
Ps. 103:13
Prov. 22:6
Job 1:5
1 Sam. 3:13
Eph. 6:4
Prov. 31:1
Gen. 18:19

Peace and joy
Lev. 26:6
Judg. 19:20
1 Kings 4:24
Ezra 3:13
Neh. 8:10
Ps. 30:5
Ps. 43:4
Ps. 55:18
Ps. 72:7
Ps. 126:1, 5
Isa. 29:19
Isa. 32:18
Isa. 48:18
Isa. 51:11
Isa. 60:15, 17
Isa. 66:12
Jer. 31:13
Dan. 10:19
Mal. 2:5
Phil. 4:7
James 3:17
Gen. 43:23
Exod. 4:18
Deut. 2:26
Deut. 20:10
Num. 6:26
Num. 25:12

1 Chron. 22:9
1 Sam. 1:17
1 Sam. 25:6
Judg. 6:23–24
Esther 10:3
Ps. 4:8
Ps. 29:11
Ps. 34:14
Ps. 55:18
Ps. 72:7
Ps. 85:10
Ps. 119:165
Ps. 122:7
Prov. 3:2
Isa. 26:12
Isa. 48:18
Isa. 55:12
2 Pet. 1:2
2 Pet. 3:14
Isa. 32:18
1 John 4:18
Ps. 116:7

Persecution
Ps. 69:26
Luke 21:12
John 16:3
Gal. 4:29
1 Cor. 4:12
John 5:16
John 15:20
Gal. 5:11
Matt. 5:12
Isa. 50:6
Jer. 15:15
Matt. 13:21
Ps. 7:1
2 Cor. 4:9
Isa. 53:7
Zech. 2:8
Ps. 10:2
Rom. 8:35
Ps. 119:86
Mark 10:30
Acts 9:4, 5
Acts 13:50
Matt. 2:13
Rom. 12:14

2 Tim. 3:12
Matt. 26:52
1 Pet. 4:19
1 Cor. 15:19
Ps. 69:24

Perseverance
Ps. 40:1
Eccles. 7:8
Luke 8:15
Luke 21:19
Acts 26:3
Rom. 5:3–4
Rom. 8:25
Rom. 12:12
Rom. 15:4–5
1 Thess. 1:3
1 Thess. 5:14
2 Thess. 1:4
1 Tim. 3:3
2 Tim. 2:24
Titus 2:2
Heb. 6:12
Heb. 10:36
Heb. 12:1
James 1:3–4
James 5:7–8
James 5:10–11
2 Pet. 1:6
Rev. 2:2

Persistence
Rom. 12:12
Heb. 6:12
James 1:3
Josh. 1:6
Judg. 20:22
1 Sam. 30:6
Ps. 27:14
Ps. 31:24
Ps. 38:15
Ps. 39:7
Ps. 44:5
Ps. 71:14
Ps. 146:5
Ps. 100:3
Ps. 123:1–2
Prov. 3:5

Mark 9:23–24
Mark 11:24
Rom. 8:25
Rom. 8:35–39
Phil. 4:13
Col. 1:11–12
Heb. 11:1

Pleading the blood of Jesus
Exod. 12:7
Exod. 12:13
Heb. 9:6–14
Lev. 17:11
1 John 1:7
Heb. 13:20

Possessing the future
Ps. 1:6
Ps. 128:6
Isa. 34:14
Matt. 6:30
Matt. 6:34
Rom. 8:28
2 Cor. 10:4–5
Phil. 1:6
Phil. 3:14
Heb. 12:2
Heb. 13:5

Power
Deut. 4:37
Deut. 8:18
Josh. 17:17
Ps. 68:35
Ps. 110:3
Eccles. 8:4
Isa. 40:29
Dan. 6:27
Zech. 4:6
Mic. 3:8
Nah. 2:1
Matt. 10:1
Mark 3:15
Mark 6:7
John 1:12
Acts 1:8

Eph. 3:20
Rev. 11:6

Prayer for all around success
Ps. 1:3
Deut. 3:9
Eccles. 3:13
Job 22:24–25
Isa. 30:23
Ps. 112:3
Deut. 28:2–6
Deut. 28:11–13
Deut. 11:15
Phil. 4:19
Prov. 15:6
Isa. 65:21–23
Ps. 128:12
Eph. 3:20

Prayer for an unsaved person
Gen. 49:18
Rom. 10:2
Job 13:16
Rom. 10:17
Ps. 25:5
Ps. 106:4
Ps. 119:166
Isa. 17:10
Isa. 59:16
Isa. 62:1
Dan. 12:3
Luke 2:30
Acts 4:12
Rom. 6:23
Rom. 10:1
2 Cor. 4:4
Gal. 3:13
Eph. 2:8
Phil. 1:19
Rev. 12:11

Prayer for businessmen and women
Deut. 8:18
Deut. 28:13

209

2 Chron. 15:7
Esther 4:14b
Prov. 10:5
Prov. 12:24
Prov. 13:4
Prov. 21:5
Prov. 22:29
Dan. 5:12
Hab. 3:19
Hag. 1:6–7
John 4:35–36
Gal. 6:10
2 Pet. 1:3–4
Heb. 6:11
James 1:5
Rev. 3:8

Prayer for godson, goddaughters, and adopted children
2 Cor. 6:18
Rom. 4:16
Exod. 2:10
Eph. 3:6
Eph. 1:5
Esther 2:7
Num. 6:27
Gal. 3:29
Eph. 1:6
Eph. 1:11
Exod. 4:22
Isa. 62:2
Gal. 3:27
Rom. 8:29
Matt. 13:43
1 Chron. 28:6
Ezek. 16:3–6
Matt. 6:25–34
Rom. 8:17
Rom. 8:14
Gen. 48:5
Gen. 48:14
Gal. 3:29

Prayer for orphans and children of single parents
Lam. 5:3
Deut. 24:17
Job 24:3
Ps. 10:18
Mal. 3:5
Exod. 22:24
Deut. 24:19
Deut. 24:20
Job 24:9
Ps. 109:9
Ps. 109:12
Jer. 5:28
Deut. 10:18
Deut. 26:12
Deut. 26:13
Job 29:12
Ps. 146:9
Hos. 14:3
Deut. 16:11
Deut. 6:14
Deut. 27:19
Job 31:17
Prov. 23:10
Ezek. 22:7
Job 22:9
Job 22:10
Ps. 10:14

Prayer for someone retiring
Isa. 46:4
Prov. 17:6
Ps. 71:17
Ps. 81:18
Deut. 5:33
Prov. 10:27
Job 12:12
Job 12:13
Job 5:26
Ps. 39:5
Deut. 6:2
Job 11:17
Ps. 91:16
Prov. 20:29

Titus 2:1–5
Ps. 39:4
Prov. 3:1
Prov. 3:2
Prov. 10:27
Prov. 9:11

Prayer for the nations
1 Tim. 2:1
1 Tim. 2:2
Prov. 16:12
Prov. 16:13
Prov. 2:10–15
Prov. 28:2
Prov. 2:21
Prov. 2:22
Prov. 29:2
Ps. 68:11
Prov. 20:26
Prov. 20:28
Prov. 16:10

Prayer for the New Year
Ps: 65:11
Ps. 90:4
John 14:26
Lev. 25:13
Prov. 16:3
Isa. 61:2
Phil. 4:6
Luke 2:41

Prayer for when facing danger
Zech. 2:5
2 Sam. 22:31
Ps. 34:7
Ps. 91:8–11
Ps. 91:14–16
2 Tim. 1:12
Ps. 91:1–2
Ps. 91:4–5
Luke 21:18
Jude 24
Ps. 32:6–7
Ps. 46:1–2

Prayer for your nation's needs
1 Tim. 2:1
Prov. 20:26
Prov. 29:2
1 Tim. 2:2
Prov. 20:28
Prov. 28:2
Prov. 2:10–15
Prov. 16:10
Ps. 68:11
Prov. 2:21–22
Prov. 16:12–13

Prayer for your President or Prime Minister
Rom. 13:1–3
1 Tim. 2:2
Titus 3:1
Prov. 10:21

Prayer for your staff
Col. 1:13
Eph. 5:1–2
Ps. 118:24
Deut. 30:19
James 5:7
Isa. 10:27
1 Pet. 5:10
Matt. 6:10
1 John 2:27
Esther 4:14
1 Cor. 6:20
Acts 2:17

Prayer for your wedding anniversary
Prov. 5:15–20
Prov. 11:16
Ps. 65:11
Ruth 1:16–17
Prov. 19:14
Prov. 31
Gen. 24:67

Prov. 21:9
Prov. 21:19
Prov. 12:4
Prov. 18:22
1 Cor. 7:39
Heb. 13:4
Eph. 5:22–33
Col. 3:18–19
1 Pet. 3:1–7

Prayer of repentance from national sins
Amos 3:3
2 Chron. 7:14
Neh. 8:9–11
1 Tim. 2:1
Prov. 20:26
Prov. 16:12–13
Prov. 28:2
Prov. 2:21
Prov. 29:2
Ps. 68:11
Jer. 18:8
Ezek. 14:6
Joel 2:14

Praying for a compassionate heart
Exod. 2:6
Deut. 13:17
Deut. 30:3
1 Sam. 23:21
1 Kings 8:50
2 Kings 13:23
2 Chron. 30:9
2 Chron. 36:15
Ps. 78:38
Ps. 86:15
Ps. 111:4
Ps. 145:8
Isa. 49:15
Jer. 12:15
Lam. 3:22
Lam. 3:32
Mic. 7:19
Zech. 7:9

Matt. 9:36
Matt. 18:27
Matt. 18:33
Mark 5:19
Luke 15:20
Rom. 9:15
Heb. 10:34
1 Pet. 3:8
Jude 22
Mark 6:34
Isa. 58:9–11
Prov. 21:21
Luke 7:12–13
Ps. 25:10
Luke 7:13
Ps. 37:21
1 Cor. 13:4–7

Praying for a job
Matt. 6:8
Isa. 30:21
Matt. 6:26
Isa. 48:17
Mark 9:23
Jer. 17:7
2 Cor. 9:8
Prov. 29:25

Praying for a rebellious child
1 Cor. 5:18–19
Ps. 37:4
Prov. 15:31
Mal. 4:6
John 14:6
Eph. 6:1–3
Prov. 13:1
Ezek. 22:30
Mark 10:13–16
1 John 1:9
Ps. 127
Prov. 22:6
Ps. 128
Luke 2:50
Luke 2:51
Luke 2:52
1 Pet. 5:7
Jer. 1:5–10

Prov. 8:6–7
Prov. 3:1
Prov. 3:2

Praying for divine ideas
Exod. 4:12
Ps. 32:8
Prov. 8:17
Isa. 48:6
Job 32:8
Ps. 36:9
Prov. 12:5
Isa. 48:7
Ps. 40:5
Prov. 24:14
Jer. 29:11
Ps. 138:8
Isa. 42:9
Isa. 43:19

Praying for exam success
Isa. 2:3
Ps. 51:6
Isa. 30:21
Ps. 32:8
Prov. 28:5
John 16:3
Ps. 16:7
2 Tim. 1:7
2 Cor. 4:6
Prov 2:5
Prov. 2:6
Prov. 2:7
James 1:5
Jer. 33:3
Prov. 1:2
1 John 5:20

Praying for hurting people
Deut. 10:18
Acts 20:35
2 Cor. 1:4
Isa. 50:4
Matt. 25:34
Rom. 12:15

2 Cor. 1:5
Isa. 58:5–7
Matt. 25:35
Rom. 15:1
Heb. 13:3
Matt. 7:12
John 13:35
2 Cor. 1:3
Gal. 6:2
Heb. 13:16
James 2:8
1 Pet. 3:8

Praying for people who are going through a personal crisis
Ps. 141:1
Gal. 6:1
Heb. 13:16
2 Cor. 9:10
James 2:8
Prov. 3:28
1 John 3:17
Matt. 5:45
Gal. 6:2
1 John 3:18
2 Cor. 9:8
Gal. 6:10
Gal. 6:8

Praying for leaders
1 Tim. 2:1–3
Deut. 28:10
Prov. 2:10–12
Deut. 28:18
Prov. 2:21–22
Rom. 8:37
Ps. 33:12
Prov. 21:1
Acts 12:24

Praying for teenagers
Ps. 34:11
Isa. 45:16
Ps. 115:16

Ps. 128:3
Ps. 127:3–4
Deut. 29:29
Ps. 78:6
Ps. 147:13
Ps. 144:7
Deut. 11:21
Ps. 144:11
Neh. 9:23
Prov. 17:6
Prov. 20:7

Praying for the backslidden
1 Kings 11:9
Num. 14:43
Ps. 37:24
Isa. 26:3
Rev. 2:4
Ps. 125:5
Prov. 16:18
Jer. 3:13–14
2 Cor. 11:3
Isa. 59:2, 9–11
Prov. 24:16
2 Chron. 7:14
Gal. 3:1
Jer. 5:6
Hos. 11:7; 14:4
Gal. 5:4, 7
Jer. 8:5
Hos. 5:15
Ps. 78:57
Luke 9:2
Gal. 6:1
Prov. 28:14
Ps. 85:8
Jer. 2:19
James 5:19
Col. 1:21–23
1 Cor. 10:12
Prov. 14:14
Isa. 59:12–14
Ps. 103:3
Exod. 32:8

Praying for the presence and the power of the Holy Spirit
Job 22:28
Job 37:23
Ps. 59:11
Ps. 145:11
Ps. 106:8
Isa. 11:2
Isa. 54:11
Jer. 16:21
Matt. 16:18–19
Mark 10:27
Mark 16:8, 16–20
Luke 9:43
Luke 22:69
1 Cor. 12:8–10
Eph. 1:21
Eph. 3:20
1 Pet. 1:5

Praying for those in courtship
Eph. 5:22–25
Phil. 2:2
Col. 2:10
Prov. 18:22
James 3:17
Prov. 19:14
Isa. 62:5
Prov. 8:8

Praying for your boss or employer
Eph. 6:5–8
Col. 3:22–24
1 Tim. 6:1–2
Titus 2:9
1 Pet. 2:18
Prov. 17:2
Prov. 27:18
Matt. 24:45–48
Luke 12:37
Luke 16:10, 12
John 13:16
1 Cor. 4:2

Exod. 21:20–21
Lev. 19:13
Deut. 24:14
Deut. 24:15
Jer. 22:13
Matt. 10:10
Rom. 4:4

Praying for your children
Gen. 33:5
Gen. 49:8
Exod. 2:2
Exod. 20:5
Deut. 14:1
Ps. 128:3
Ps. 144:7
Isa. 54:13
Prov. 13:22
Prov. 17:6
Prov. 20:11
Prov. 22:6
Prov. 22:15
Prov. 29:15
Prov. 29:21
Eccles. 4:13
Rom. 8:26
1 Cor. 13:11
Gal. 4:1
Eph. 5:8
1 John 3:10

Praying for your husband
James 5:7
Titus 2:4
Deut. 22:24
Eph. 5:22–23
Jer. 31:32
1 Pet. 3:1
1 Cor. 7:2–39
Exod. 20:17
Luke 16:18
Prov. 31:11
Prov. 31:23, 28
Job 19:17
Matt. 6:33
2 Cor. 5:17

Prov. 12:4
Ps. 128:3
Col. 3:19
Eccles. 9:9
Mark 10:12
1 Tim. 3:2
Prov. 19:13–14

Praying for your pastors and ministers
1 Chron. 15:2
1 Chron. 23:13
2 Chron. 15:7
Ps. 23:1
Prov. 8:14
Isa. 35:3–4
Isa. 40:11
Jer. 23:4
Ezek. 34:5
Hab. 3:19
1 Cor. 12:8
2 Cor. 4:8
2 Cor. 6:3–4
2 Cor. 9:8
2 Cor. 12:9
Eph. 3:20
2 Cor. 2:12, 14, 17
2 Cor. 3:2–3
2 Cor. 3:17
1 Pet. 4:11

Praying for your wife
Gen. 12:3
Deut. 28:11
1 Cor. 7:2–39
1 Pet. 3:1
Ps. 127:1, 3
Ps. 128
1 Tim. 3:2, 11–12
Prov. 5:15
Prov. 8:33–34
Col. 3:18
Prov. 9:13
Lev. 20:11
Prov. 11:11
Prov. 11:16, 29

Num. 30:6–24
Prov. 12:4
Prov. 14:1
Exod. 22:16
Prov. 15:17
Prov. 18:22
Prov. 19:13
Prov. 19:14, 20
Prov. 31:10
Prov. 31:30
Jer. 31:3
Eph. 5:25–30

**Praying to know
and do the will of
God**
Exod. 19:5
Ps. 1:2
Matt. 12:50
Exod. 19:6–9
Ps. 25:10
John 14:15
Ps. 111:10
John 14:23
Ps. 1:1
Isa. 1:19
John 15:10
John 15:14
1 John 3:22

Prosperity
Gen. 26:1–2
Gen. 39:3
Josh. 1:7
Judg. 4:24
1 Kings 10:7
1 Kings 2:3
2 Chron. 14:7
2 Chron. 18:11
2 Chron. 20:20
2 Chron. 26:5
Neh. 2:20
Job 36:11
Ps. 1:3
Ps. 35:27
Ps. 122:7
Prov. 17:8
Zech. 1:7

Zech. 8:12
1 Cor. 16:2
3 John 2
Gen. 24:40
Josh. 24:13
Ps. 30:6
Ps. 118:25
1 Chron. 22:11
2 Chron. 32:30
1 Kings 22:15
Isa. 53:10
Isa. 55:11
Neh. 1:11

Protection
Lev. 26:5–6
Deut. 1:30
Deut. 12:10
Ps. 91:10
Judg. 20:28
Ps. 91:11
2 Sam. 22:3, 31
Job 1:10
Ps. 3:3
Ps. 32:7
Ps. 34:7
Ps. 64:2
Ps. 91:9
Ps. 91:2
Ps. 91:3
Ps. 125:2
Prov. 3:24
Prov. 18:10
Isa. 43:2
Zech. 2:5
Luke 21:18
2 Tim. 1:7
2 Tim. 1:12

Prudence
1 Sam. 16:18
Prov. 8:12
Prov. 12:16
Prov. 14:18
Prov. 15:5
Prov. 18:15
Prov. 19:14
Prov. 22:3

Isa. 10:13
Isa. 29:14
Isa. 52:13
Amos 5:13
Eph. 1:8

**Pulling down
strongholds**
Exod. 11:7
2 Sam. 5:7
Ps. 35:1–10
Ps. 89:40
Isa. 10:27
Isa. 23:11
Isa. 54:14–17
Isa. 41:11
Isa. 41:12
Nah. 1:7
Mal. 3:18
Matt. 8:16–17
Matt. 10:19
Luke 9:1
Luke 10:19
2 Cor. 10:4
2 Cor. 10:5
Eph. 1:22
Eph. 6:12
2 Tim. 1:7
Rev. 12:8–11
Rev. 12:13
Gen. 49:19
Num. 13:30
2 Chron. 32:22
Isa. 49:26
Isa. 58:6
Acts 19:16
John 16:33
1 John 2:13
1 John 4:4
1 John 5:4
Rev. 2:7
Rev. 2:11
Rev. 2:26
Rev. 3:5
Rev. 3:12
Rev. 3:21
Rev. 12:11
Rev. 21:7

Purpose
Prov. 15:22
Prov. 20:18
Isa. 14:24
Isa. 46:11
Dan. 1:8
Jer. 51:29
Acts 11:23
Rom. 8:28
Rom. 14:7
Rom. 14:8
Rom. 15:20
Phil. 4:13
Eph. 1:11
Eph. 3:11
2 Cor. 5:9
Col. 3:23
2 Tim. 3:10

**Renewing your
zeal**
Deut. 4:9
Deut. 13:14
Deut. 24:8
Josh. 22:5
Ezra 7:23
Prov. 4:23
Prov. 10:4
Prov. 12:24
Prov. 12:27
Prov. 13:4
Prov. 21:5
Prov. 22:29
Prov. 27:23
Acts 18:2–5
Rom. 12:8
Rom. 12:11
2 Cor. 8:7
Heb. 6:12
2 Pet. 1:5
2 Pet. 3:14

**Repossessing
your land**
Jer. 16:14–15
Deut. 2:31; 4:5
Deut. 11:23
Amos 9:14–15

Num. 24:18
2 Sam. 7:10
Deut. 6:18
Josh. 1:3
Neh. 5:11
Ps. 2:8; 44:3
Deut. 2:24
Ps. 69:35

**Repossessing
your properties**
Exod. 22:7
Exod. 22:1
Num. 14:30
Deut. 1:21
Exod. 1:21
Neh. 5:11
Neh. 9:25
Job 21:9
Job 22:8
Isa. 65:21
Jer. 29:5
Jer. 32:15
Ezek. 28:26

**Resisting Satan's
lies**
2 Cor. 10:3–5
1 Cor. 13:7a
Ps. 103:1
Col. 3:2
1 Cor. 6:20
Phil. 4:8
1 Cor. 13:5b
1 Cor. 2:16
1 Pet. 1:13
Phil. 4:9

Rest
Job 3:17
Ps. 37:7
Ps. 116:7
Song of Sol. 1:7
Isa. 11:10
Isa. 28:12
Isa. 34:14
Jer. 30:10
Matt. 11:28

Matt. 11:29–30

Restoration
Gen. 40:13
Ruth 4:15
2 Kings 8:5
2 Kings 8:6
Job 20:18
Job 20:10
Ps. 23:3
Ps. 51:12
Isa. 58:12
Neh. 5:12
Jer. 27:22
Jer. 30:17

Revival
Exod. 3:8
Num. 11:17
1 Kings 18:41
2 Kings 13:21
Neh. 4:2
Ps. 85:6
Ps. 138:7
Isa. 11:10
Isa. 57:15
Isa. 64:1–3
Hos. 6:2
Hos. 10:12
Hos. 14:7
Hab. 3:2
Mal. 3:10
Luke 1:78
John 4:24
Exod. 31:3
Ezra 9:8–10
Ps. 27:4, 8–9
Ps. 42:1
Ps. 85:4–6
Ps. 126:1
Ps. 138:7
Isa. 6:1–3
Isa. 57:15
Isa. 58:8
Hab. 3:1–3
Matt. 5:6
2 Cor. 5:17
Rom. 8:37

Eph. 3:20
Phil. 4:13
Col. 3:1–4
2 Pet. 1:2–3

Reward
Gen. 15:1
Exod. 11:3
Ruth 2:12
Ps. 19:11
Ps. 58:11
Ps. 127:3
Ps. 137:8
Prov. 13:13
Prov. 11:18
Prov. 24:14
Eccles. 4:9
Dan. 2:6
Matt. 6:4
Matt. 6:6
Matt. 6:18
Matt. 10:41
Matt. 16:27
Luke 6:23

Salvation of souls
Isa. 58:12
Isa. 6:1
Isa. 61:3
Luke 19:9
Acts 16:30–32
Rom. 1:16
Rom. 13:12
2 Cor. 1:6
2 Cor. 6:2
2 Cor. 7:10
Gal. 5:19–25
Phil. 1:19
Phil. 1:28
Phil. 2:12
1 Thess. 5:8–9
2 Thess. 2:13
2 Tim. 2:10
2 Tim. 3:15
Heb. 1:14
Heb. 2:3
Heb. 2:10
Heb. 5:9

Heb. 6:9
Heb. 9:12
1 Pet. 1:5
1 Pet. 1:10
2 Pet. 3:15
Rev. 12:10

Satisfaction
Deut. 14:29
Deut. 33:23
Ps. 17:15
Ps. 22:26
Ps. 37:19
Ps. 48:14
Ps. 63:5
Ps. 65:4
Ps. 90:14
Ps. 81:13–16
Ps. 91:6
Ps. 103:5
Ps. 104:13
Ps. 105:40
Ps. 107:9
Ps. 132:15
Ps. 145:16
Prov. 12:11
Prov. 18:20
Prov. 19:23
Prov. 20:13
Isa. 53:11
Isa. 66:11
Isa. 58:10
Isa. 58:11
Jer. 31:14
Jer. 31:25
Joel 2:14
Joel 2:26
John 4:14

Security
Lev. 25:18
Lev. 25:19
Deut. 12:10
Deut. 33:12
Deut. 33:28
1 Sam. 12:11
1 Kings 4:25
Judg. 18:7

Judg. 18:10
Job 11:18
Job 12:6
Ps. 12:5
Ps. 91
Ps. 94:22
Ps. 119:117
Prov. 3:29
Prov. 11:14
Prov. 11:21
Prov. 18:10
Prov. 29:25
Hos. 2:18
Luke 15:27

Self-esteem
Prov. 3:26
Prov. 14:26
Prov. 28:1
Isa. 30:15
Isa. 41:13
2 Cor. 5:21
2 Cor. 7:16
Gal. 5:10
Rom. 8:31
Rom. 8:37
Rom. 8:26
Eph. 1:17–20
Phil. 3:3
Heb. 4:16
Heb. 13:6
1 John 5:4
1 John 5:14

Serving the Lord
Gen. 39:4
Num. 4:37
Num. 8:15
1 Sam. 2:20
1 Chron. 22:11
1 Chron. 29:5
2 Chron. 20:20
Ps. 101:6
Ps. 137:8
Isa. 11:10
Isa. 56:6–7
Zeph. 3:9
Mal. 3:17

Luke 1:74
Luke 2:37
Luke 4:8
Luke 16:13
Luke 22:27
John 12:26
Acts 27:23
Rom. 1:9
Rom. 7:6
Rom. 12:1
Eph. 6:5
Eph. 6:6
Eph. 6:7
1 Tim. 6:2
2 Tim. 1:3
Heb. 6:12
Rev. 2:19

Special anniversaries
Isa. 38:18–19
Nah. 2:15
Lev. 23:41
Isa. 61:7
Acts 18:21
Isa. 25:1
Ps. 109:30

Spiritual gifts
Acts 2:38
Eph. 4:11–14
Acts 11:17
1 Cor. 12:31
Rom. 1:11
Rom. 11:29
Rom. 12:6
Rom. 12:7
Rom: 12:8
1 Cor. 1:7
1 Cor. 12:8
1 Cor. 12:9–10
1 Cor. 13:2
1 Cor. 14:12
2 Cor. 9:15
Eph. 3:7
Eph. 4:7
1 Tim. 4:14
2 Tim. 1:6

Heb. 6:4
James 1:17

Steadfastness
Ruth 1:18
Job 11:15
Dan. 6:26
Acts 1:10
Acts 14:9
1 Cor. 7:37
1 Cor. 15:58
2 Cor. 1:7
Col. 2:5
1 Tim. 6:12
Heb. 2:2–3
Heb. 3:14
Heb. 6:19
1 Pet. 5:9
2 Pet. 3:17
Rev. 3:11

Strength
Gen. 49:4
Gen. 49:24
Exod. 13:3
Exod. 15:2
Deut. 3:28
Deut. 33:25
Josh. 14:11
Judg. 16:28
1 Sam. 23:16
2 Sam. 22:33
1 Chron. 16:28
1 Chron. 29:12
2 Chron. 11:17
Ezra 1:6
Ezra 6:22
Neh. 2:18
Neh. 6:9
Job 4:3–4
Job 12:13
Ps. 8:2
Ps. 21:1
Ps. 21:13
Ps. 22:19
Ps. 27:1
Ps. 28:7
Ps. 31:4

Ps. 37:39
Ps. 43:2
Ps. 46:1
Ps. 68:35
Ps. 54:1
Ps. 84:5
Ps. 89:21
Ps. 93:1
Ps. 118:14
Ps. 147:13
Prov. 8:14
Prov. 20:29
Prov. 24:5
Prov. 24:10
Prov. 31:17
Eccles. 9:16
Isa. 28:6
Isa. 30:15
Isa. 35:3
Isa. 41:10
Isa. 54:2
Jer. 1:18
Jer. 16:19
Hos. 12:3
2 Cor. 12:9–10
Col. 1:10–11
2 Tim. 2:1

Students
Deut. 31:13
Ps. 32:8
Prov. 1:5
1 Thess. 4:11
Prov. 2:10–11
Prov. 16:21
Prov. 15:28
Prov. 16:23
Eccles. 12:12
Isa. 29:11
Isa. 50:4
Dan. 1:17
Matt. 11:29
Acts 7:22
Rom. 15:4
Rom. 16:17
2 Tim. 3:7
2 Tim. 2:15
2 Tim. 3:14

Thanksgiving and praise
2 Chron. 33:16
Ps. 26:7
Ps. 50:14
Ps. 69:30
Ps. 95:2
Ps. 100:4
Ps. 147:7
Eccles. 9:7
Isa. 51:3
1 Cor. 15:57
2 Cor. 2:14
2 Cor. 8:16
2 Cor. 9:15
Phil. 4:6
Col. 2:7
Col. 4:15
1 Thess. 5:18
1 Tim. 1:12
2 Tim. 1:3
Heb. 13:15
1 Pet. 2:19
Rev. 4:9–11
Rev. 7:11–12
Lev. 7:12
2 Chron. 20:21
2 Chron. 20:23
Neh. 12:46
Ps. 26:7
Ps. 34:1–3
Ps. 69:30
Ps. 95:1–7
Ps. 107
Ps. 116:17
Ps. 148
Ps. 150
Amos 4:5
Jonah 2:9
Acts 16:25–26
Col. 4:2
1 Tim. 2:1
Rev. 4:11
Rev. 7:12

The bereaved
Isa. 61:3
2 Cor. 1:4

Heb. 4:14–15
Matt. 5:4
1 Thess. 4:13b
Heb. 4:16
Luke 4:18
1 Thess. 4:1
1 Thess. 4:4
2 Thess. 2:16
2 Cor. 1:3

The inner life
Ps. 4:8
Ps. 85:8
Prov. 13:20
Matt. 5:48
Luke 6:45
John 13:15
John 13:16
John 13:34
Rom. 12:1–2
Rom. 15:5–7
1 Cor. 4:2
1 Cor. 15:58
Gal. 6:2, 10
Eph. 5:1–2
Eph. 5:8
Eph. 6:5–7
Phil. 2:5–8
Col. 3:13, 17
1 John 2:16
3 John 2

Those in authority
Gen. 41:43
Exod. 22:28
Exod. 32:34
Lev. 4:22–24
2 Chron. 30:9
Ps. 67:4
Prov. 28:15, 16
Prov. 19:2, 12
Isa. 9:6–7
Isa. 63:14
Matt. 8:9
Rom. 13:1, 3
1 Cor. 12:28
1 Tim. 2:2

1 Pet. 2:14

Those in hospital
Deut. 7:15
Ps. 103:2–3
Isa. 53:4
Isa. 53:5
Jer. 17:14
Jer. 30:17a
Matt. 8:7
James 5:13–16
3 John 2
Matt. 8:16
Matt. 8:17
1 Pet. 2:24
Gal. 3:13
Exod. 15:26
Ps. 41:3
Ps. 91:10–16
Ps. 107:20
Prov. 4:22
Mal. 4:2
Prov. 14:30
Job. 37:23

Those in prison
Matt. 25:36
Eph. 4:32
Eph. 5:2
Ps. 91:1–2
Ps. 91:4
Ps. 91:9–11
Ps. 91:15–16

Transition
Gen. 1:14
Lev. 26:4
Josh. 24:7
2 Chron. 15:3
Ps. 1:3
Prov. 15:23
Eccles. 3:1
Isa. 40:31
Jer. 5:24
Dan. 2:21
Zech. 4:6
Luke 1:20
Luke 12:42

John 5:35
Acts 1:7
2 Cor. 7:8
Gal. 6:9
2 Tim. 4:2
Heb. 11:25
1 John 1:9

Traveling
Gen. 26:3
Lev. 25:35–40
Deut. 32:12–13
Josh. 1:11
Josh. 20:9
1 Chron. 29:1
1 Chron. 29:16
Ps. 37:3
Ps. 39:12
Ps. 91:5
Ps. 105:23
Prov. 2:21
Jer. 7:3, 5–7
Matt. 28:19
Acts 27:10–1
Heb. 11:9
1 Pet. 1:17
Rev. 3:8

Triumph
Exod. 15:1
Exod. 15:21
Deut. 11:24–25
Josh. 1:3
Ps. 25:2
Ps. 41:11
Ps. 44:5
Ps. 60:12
Ps. 91:13
Ps. 92:4
Ps. 106:47
Ps. 108:13
Zech. 10:5
Luke 10:19
1 Cor. 10:13
1 Cor. 15:57
2 Cor. 1:4
Col. 2:15

Trust

Ps. 9:10
Ps. 22:4
Ps. 25:2
Job 13:15
Ps. 28:7
Ps. 37:3
Ps. 49:6
Ps. 56:3
Ps. 62:8
Ps. 84:12
Ps. 86:2
Ps. 91:4
Ps. 112:7
Ps. 125:1
Ps. 143:8
Prov. 3:5
Prov. 16:20
Prov. 28:26
Isa. 12:2

Understanding

Exod. 31:3
1 Sam. 25:3
1 Kings 3:9
1 Chron. 12:32
1 Chron. 28:19
Job 32:8
Job 34:34
Ps. 111:10
Ps. 119:34
Ps. 119:99
Ps. 119:104
Ps. 119:130
Ps. 139:2
Prov. 3:4–5
Prov. 4:7
Prov. 7:4
Prov. 8:9
Prov. 14:33
Prov. 16:16
Prov. 19:25
Prov. 28:5
Prov. 28:11
Isa. 11:3
Isa. 32:4
Dan. 5:14
Dan. 9:13

Matt. 13:23
Luke 24:45
Eph. 5:17
Phil. 4:7
Col. 1:9
Col. 2:2
2 Tim. 2:7
1 John 5:20
Rev. 13:18

Unity

Gen. 2:24
1 Chron. 17:21
1 Chron. 17:22
Matt. 19:6
Mark 10:9
1 Cor. 6:19
1 Cor. 12:4–7
1 Cor. 12:12
Eph. 4:2–4
Eph. 4:16
Eph. 4:32
Eph. 5:19
Ps. 133:1
Amos 3:3

Victory over intimidation

John 8:32
Isa. 26:3
Phil. 4:13
Heb. 13:5
Matt. 6:33
Prov. 24:3–4
1 Pet. 5:8–9
John 16:33
1 John 4:4

Victory over lack

Josh. 1:8
Matt. 6:33
Deut. 8:18
3 John 2
Phil. 4:19
Deut. 28:12
Isa. 48:17
Ps. 34:10
Rom. 8:32

Gal. 3:13–14
Isa. 45:2–3
Isa. 1:19
2 Cor. 8:9
Prov. 13:22
Prov. 28:20
Ps. 37:4
Eph. 3:20
2 Pet. 1:3
Luke 6:38
Heb. 6:12
John 10:10
Heb. 8:6
Luke 12:32
Prov. 10:22
Gal. 6:9
Gen. 14:18–20
Gen. 26:12
Deut. 14:28
2 Chron. 20:20
Job 42:14–15

Victory over worries and burdens

Ps. 42:11a
Ps. 37:7
Exod. 33:14
James 4:6–7
Ps. 42:11b
1 Pet. 5:9a
Ps. 127:1a
Matt. 11:28–30
John 14:27b
Ps. 55:22
Heb. 4:10–11

Walking in discernment

Job 32:8
Ps. 43:3
Prov. 16:22
Isa. 55:8
Col. 1:9–10
Ps. 16:7
Ps. 128:8
Prov. 16:23
Prov. 8:14

Eph. 5:17
Ps. 18:30
Prov. 3:5
Prov. 24:3
Isa. 55:9
1 Kings 3:9
Ps. 27:11
Prov. 3:6
Prov. 24:4
Jer. 33:3
Josh. 1:5

Walking in love

Josh. 22:5
Ps. 91:14
Prov. 10:12
Prov. 17:9
Song of Sol. 8:6–7
John 13:34–35
John 15:10
Rom. 5:5
Eph. 3:17
Phil. 1:9–11
1 Thess. 3:12–13
1 Thess. 4:9–10
1 Pet. 4:8
1 John 2:10
1 John 4:10–12
1 John 4:16–18
Gen. 29:20
Lev. 19:18
2 Sam. 1:26
Prov. 16:17
Prov. 27:5
Song of Sol. 1:2
Song of Sol. 2:4
Matt. 24:12
John 13:35
John 15:9
Rom. 8:35
Rom. 12:9–10
Rom. 13:10
1 Cor. 13:4–8
1 Cor. 13:13
Gal. 5:6
Eph. 1:15–16
Eph. 4:2
Eph. 4:15

Eph. 5:2
Col. 3:14
1 Tim. 1:5
2 Tim. 1:7
Titus 2:4
Philem. 7
Heb. 6:10
Heb. 10:24
Heb. 13:1
1 John 2:15
1 John 3:18
1 John 4:7–8
1 Pet. 1:22

**Walking in
obedience**
Gen. 22:18
Exod. 23:21
Exod. 24:7
Exod. 30:29
Num. 27:20
Deut. 4:30
Deut. 11:27
Deut. 28:2
Prov. 25:12
Isa. 1:19
Hos. 10:12
Hag. 1:12
Zech. 6:15
Rom. 1:5
Rom. 5:19
Rom. 10:15
Rom. 12:1
Rom. 15:18
Rom. 16:19
2 Cor. 2:9
2 Cor. 7:15
2 Cor. 10:5–6
Phil. 2:8
Col. 3:20
Titus 2:5
Titus 2:9
Philem. 1:21
Heb. 5:8
Heb. 5:9
Heb. 11:8
1 Pet. 1:2
1 Pet. 1:22

1 Pet. 3:1
1 Pet. 1:14
1 John 5:3

Walk of victory
Exod. 31:3
Num. 13:30
2 Sam. 5:20
2 Sam. 23:10
Ps. 18:29
Ps. 34:6
Ps. 98:1
Ps. 126:1
Ps. 144:1
Phil. 4:13, 19
Rom. 8:37
1 Cor. 15:55
1 Pet. 4:10, 11
2 Pet. 1:2–3
1 John 4:4
1 John 5:4
Rev. 2:26
Rev. 21:7

**War against
territorial spirits**
Gen. 39:7–23
Exod. 3:9
Num. 16:3–40
1 Sam. 28:7
1 Kings 18:19
1 Kings 22:21–23
Ps. 43:2
Ps. 56:1
Ps. 69:20
Ps. 119:28
Prov. 6:34
Prov. 12:20
Prov. 16:18–19
Prov. 25:28
Prov. 26:24
Song of Sol. 8:6
Isa. 45:16
Isa. 60:20
Isa. 61:3
Mark 1:24
Mark 9:25
Luke 13:11–13

John 8:36
Acts 10:38
Acts 16:16
Rom. 8:15
Rom. 11:8
Eph. 4:31
Eph. 5:36
1 Thess. 2:2
1 Tim. 4:1
2 Tim. 4:3–4
Heb. 12:15
1 John 1:7
1 John 4:3, 6
Rev. 6:8

**When faced with
court matters**
Jer. 33:3
Col. 4:6
Prov. 3:5–6
1 Cor. 1:8
Jer. 1:12
Isa. 49:25
Prov. 14:25
Matt. 18:18
Isa. 30:21
Isa. 43:26
Ps. 138:8
Prov. 8:8
Eph. 6:10
Isa. 54:14
Ps. 91:1
Prov. 25:15
Eph. 6:16
Luke 21:15
Isa. 54:17
Ps. 31:20
Luke 12:11–12
Luke 2:52
2 Tim. 1:7

**When you are
tempted to give
up**
Ps. 27:14
Ps. 39:7
Prov. 13:12
Mark 9:23

Rom. 12:12
Ps. 31:24
Ps. 71:14
Prov. 24:14
Mark 9:24
Rom. 15:13
Ps. 38:15
Prov. 3:5
Jer. 17:7
Mark 11:24
Heb. 11:1
Ps. 146:5
Rom. 8:25
Lam. 3:26

**When you face a
hostile board**
Ps. 39:1
Prov. 12:18
Prov. 17:27
James 3:17
Ps. 50:23
Prov. 12:19
Prov. 17:28
Col. 4:6
James 3:16
Ps. 141:3
Prov. 12:20
Prov. 21:23
James 1:18
Prov. 16:24
Prov. 10:11
Prov. 15:2
Matt. 12:37
James 3:13
Luke 6:45
James 3:18

**When you have
been slandered**
Prov. 6:16, 19
Jer. 20:10
Matt. 12:36
Exod. 23:1
Eccles. 10:11
1 Cor. 4:13
Prov. 16:28
Eph. 4:31

James 4:11–12
1 Sam. 24:9
Rom. 1:29, 32
Ps. 41:5, 11–12
Prov. 25:23
2 Cor. 12:20
Ps. 109:20
Prov. 17:9
Prov. 26:20
James 1:26
Ps. 140:3
Matt. 15:19
Jer. 38:4
Ps. 38:12–15
Ps. 34:13
Titus 3:1–2

**When you need a
breakthrough**
Gen. 26:1–12
Exod. 15:26–27
Num. 13:30
1 Chron. 4:10
2 Chron. 20:20
2 Sam. 5:20
Job 14:14
Job 42:10–13
Ps. 1:3
Ps. 32:8
Ps. 92:4
Ps. 126:1
Isa. 40:4
Isa. 42:16
Isa. 42:9
Isa. 43:19
Isa. 48:6
Joel 3:10
Matt. 17:20
Matt. 19:26
Acts 12:10
Rom. 8:31–32
1 Cor. 15:57
1 Pet. 1:7
Exod. 19:4

**When you need
motivation**
Deut. 11:25

Isa. 40:29–31
2 Pet. 3:1
Isa. 54:17
Deut. 28:7
2 Cor. 12:9
Judg. 20:22
Matt. 7:7–8
Josh. 23:9
2 Tim. 1:7
Acts 27:22
1 Pet. 3:11
Prov. 10:5
Phil. 4:13
1 Sam. 30:6
1 Pet. 3:12
Prov. 12:24
2 Tim. 1:6
Prov. 21:25
Prov. 18:9
2 Pet. 1:13
Prov. 22:13

**When you need
to be watchful**
Ps. 102:7
Prov. 8:34
Dan. 9:14
Matt. 24:42
Matt. 26:38
Mark 13:33–34
Mark 13:37
Mark 14:37, 38
Acts 20:31
Eph. 6:18
Col. 4:2
1 Thess. 5:6
2 Tim. 4:5
Heb. 13:7
1 Pet. 4:7
Rev. 16:15

**When you need
to forget the past**
Phil. 3:7–9
Prov. 3:5
John 1:12
Prov. 3:6
Ps. 32:5

Phil. 3:10
Phil. 3:13
Phil. 3:11
Gal. 2:20
Phil. 3:12–14

**When you need
to forgive**
Num. 14:18
Deut. 21:8
Ps. 25:18
Ps. 32:1
Ps. 32:5
Ps. 78:38
Ps. 99:8
Jer. 31:34
Amos 7:2
Matt. 6:12
Matt. 6:14
Mark 2:5
Mark 11:25
Luke 7:43
Luke 7:48
Luke 11:4
Rom. 4:7
Rom. 12:14
2 Cor. 2:10
Eph. 1:7
Eph. 4:32
Col. 1:14
Col. 2:13
James 5:15
1 John 1:9
1 John 2:12

**When you need
to make decisions**
Prov. 1:23
Ps. 32:8
Ps. 36:9
Ps. 18:30
Ps. 27:11
Ps. 43:4
Ps. 119:125, 130
Ps. 119:169
Prov. 3:5–6
Prov. 3:13
Prov. 4:18

Prov. 8:14
Prov. 25:8–9
Jer. 33:3
Isa. 30:21
Luke 24:45
Eph. 5:17
2 Tim. 2:7
1 John 2:20
Prov. 24:6
Acts 2:23
Acts 4:28
Acts 5:38
Prov. 11:14
Acts. 17:26
1 Cor. 2:2
1 Cor. 4:5
Eph. 1:11
Heb. 6:17
1 Pet. 5:10
Deut. 30:19
2 Chron. 2:1
Job 14:5

**When you need
vision**
1 Chron. 17:11–15
2 Chron. 26:5
Ps. 92:10–11
Prov. 29:18
Ezek. 11:24
Dan. 7:15
Dan. 8:16
Dan. 8:26
Dan. 10:1
Dan. 10:7
Dan. 10:16
Joel 2:28
Hab. 2:2–3
Luke 1:22
Luke 24:23
Acts 2:17
Acts 9:10
Acts 9:12
Acts 10:17
Acts 18:9
Acts 26:19

Winning
Gen. 49:19
Exod. 14:27
Exod. 15:7
Exod. 23:24
Num. 13:30
Deut. 12:3
2 Chron. 32:22
Job 12:19
Ps. 8:3–5
Ps. 98:1
Ps. 106:26–27
Ps. 112
Ps. 136:15
Ps. 140:11
Ps. 141:6
Prov. 13:6
Prov. 14:11
Jer. 18:23
Dan. 11:41
John 16:33
Acts 5:39
Acts 27:22
1 Cor. 9:24
1 John 2:13–14
1 John 4:4
1 John 5:4
Rev. 2:7
Rev. 2:11
Rev. 2:17
Rev. 2:26
Rev. 3:5
Rev. 3:12
Rev. 3:21
Rev. 12:11
Rev. 21:7

Wisdom
1 Chron. 22:12
Ps. 37:30
Ps. 90:12
Prov. 2:7
Prov. 1:2
Prov. 1:7
Prov. 2:2
Prov. 8:5
Prov. 9:10
Prov. 10:31

Eccles. 1:17
Eccles. 2:13
Eccles. 8:1
Isa. 33:6
Dan. 1:4
Dan. 2:21
Eph. 1:17–19
Col. 1:9

Word of God
Ps. 18:3
Ps. 119:11
Ps. 119:67
Ps. 119:103
Ps. 119:116
Ps. 119:133
Ps. 119:140
Ps. 119:154
Ps. 119:158
Ps. 119:170
Ps. 138:2
Prov. 30:5
Matt. 4:4
Matt. 26:75
Luke 1:38
John 5:47
John 6:63
John 6:68
John 8:47
John 12:47–48
John 14:10
John 15:7
John 17:8
Acts 11:16
Rom. 10:8
Rom. 10:17
2 Cor. 2:17
2 Cor. 4:2
2 Cor. 5:19
Eph. 5:26
Eph. 6:17
Phil. 1:14
Col. 3:16
1 Thess. 4:18
2 Thess. 2:17
1 Tim. 4:5
1 Tim. 4:12
2 Tim. 1:13

2 Tim. 4:2
2 Tim. 4:15
Titus 1:9
Titus 2:5
Heb. 1:3
Heb. 4:2
Heb. 4:12
Heb. 5:13
Heb. 6:5
Heb. 11:3
James 1:21–22
1 Pet. 1:23
1 Pet. 2:8
1 Pet. 3:1
2 Pet. 1:19
1 John 1:1
1 John 1:10
1 John 2:14
Rev. 3:10
Rev. 12:11
Rev. 22:19

Work
Exod. 5:13
Deut. 2:7
Deut. 14:29
Ps. 15:2
Hab. 1:5
Zech. 4:6
Matt. 10:10
Matt. 11:28
John 6:28
Rom. 13:10
1 Cor. 4:12
1 Cor. 9:10
Eph. 4:28
Phil. 2:13
Col. 1:10
1 Thess. 4:11
2 Thess. 3:10
1 Tim. 5:8
2 Tim. 2:15

Worry-free living
Gen. 15:15
Gen. 43:23
Exod. 4:18
Lev. 26:6

Num. 6:26
Num. 25:12
Deut. 29:19
Judg. 6:23
Judg. 19:20
1 Sam. 25:6
1 Kings 4:24
1 Chron. 12:22
2 Chron. 15:4
Esther 9:30
Esther 10:3
Job 5:24
Ps. 4:8
Ps. 29:11
Ps. 34:14
Ps. 55:18
Ps. 60:6–7
Ps. 66:12
Ps. 72:3
Ps. 72:7
Ps. 85:10
Ps. 119:165
Ps. 122:7
Ps. 128:6
Ps. 147:14
Prov. 3:2
Prov. 12:20
Eccles. 3:8
Isa. 9:6
Isa. 26:12
Isa. 32:17
Isa. 39:8
Isa. 48:18
Jer. 29:11
Jer. 30:10
Jer. 33:6
Hag. 2:9
Mal. 2:5
Luke 1:79
John 20:19
John 20:21
Heb. 12:14
Heb. 13:20
1 Pet. 1:2

Worship
Gen. 22:5
Deut. 26:10

Isa.12:2
Mark 5:6
Luke 4:8
John 4:22–24
John 9:38
1 Cor. 14:25
Phil. 3:3
Heb. 1:6
Rev. 7:11
Rev. 14:7
Rev. 15:4
Rev. 19:10
Rev. 22:8–9

Notes

CHAPTER 4
THE PLACE OF SACRIFICE: THE BRAZEN ALTAR

1. *Biblesoft's New Exhaustive Strong's Numbers and Concordance With Expanded Greek-Hebrew Dictionary* (Seattle, WA: Biblesoft and International Bible Translators, Inc., 1994), s.v. *mizbeach*, 4196, and *zabach*, 2076, "kill, offer, (do) sacrifice, slay."

2. Ibid., s.v. *thusiasterion*, 2379, "altar"; *thusia*, 2378, "sacrifice"; and *thuo*, 2380, "kill, (do) sacrifice, slay."

3. *The Chumash,* The Stone Edition, ArtScroll Series, Rabbi Nosson Scherman and Rabbi Meir Zlotowitz, general editors (New York: Mesorah Publications, 1993, 1994), 591, commentary on Leviticus 9:24.

CHAPTER 6
THE GARMENTS OF COMPLETION

1. *Merriam-Webster's Collegiate Dictionary,* 11th edition (Springfield, MA: Merriam-Webster, Inc., 2003), s.v. "loins."

2. *Nelson's Illustrated Bible Dictionary* (Nashville, TN: Thomas Nelson Publishers, 1986), s.v. "Urim and Thummim," in PC Study Bible, version 3 (Seattle, WA: Biblesoft Publishers).

CHAPTER 9
DIVINE PROTECTION: THE TABERNACLE COVERING

1. *The Chumash,* 458–459, commentary on Exodus 26:31–33, 37.
2. Ibid., 453, commentary on Exodus 26:1.
3. Ibid., 25.
4. Ibid., 477, commentary on Exodus 29:22.

CHAPTER 10
THE HOLY PLACE

1. *The Chumash,* 458–459, commentary on Exodus 26:31–33.
2. Ibid., 431, commentary on Exodus 30:31.

3. *The International Standard Bible Encyclopedia*, s.v. "olive tree," in PC Study Bible, version 3 (Seattle, WA: Biblesoft Publishers, 1996).

4. The word studies in the paragraphs to follow were taken from *Webster's American Family Dictionary* (New York: Random House Reference, 1997), s.v. "inter," "cession," and "cede."

5. *Nelson's Illustrated Bible Dictionary* (Nashville, TN: Thomas Nelson Publishers, 1986), s.v. "plants of the Bible: stacte," in PC Study Bible, version 3 (Seattle, WA: Biblesoft Publishers).

CHAPTER 12

ETERNAL COMMUNION: THE ARK OF THE COVENANT

1. Juanita Bynum, *Matters of the Heart* (Lake Mary, FL: Charisma House, 2002), see chapter six, "A Scientific Point of View."

2. *The Chumash*, 449, commentary on Exodus 25:21.

You can contact the author or purchase other
great ministry products through:

Juanita Bynum Ministries

P. O. Box 939

Waycross, GA 31502-0939

Phone: 877.4JBYNUM (877.452.9686)

Web site: www.juanitabynum.com

Damage Noted:
Brown spots
corner pages

By: *dsp* Date: Z